**W9-BRY-727**

 *Contents*

# ☙ *Acknowledgments*

𝒪 am so grateful for the support of many people in bringing this project from idea to reality. Heartfelt thanks to

My work home, Texas Woman's University, for grant support

My colleagues in the School of Library and Information Studies, including my director, Ling Hwey Jeng, for time and support

Special colleagues who support and encourage my every writing endeavor: June Jacko, Nancy Hadaway, Terrell Young, and all collaborators on many previous poetry pieces

Colleagues from professional associations, committees, and electronic discussion lists who have shared their ideas, insights, and quotes with me

Current and former graduate students (librarians and teachers) for sharing their insights and comments, particularly the practitioners quoted in this book: Kay Hardy, Pam McWhorter, Melanie Letendre, Stacey Noble, Lauren Yarbrough, Jean Collier, Renee Newry, Cristal Isaacks, Nicki Blake, S. Zulema Silva Bewley, Amy Autin Nolan, Asha Patel, Sarah Dornback, Charry Lackey, Mary Wegher, Bonnie Boyd McCormick, Lindsey Mendrop, Wendy Watson Fox, Jackie Chetzron, Kirsten Murphy, Ashley Stephenson, Clarice Howe-Johnson, Rhonda Brockett, Cristal Isaacks, and Hilary Haygood

Graduate assistants who diligently assisted with research and bibliographic support: Donna Van Cleve, Ann Sloan, and Rose Brock

Texas Poetry Festival colleagues who work so hard to make poetry come alive for children, families, and educators in my community

The Texas Library Association for supporting the "Poetry Round-up" session at the annual conference and for grant support through DEMCO for my early poetry research

*Book Links* editor Laura Tillotson for early opportunities and encouragement to write about poetry for children

The Association for Library Service to Children (ALSC) for their endorsement and support, the inspiration of the ALSC Poetry Blast, and particularly the ALSC Publications Committee, chaired by Jennifer Duffy, for the early vote of confidence

The wonderful people at ALA Editions who answer endless questions and provide encouragement and understanding, especially my generous editor, Laura Pelehach

The amazing and generous poets who shared their thoughts and words in the Poet Profiles throughout the book: Brod Bagert, Douglas Florian, Nikki Grimes, Lee Bennett Hopkins, J. Patrick Lewis, Pat Mora, Naomi Shihab Nye, Jack Prelutsky, Marilyn Singer, and Janet Wong

My supportive friends who keep me honest, especially Susan Garner, Arlene and Lee Graham, Bill and Diana Lawson, and Diane Dela-Torre, and my church family at Our Saviour's Lutheran Church of Durant, Oklahoma, for their understanding

My wonderful family, who continues to believe in me and give me time and space away when needed: my mom, Ingrid Mergeler; my faithful husband, Russell Vardell; my son, Alex Vardell, and daughter, Emily Vardell; and my brother and sister-in-law, Robert and Sophie Mergeler

My husband—believe me, this bears repeating—for all the roses, real and metaphorical, thank you

# Poetry Aloud Here!

## Sharing Poetry with Children in the Library

SYLVIA M. VARDELL

American Library Association
Chicago    2006

ne paper used in this publication meets the minimum requirements of
American National Standard for Information Sciences—Permanence of Paper
for Printed Library Materials, ANSI Z39.48-1992. ∞

**Library of Congress Cataloging-in-Publication Data**

Vardell, Sylvia M.
    Poetry aloud here! : sharing poetry with children in the library /
Sylvia M. Vardell.
        p.    cm.
    Includes bibliographical references and index.
    ISBN 0-8389-0916-7
    1. Children's libraries—Activity programs. 2. School libraries—Activity
programs. 3. Poetry and children. 4. Poetry—Study and teaching
(Elementary) 5. Language arts (Elementary) I. Title.
    Z718.1.V338 2006
    372.64—dc22                                             2005032866

Printed in the United States of America

10   09   08   07   06          5   4   3   2   1

## Chapter One

# ∽ Why Make Poetry a Priority?

*We have no borders when we read.*

—Naomi Shihab Nye, Poet

## Poetry Is Everywhere

I was in Yemen on a study tour a few summers ago and discovered that poetry was a big part of everyday life there. People recited long poems at nearly every public event, including government functions. Poems were printed in the daily newspaper, and the president of the major university was a poet. Poetry was everywhere—natural, expressive, and highly valued.

More recently I reread the classic novel *Animal Farm* with my teenage son (it is required summer reading for ninth grade in my community). I had forgotten that the lead pig in the story was a poet who composed propagandist verses to keep the people in line.

Then, as this project got under way, my selective attention found poetry all over the map. Clearly, I was now on the lookout for poetry, but I was still surprised when I encountered the following examples of poetry and poetic language all in a single day:

- I heard a wedding toast (in rhyme) on a TV morning show.

- I found a penny on the ground and spontaneously recited the rhyme "See a penny, pick it up, all day long, you'll have good luck" and remembered the teen version that I have seen on a T-shirt and that always makes me laugh: "See a penny, pick it up, all day long, you'll have . . . a penny."

- I listened to a music CD on the car radio (with rhyming lyrics).

- I reviewed a biography of Ben Franklin that ended with one of his proverbs told in rhyme.

I scanned a magazine in a doctor's waiting room and found an ad that used rhyme ("the potion's in the lotion").

I stumbled upon the middle of a cable television movie, *Desk Set*, in which Katharine Hepburn's character spouted multiple stanzas of several classic poems.

On an electronic discussion list I read a posting about a friend who had a loved one in hospice care who wanted to hear poetry read aloud.

As we stop and think about the language we encounter in our everyday lives, it is interesting to observe how often that language takes poetic form. It may not always be in the form of a published poem on a piece of paper, but the presence of poetry is interwoven throughout our lives.

## Life without Poetry

Or to approach things from another angle, gadfly poet Charles Bernstein shared this opinion about poetry's place in society:

> As an alternative to National Poetry Month, I propose that we have an International Anti-Poetry month. As part of the activities, all verse in public places will be covered over—from the Statue of Liberty to the friezes on many of our government buildings. . . . Parents will be asked not to read Mother Goose and other rimes to their children but only . . . *fiction*. Religious institutions will have to forego reading verse passages from the liturgy and only prose translations of the Bible will be recited, with hymns strictly banned. . . . Poetry readings will be replaced by self-help lectures. Love letters will have to be written only in expository paragraphs. . . . No vocal music will be played on the radio or sung in the concert halls. Children will have to stop playing all slapping and counting and singing games and stick to board games and football (http://www.press.uchicago.edu/Misc/Chicago/044106.html).

An interesting prospect. . . . Clearly, the world would be far less interesting if poetry were absent!

## What Does Poetry Do?

Poetry is all around us. Published poetry and classic poetry are more present than you might think—and informal verses and rhyming language are so ubiquitous that we take them for granted. We are experiencing a renaissance in poetry publishing in recent years with greater general interest in poets, poetry books, poetry jams and slams, poetry websites, National Poetry Month, and the like. Why? What does poetry do for us? In her recent essay, "Spiral Staircase," poet Naomi Shihab Nye writes, "Poetry wasn't trying to get us to DO anything, it was simply inviting us to THINK, and FEEL, and SEE" (2005, 253). Booth and Moore put it this way:

> Like film makers or photographers, poets manipulate our ears and eyes at the same time, using close-ups, long shots, slow motion, fast-forward, and soft focus; they juxtapose sound and image to make new meanings; they weave in subplots and overlap scenes; and they do it at lightning speed, in a few lines, in one word (2003, 12).

Through the ages, great minds have hypothesized where the power of poetry lies. The words? The sounds of words? The structure and shape? Meaning? Emotion? Effect? The philosopher Plato wrote, "Poets utter great and wise things which they do not themselves understand." Poet Robert Frost noted that "Poetry is the renewal of words forever and ever. Poetry is that by which we live forever and ever unjaded. Poetry is that by which the world is never old." Years later, at the dedication of a library named for Robert Frost, President John F. Kennedy said:

> When power leads man towards arrogance, poetry reminds him of his limitations. When power narrows the areas of man's concern, poetry reminds him of the richness and diversity of his existence. When

---

**PRACTITIONER PERSPECTIVE**

As a relatively new librarian. I have been amazed at the power we have to open up new avenues of readership for children. This April during Poetry Month, I read a variety of poems to all classes, prekindergarten through grade 5. Of course, they responded to the humorous ones, but they were also fascinated by the shape poems and wanted to hear and see more. There was a definite stampede to the 800 section (where most of the poetry lives). Because I have not been in the field long, I am discovering these works, too.

Jean Collier
Librarian
Foster Village Elementary School
North Richland Hills, Texas

> power corrupts, poetry cleanses. For art establishes the basic human
> truth which must serve as the touchstone of our judgment.

Whatever the reasons, our human capacity for language has long manifested itself in poetic expression.

## Reclaiming Poetry

What is it about life's big and little moments that calls for a poem? At weddings. At funerals. On greeting cards. In church. On the radio. At moments of great happiness or deep sadness. At beginnings and endings. Cullinan, Scala, and Schroder (1995) remind us that "poetry is a shorthand for beauty; its words can cause us to tremble, to shout for joy, to weep, to dance, to shudder or to laugh out loud." Poet Emily Dickinson wrote, "If I feel physically as if the top of my head were taken off, I know that is poetry." Professor and author Charlotte Huck wrote, "Fine poetry is the distillation of experience that captures the essence of an object, feeling, or thought" (2003, 359). Poetry is brief and full of interesting language, but it is the capture of emotion or experience in a nutshell that gives poetry its power. And amazingly, poetry does this in fewer words than any other genre. And unlike with other genres, we often return to the same poems over and over and over again. We can cherish one poem throughout a lifetime, gaining new meaning from it as life experiences color our perceptions and understanding.

If this is so, why is there often such a disconnect when the topic of poetry comes up in our work life? Even the word *poetry* puts off many adults. It reminds them of forced memorization, searching for hidden symbolism, or counting meter for iambic pentameter. So many adults have had negative experiences that keep them from sharing poetry with children. Children then grow into a similar dislike or apathy for poetry. Maybe we need to remodel our poetry memories. Sara Holbrook in her book *Practical Poetry* (2005) writes:

> I believe in functional poetry. Much like functional pottery, this is po-
> etry that holds water. It makes sense to keep it around. It does some-
> thing for us. Makes a connection. It doesn't just sit there on the shelf
> and look mysterious. Art for art's sake is a silly philosophy that rele-
> gates us to that room down the hall in which we run the risk of losing
> our connection to the real world. I would argue that art is for the sake
> of everyone. Art, poetry included, should be an intramural event, not
> simply a spectator sport (xvi).

If we think about poetry in this way, we may begin to see both the beauty and the utility in this form of literature. We can reclaim poetry as something new.

## The Value of Poetry for Children

Why make poetry a priority when our shelves are full of many choices and our days are full with many tasks? Scholar Lissa Paul makes a case for the importance of children's poetry, from traditional verse to more literary poetry, in her introduction to "Verse" in the seminal work *The Norton Anthology of Children's Literature: The Traditions in English.* She reminds us that "the history of poetry written for children begins in oral tradition" (Zipes et al. 2005, 1132) and includes lullabies, baby songs, nursery verse, riddles and wordplay, playground verse, nonsense, and standard poetry collections. It is a rich tradition that has stood the test of time and nurtured us from the cradle onward. It is also a shared experience that brings adults and children together by virtue of its oral dimension. Poetry for children begs to be heard. To be shared out loud. To be talked about. It is a social connection as well as a language experience.

---

**PRACTITIONER PERSPECTIVE**

I happen to *love* the poem "Sick," by Shel Silverstein. (I even memorized it on my own in third grade and performed it. I still perform it for my first graders!) I think the reason I love that particular poem is that it makes me think of all the times I have lain in bed, not wanting to get up, and thought of all the ways I could get out of doing whatever it was that I was supposed to be doing! So the concrete meaning, emotional impact, and sense imagery of acting sick is what really does it for me. This idea is reinforced when I think of the many abstract poems I read in school that I had no emotional connection to and therefore despised. When relating to my own classroom of kids, I think that it is very important to show them how they can figure out which kinds of poetry they like and why. Part of this is, once again, exposing them to all kinds of poetry so that they can truly know for themselves what they like.

Lauren Yarbrough
Reading Specialist
Calvin Bledsoe Elementary School
Frisco, Texas

---

## Pat Mora

### *Exploring the Self*

*by Pat Mora*

Opportunities prompt creativity. I grumbled when I was a student and had to write essays, poems, or book reports; but when I finished, I had written what would probably never otherwise have arrived on the page. I'm grateful to my friend Sylvia Vardell for inviting me to write about sharing poetry aloud. I like Sylvia so much that I told her that even if I had no writing implements and had to carve the poem with a stick or rock, I'd be happy to try.

Poems incubate. I knew I had this "assignment" and wanted to write a poem that might be useful for teachers and librarians working to excite students about presenting poems, theirs or poems written by others. When I was in elementary school in El Paso, Texas, we memorized many poems, but we really didn't experience the pleasure of investing ourselves in sharing them. In high school and college, I competed in oral interpretation. I'd prepare poems I liked to share with an audience. I never thought about sharing my own poems.

In New York recently, accompanied by Sylvia's request, I just let the possibilities simmer. I love museums and folk art, so I returned to the American Folk Art Museum, where I discovered "Self and Subject," self-portraits by folk artists. "Hmmm," I thought as I strolled, "animal self-portraits by children." The tradition of the animal spirit within is an old and complex one. It's always fun to ask children (and adults), "What animal would you like to be?" but the structure of the poem below lures the reader beyond wishing to feeling, to exploring within.

In some indigenous communities in Mexico and Central America, there's the belief that at birth every infant is given a *nagual*, a guardian animal spirit. My anthropologist husband remembers that we were once in Chiapas, Mexico, and heard someone talk about how family members in such communities would search outside for animal footprints when a baby was born. If many different kinds of footprints were found, the child was assumed to be a shaman, a human with many guardian spirits. In my adult Halloween poem to my three children, "Mama Spell" (*Agua Santa / Holy Water*, 1995), I write to my son, "Discover your hidden nagual, *pan, pan* / Come, dance in the fright of the moon."

All those ideas and images simmered inside me, though not necessarily in an intellectual manner. Yes, I wanted to write a poem that would be both fun and intriguing to children and young people, that would prompt them to ponder and then to create on the page. Yes, I wanted an approach that would lend itself to presentations and dramatizations, to giggles and growls. And yes, I wanted to create an opportunity for you, teachers and librarians, to explore your inside selves too and to explore creating an affirming atmosphere that would allow all kinds of spirits to reveal and revel.

'Tis true, and yet, and yet when I wrote the poem, I was too busy playing to be that premeditated. I was exploring possibilities, images, sounds, echoes. I hope you and your students do the same.

### Who's Inside?

*by Pat Mora*

Are you a lumbering bear, *un oso*,
shoving your big ole paw
into a honey hive and licking that gold
sweetness with your thick tongue,

or are you a cheetah racing
with the wind, running so fast you

                                fly,
your spots, streaking black stars?

Are you *una águila*, an eagle screeching,
"*Eeek eeek*," over mountaintops,
each wing stretched wide to touch blue
sky, your shiny eyes roaming,

or are you a giraffe, *una jirafa*,
looking
            down
                  down
                        down

at us with round, brown eyes
and long, smiling lashes?

Listen.
Who's inside your skin?

With your magic wand, draw
that inside self, write
your inside poem, the song
of a bear, cheetah, eagle, *jirafa*,
or maybe a manatee, grazing
on grasses all day, all night;
rolling in water all day,
rolling in glimmering stars all night.

*Read "Who's Inside" out loud one or more times. Because the poem men-
tions many animal movements and sounds, it is ideal for children to act
out through pantomime. In addition, children may enjoy animal face
painting or making paper plate masks for the bear, eagle, cheetah, giraffe,
manatee, or other inner animal.*

It forms a bridge from children's oral language development to their first steps
in reading and writing language (Hadaway, Vardell, and Young 2001). It helps
children move forward in their literacy development. Indeed, children's book
author and literacy expert Mem Fox writes, "Rhymers will be readers; it's that
simple. Experts in literacy and child development have discovered that if children know eight nursery rhymes by heart by the time they're four years old,
they're usually among the best readers by the time they're eight" (2001, 85).

Poetry does so much for children still developing their language skills.

It introduces new vocabulary and figurative language.

It reinforces word sounds, rhymes, and patterns (think phonics!).

It provides practice for word recognition and word pronunciation.

It provides examples of synonyms, antonyms, puns, wordplay, and
coining of new words and expressions.

It is rich in imagery, in seeing familiar things in new ways, and in sensory language, and it stimulates the imagination.

It is an important part of our literary and cultural heritage. Remember *Beowulf*? The Psalms? "Twinkle, Twinkle Little Star"? "Hold Fast to Dreams?"

It is meant to be heard and thus provides practice for oral language development, listening, oral fluency, and choral reading and performing.

It has many pedagogical uses across the curriculum: for building science concepts, reinforcing historical themes, adding motivation to math lessons, as a "sponge" activity in transition times, and so forth.

Poetry has value for any of us at any age, but for children it offers even more specific benefit. As children are growing in their knowledge of language and literature, poetry is just right for their developing minds and hearts. Poetry is primal: it speaks to a basic human need for expression and is made from the basic building blocks of language.

---

### PRACTITIONER PERSPECTIVE

I am tutoring a child learning English this summer. Since we started, I have been using poems and some of the strategies I have read about. I can already see his confidence and his fluency improving as he reads aloud. The flow of the words, the repetition, and the introduction to new vocabulary have helped with his various reading needs. He has been more willing to read as a result. It has been a short time, but I believe that we will see great results with this child. Today we were calling out sentences about things we like. He yelled out, "I like poems!" and "I like homework!" His homework this week was to read my selected poems. What a joy! I cannot wait to share these strategies with my teachers, especially those who teach English as a second language.

Renee Newry
Library Media Specialist
Evelyn T. Clifton Early Childhood School
Irving, Texas

## Learning through Poetry

Poetry is one of the first forms of literature children experience, albeit often in oral rather than printed form. Mother Goose nursery rhymes are often the first experience a child has with literature of any kind. "Their compact structure, lyrical rhythm and rhyme, colorful characters, and clever titles not only captivate young children but also reinforce key reading skills, such as phonemic awareness and word recognition" (Cullinan 1999). From an early age, children love the rhythm and rhyme of poetry and increase their knowledge of language and its conventions without even realizing it. When we consider the recent emphasis on developing phonemic awareness, on the sound and rhythm of words and the importance of words' beginnings, endings, and middles, we see that that is exactly what children learn by experiencing and enjoying poetry and verse (Bryant et al. 1989).

A first-grade teacher uses poetry to introduce sight words—high-frequency words taught explicitly (Burleson 2002). She chooses poems and nursery rhymes based on the sight word vocabulary that appears in them and introduces each poem with the sight words highlighted. Teacher and class enjoy reading the rhymes out loud together and talk about the new words they encounter. Students get their own copies and practice the poem at home and in class and add it to their poetry anthologies at the end of the week. This provides practice with learning vocabulary in the context of poems that are appealing, memorable, and worth revisiting. Thus children learn both words that are phonetically significant and words that may be phonetically irregular through the rhyme as well as the meaning of poetry.

---

**PRACTITIONER PERSPECTIVE**

I teach first graders, and at the beginning of the year many of them are very reluctant to start reading. I never thought that poetry would be a way to help them feel that they could manage reading. Children love rhythm and rhyme, and although stories are unable to provide this, poetry can. Both my students and I benefit from the discovery that poetry can give reluctant children the confidence they need to begin trying to read.

> Stacey Noble
> Library Media Specialist
> Mathews Elementary School
> Plano, Texas

---

The use of poetry capitalizes on "the magical moment when children fall in love with words: they notice that the sounds of language fall gently on the ear, they discover double meanings, and they notice the playfulness of language" (Cullinan, Scala, and Schroder 1995). In a brief interview, Mahmud Kianush, regarded as the founder of children's poetry in Iran, said, "Poems for children are like toys that are made of words, and these words give wings to their imagination. Children want to sing them, to dance with them, and to play with them" (http://www.art-arena.com/cpoetry.html). Through poetry, children internalize word sounds and meanings in the most playful, magical contexts, from classic poems like Laura E. Richards's "Eletelephony" to contemporary gems like Douglas Florian's "The Daddy Longlegs."

But in addition to all these cognitive benefits, exposure to poetry also provides emotional benefits. Sharing poetry can reduce stress, increase laughter, provide comfort, offer inspiration, give relief, mirror emotions, and reinforce identification—even for adults. For example, a school librarian, Gail Bush (1997), initiated a Random Acts of Poetry program during the month of April. For each staff member, she chose several poems that would have special meaning. Then, each day throughout the month, she placed some of the poems, one at a time, in the mailboxes of their intended recipients. Typically, those who received poems were so pleased that they spontaneously shared the verses with their students and others, and those who did not receive poems looked forward to when they would. Needless to say, the program was a big success.

## Teaching about Poetry

"As librarians and teachers, we need to set this pattern. Don't analyze it [poetry] too much, but rather enjoy it for what it is—a unique presentation of timeless and universal topics. Think of it [poetry] as psychology without the guilt, songs without the music, art without the illustration" (Korbeck 1995). Poet Lee Bennett Hopkins says, "Don't dissect poetry, enjoy it . . . everyday! There shouldn't be a day without poetry—it fits into every area of the curriculum, every area of life" (Raymond 1999).

Pauline Harding, a homeschooling colleague, asked her own homeschooled ten-year-old son why we should study/ learn about poetry. He said, "We shouldn't." She continued:

> That kind of threw me, since he loves poetry, and we do tons of it. So I asked him to explain. "Learning poetry would be dead boring." Aha—he means "doing poetry as school." He said we should read poetry, and buy poetry books, and listen to poetry on books-on-tape,

and snuggle up on winter mornings and take turns reading poems to each other, and memorize poems we like 'cause we feel like it, and have poetry readings at our co-op, but we should NOT "learn" poetry, in the sense of doing worksheets about it or having to analyze it and so on (child_lit@email.rutgers.edu).

Clearly there is a message here. What this ten-year-old may not recognize, however, is that reading poetry, listening to poetry, sharing poetry is all part of "learning" poetry. We do not have to "butcher" poems for instructional value via lecture and exposition when poems themselves can teach us so much. Involving children in just reading, listening to, performing, and responding to poetry offers rich learning experiences in and of itself. In fact, in this context, thoughtful discussion and critical analysis often emerge quite naturally as children begin to notice patterns, new words, interesting ideas, and powerfully expressed emotions.

### Ways to Teach Kids to Hate Poetry

Read children sentimental poems that you think are wonderful.

Make the entire group memorize the same poem, and then make each child recite it in front of the class.

Tediously analyze the rhyme scheme of each poem read.

Discuss a poem until everyone in the class arrives at the same interpretation that you have predetermined.

### Ways to Encourage Kids to Love Poetry

Keep in mind that children have different tastes in poetry, and allow them to help you select the poems to share.

Ask children to respond to poetry, but avoid picking each line apart.

Allow listeners to express their own interpretations.

Keep a variety of poetry books available at all times.

Source: Based on Nancy A. Anderson, *Elementary Children's Literature: The Basics for Teachers and Parents*, 2nd ed. (New York: Pearson, 2006), 310–11.

# How to Begin

How do we begin? In their literature textbook *Children's Literature, Briefly*, Jacobs and Tunnell (2004) give very clear-cut advice on how to create a community of readers. I find their list of tips for learning from motivated readers particularly intriguing and applicable to promoting poetry. Specifically:

> Be an adult who reads poetry.
>
> Make poetry books accessible (at arm's length, if possible).
>
> Put poetry books and poems on the agenda every day.
>
> Model joy and enthusiasm for poetry.
>
> Begin where the children are, with their interests, concerns, and experiences.
>
> Provide opportunities for choral reading and active participation.
>
> Feature notable poets and access to quality poetry books.
>
> Focus on meaning, cross-curricular connections, and children's responses.

These variables remind us of what is important in any attempt to encourage reading in any genre. Typically we are fairly diligent about using these strategies to promote the reading of fiction: we read aloud, display books, share booklists, and develop programs. How often do we apply this same full-court press to promoting poetry for children? What would happen if we gave poetry this same royal treatment?

This book is intended as a guide for librarians, teachers, and others who want to share poetry with children in ways that are inviting, meaningful, and participatory. It is drawn from my experiences with librarians and teachers who agree that young people should be introduced to poetry they will enjoy but whose own familiarity with poetry is often limited to a handful of poets and poetry books, and only a few strategies for presenting those materials. My approach is focused on helping adults share a variety of poetry with children aged five to twelve years in innovative ways in an atmosphere that encourages participation and exploration. Grounded in the current renaissance of interest in poetry and spoken-word events evidenced by the growing celebration of National Poetry Month, this book offers an overview of major poets writing for children, an update on the latest poetry books published for children, an outline of effective poetry promotion activities, a tool kit of poetry presentation strategies, and a repertoire of follow-up possibilities.

Although the last chapter includes several ways to involve children in brief poetry-writing exercises, this book is not about poetry writing per se. Child writers need ongoing time and support to draft and revise their poems, and there are many excellent resource books on how to guide children through the process of writing original poetry. Instead, the emphasis of this book is on the oral dimensions of poetry, on sharing poems out loud and reveling in the spoken word. If you work primarily with teens or with preschoolers, you will have to be somewhat creative in adapting these ideas for your audience. However, you will find a wide continuum of poetry included in the lists and examples provided, from light verse to serious poetry, from nonsensical rhymes to ageless classics. Fortunately, poems are generally less age-bound than any other genre, and you should find poems cited here that children (and adults) across the spectrum will enjoy. I am never too proud to share an odd nursery rhyme with teens or a favorite classic with kindergarteners!

In these pages you will find noteworthy quotes about poetry, perspectives from practitioners in the field, and poet essays and original poems generously shared by well-known poets writing for young people, including Brod Bagert, Douglas Florian, Nikki Grimes, Lee Bennett Hopkins, J. Patrick Lewis, Pat Mora, Naomi Shihab Nye, Jack Prelutsky, Marilyn Singer, and Janet Wong. Children who are immersed in poetry and poets, hear poems read aloud every day, jump in and participate in poem read-alouds, experience poetry in all curricular subjects, and talk about and share their responses to poetry will quite naturally engage in a great deal of verbal interaction, higher-level thinking,

---

### PRACTITIONER PERSPECTIVE

Language is the poet's paint, but some kids who never leave their town and do not own a book hear very little rich language. One way librarians can help these students is to immerse them in poetry. The more poetry they hear, the better they will understand it and the more they will use such language themselves. As a librarian, I will continue to use poetry to help students feel, visualize, and learn about the world outside our small community with the hope that they will ultimately become more productive citizens and lifelong learners and lovers of poetry.

Cristal Isaacks
Librarian
South Elementary School
Levelland, Texas

and critical analysis. They may even unknowingly memorize favorite poems that they have asked to hear again and again. But analysis and memorization are not my primary focus. My approach is to provide children access to poetry in all its variety, hoping that everyone will find poems that become a special part of his or her literate life.

> *Every poet is a big child.*
> *And every child is a little poet.*
> *Childhood is the poetry of life.*
> *Poetry is the childhood of the world.*
>
> —Boris Novak, Poet

*Chapter Two*

## ∞ Which Poets Are Popular?

*There's no money in poetry, but there's no poetry in money either.*
—Robert Graves, Poet

W hich poets are worth knowing about? In this chapter we will look at the leading awards given to poetry for children, the classic poets and poems still worth sharing, notable anthologists, and poets from many cultures. We will briefly consider fifty contemporary poets who write for young people, and we will discuss the value of websites and biographical resources that can help provide background information as well as strategies for promoting poets.

Poetry award winners are certainly a good place to begin, but they are not the only poets children will enjoy. We can also rely on classic poets whose work has stood the test of time. And reputable anthologists can be relied upon for thematic collections. But there are many other wonderful writers creating poetry for young people today, including many poets from different cultures and countries around the world. Try to discover as many new names as possible as you choose poems to read and share with children. This seems to be a golden age for publishing poetry for children, with more variety of poets and poetry formats than ever (Barton and Booth 2004). Today's selection of poetry for young people is so varied, with styles, topics, themes, and names ranging from Shel Silverstein to Valerie Worth, from girl bullies (in "The New Kid on the Block," by Jack Prelutsky) to racism ("The Incident," by Countee Cullen). Every reader can surely find poems that speak to him or her, given the proper introduction. That is the key: providing open access to poetry, free from the roadblocks of formal analysis. Opportunity for in-depth responding and understanding can follow when we create an environment for spontaneous pleasure in poetry. Poet and teacher Georgia Heard puts it this way: "Kids need to become friends with poetry as well. They need to know that poems can comfort them, make them laugh, help them remember, nurture them to know and understand themselves more completely" (1999, 20).

# Poetry Awards

How do we identify which poems are the best for children and young adults? One of the best places to begin is by looking at award winners.

## *The NCTE Award for Excellence in Poetry for Children*

One major award for poetry for children is given by the National Council of Teachers of English (NCTE). This award is given to a poet for her or his entire lifetime of poetry writing for children. Thus there is name recognition—you can bet that any book of poetry by one of these award winners will be well worthwhile.

The National Council of Teachers of English established its Award for Excellence in Poetry for Children in 1977 to honor a living American poet for his or her lifetime achievement in works for children aged three to thirteen years. The award was given annually until 1982, at which time it was decided that the award would be given every three years. The National Council of Teachers of English wanted to recognize and foster excellence in children's poetry by encouraging its publication and by exploring ways to acquaint teachers and children with poetry through such means as publications, programs, and displays. As one means of accomplishing this goal, NCTE established its Award for Excellence in Poetry for Children to honor a poet for his or her aggregate work. Over a dozen leading poets have since been recognized. Each met the following criteria:

NCTE POETRY AWARD CRITERIA

Literary merit (art and craft of aggregate work)
- Imagination
- Authenticity of voice
- Evidence of a strong persona
- Universality; timelessness

Poet's contributions
- Aggregate work
- Evident potential for growth and evolution in terms of craft
- Excellence

Evolution of the poet's work
- Technical and artistic development as evidenced in the poetry
- Evidence of risk, change, and artistic stamina
- Evidence of different styles and modes of expression

Appeal to children

- Evidence of childlike quality; yet poem's potential for stirring fresh insights and feelings should be apparent. Although the appeal to children of a poet's work is an important consideration, the art and craft must be the primary criterion for evaluation.

### Recipients of the NCTE Poetry Award

| | | | |
|---|---|---|---|
| 2006 | Nikki Grimes | 1985 | Lilian Moore |
| 2003 | Mary Ann Hoberman | 1982 | John Ciardi |
| 2000 | X. J. Kennedy | 1981 | Eve Merriam |
| 1997 | Eloise Greenfield | 1980 | Myra Cohn Livingston |
| 1994 | Barbara Esbensen | 1979 | Karla Kuskin |
| 1991 | Valerie Worth | 1978 | Aileen Fisher |
| 1988 | Arnold Adoff | 1977 | David McCord |

Look for *A Jar of Tiny Stars*, edited by Bernice Cullinan, an anthology of poems by NCTE Poetry Award recipients (up to the year of the book's publication). It is an excellent resource, based on children's votes for their favorite poems by each award winner. It is a very child-friendly collection of some of the best poetry by some of the best poets who have ever written poetry for children. Plus, it includes biographical information about, sketches of, and quotations from the award-winning poets.

## The Lee Bennett Hopkins Promising Poet Award

Other sources of quality poetry for children are books by recipients of a fairly new award given to up-and-coming poets. The Lee Bennett Hopkins Promising Poet Award was established in 1995 by Hopkins along with the International Reading Association to encourage new poets in their writing. Although the award winners cannot have published more than two books, their work has already proved to be of high quality.

As the award's website reports, the Lee Bennett Hopkins Promising Poet Award is a monetary prize given every three years to a promising new author of poetry for children and young adults up to grade 12 who has published no more than two books of children's poetry. A book-length single poem may be submitted. *Children's poetry* is defined as poetry rather than light verse, and the award is for published works only. More information about the award can be found at http://www.reading.org/association/awards/childrens_hopkins.html. Readers, besides enjoying the award winners' current titles, should watch for their future works.

### Recipients of the Lee Bennett Hopkins Promising Poet Award

2004      Lindsay Lee Johnson, for *Soul Moon Soup*

2001      Craig Crist-Evans, for *Moon over Tennessee: A Boy's Civil War Journal*

1998      Kristine O'Connell George, for *The Great Frog Race, and Other Poems*

1995      Deborah Chandra, for *Rich Lizard, and Other Poems*

## *The Lee Bennett Hopkins Award for Children's Poetry*

As we seek out new books of poetry, it is helpful to know about awards for specific titles. The Lee Bennett Hopkins Award for Children's Poetry, established in 1993, is presented annually to an American poet or anthologist for the most outstanding new book of children's poetry published in the previous calendar year. The award is made possible by a gift from Lee Bennett Hopkins himself and is administered by the Pennsylvania State University College of Education and the Pennsylvania State University Libraries. The winning poet or anthologist receives a handsome plaque and a $500 honorarium made possible by Mr. Hopkins, himself a poet and anthologist. In recent years, the committee has also cited several honor books each year. As specified on the award's website, the award shall be granted annually to an anthology of poetry or a single-volume poem published for children in the previous calendar year (per copyright) by a living American poet or anthologist. The criteria state:

> Good poetry is imaginative. It deals with emotion and has significance beyond the act of creation. It uses figurative language, yet is compact in thought and expression. Good poetry has an element of beauty and truth which appears unstable outside of the poem. The

book which wins the Lee Bennett Hopkins Award for Children's Poetry must be accessible to children and its presentation must serve the poem or poems in an attractive and appropriate manner (http://www.pabook.libraries.psu.edu/activities/hopkins/).

---

### Recipients of the Lee Bennett Hopkins Award for Children's Poetry

2005  *Here in Harlem*, by Walter Dean Myers

2004  *The Wishing Bone, and Other Poems*, by Stephen Mitchell

2003  *Splash! Poems of Our Watery World*, by Constance Levy

2002  *Pieces: A Year in Poems and Quilts*, by Anna Grossnickle Hines

2001  *Light-Gathering Poems*, by Liz Rosenberg

2000  *What Have You Lost?* by Naomi Shihab Nye

1999  *The Other Side*, by Angela Johnson

1998  *The Great Frog Race*, by Kristine O'Connell George

1997  *Voices from the Wild*, by David Bouchard

1996  *Dance with Me*, by Barbara Esbensen

1995  *Beast Feast*, by Douglas Florian

1994  *Spirit Walker*, by Nancy Wood

1993  *Sing to the Sun*, by Ashley Bryan

---

## The Claudia Lewis Award

One other well-known poetry award recognizes a single title each year. That is the Claudia Lewis Award, given by Bank Street College in New York. Presented for the first time in 1998, this award honors the late Claudia Lewis, a distinguished children's book expert and longtime member of the Bank Street College faculty and Children's Book Committee. According to the award's website, Lewis conveyed her love and understanding of poetry with humor and grace, and this award is a tribute to her legacy. The award is presented annually for the best poetry book of the year. Given Bank Street College's long and distinguished history in teaching and literature, this award is worth noting.

### Recipients of the Claudia Lewis Award

2003  *The Way a Door Closes*, by Hope Anita Smith, and
       *Yesterday I Had the Blues*, by Jeron Ashford Frame

2002  *Little Dog and Duncan*, by Kristine O'Connell George

2001  *Love That Dog*, by Sharon Creech, and *Amber Was
       Brave, Essie Was Smart*, by Vera B. Williams

2000  *Mammalabilia*, by Douglas Florian

1999  *Stop Pretending*, by Sonya Sones

1998  *I, Too, Sing America*, by Catherine Clinton

1997  *The Invisible Ladder*, edited by Liz Rosenberg

As we strengthen the poetry holdings in our library collections, one extra step that may help patrons find more award-winning poetry is to note the awards a title has received on its circulation records. Such notations can also assist us in compiling bibliographies and recommended reading lists.

As we seek out the best new poetry books for children each year, other sources of recommendations can also be helpful. For example, you can count on the annual Horn Book Fanfare List to identify the poetry titles that the magazine's editors have selected as the year's best in children's literature. In addition, the distinguished journal *Lion and the Unicorn* established its Award for Excellence in North American Poetry in 2005. And we should note the Signal Poetry Award, given in England from 1979 to 2001 for single-poet collections, poetry anthologies, the body of work of a contemporary poet, or a critical or educational activity that promotes poetry for children. The journal *Signal* published an annual article reviewing the state of poetry publishing for the year. The Centre for Literacy in Primary Education in England initiated a new prize for children's poetry in 2003, hoping "the Prize will place children's poetry firmly in the literary limelight, imbuing it with some long overdue prestige and encouraging the growth of a knowledgeable, critical, enthusiastic poetry readership of the future." Those are worthy goals for all of us who care about children's poetry. Other local and regional organizations offer poetry prizes of one kind or another from time to time, too. In fact, there is no reason you cannot initiate your own local celebration and recognition of new poets and poetry books—and even involve children in voting for their favorites.

## Classic Poets

When we look for poetry to share with children we often remember the poems of the past that were shared with us in our own childhoods. Many of us have fond memories of hearing classic poems read aloud by loving family members. We may even be able to recite "Jabberwocky," by Lewis Carroll, or "The Swing," by Robert Louis Stevenson, or "Eletelephony," by Laura E. Richards without missing a beat. Or we may recall the poetry anthologies of Walter de la Mare, Robert Graves, or Charles Causley with great fondness. These are further reminders of how powerful an enthusiastic model of reading can be in fostering a love of poetry. Unfortunately, the opposite is also true. For some people, classic poems conjure up memories of forced memorization or puzzled analysis. Classic poems may seem abstract or old fashioned. But this need not be the case. For example, books such as A. A. Milne's *When We Were Very Young* and Robert Louis Stevenson's *A Child's Garden of Verses* are still in print and include poems of childhood experiences that kids today can still relate to.

## Classic Poems Worth Sharing

Many classic poems are still popular with young people. The subject matter, language, rhythm, and imagery of these poems are still inviting for today's

---

### PRACTITIONER PERSPECTIVE

A poem should have an impact on you. You should be moved in some way by experiencing it. This impact is what I am always searching for in any form of art, whether it be a poem, a song, a movie, or a painting. But the fascinating thing about art is that what makes an impression on one person may not make an impression on another person. Art is such a personal thing.

This is why I believe that offering students the opportunity to make their own selections as often as possible for arts-related assignments and activities is of critical importance. If we want to turn kids on to a variety of art forms, we should not force feed them what we think is good without letting them discover what they personally appreciate.

Amy Autin Nolan
Teacher
Medlin Middle School
Trophy Club, Texas

readers and listeners. Most of the selections below continue to be included in current anthologies of popular children's poetry.

## *Twenty Classic Poems Not to Be Missed*

William Blake, "The Tyger"

Gwendolyn Brooks, "We Real Cool"

Lewis Carroll, "Jabberwocky"

Emily Dickinson, Poem: 288, "I'm Nobody! Who Are You?"

Eugene Field, "Wynken, Blynken, and Nod"

Robert Frost, "Stopping by Woods"

Langston Hughes, "Dreams"

Rudyard Kipling, "If"

Edward Lear, "The Owl and the Pussycat"

Henry Wadsworth Longfellow, "Paul Revere's Ride"

A. A. Milne, "If I Were King"

Clement Moore, "A Visit from St. Nicholas"

Ogden Nash, "The Tale of Custard the Dragon"

Laura E. Richards, "Eletelephony"

Christina Rossetti, "The Wind"

Carl Sandburg, "Fog"

Robert Louis Stevenson, "My Shadow"

Edna St. Vincent Millay, "Afternoon on a Hill"

Ernest Thayer, "Casey at the Bat"

Walt Whitman, "O Captain! My Captain!"

Classic poems are often available in picture book format, which can provide fresh, new interpretations of these familiar verses and make them even more accessible for younger readers. Susan Jeffers, for example, illustrated the Robert Frost poem "Stopping by Woods" in a beautiful picture book. The Thayer poem "Casey at the Bat" has been illustrated several times over, most recently by Christopher Bing, whose version won Caldecott honors. Both Jan Brett and James Marshall created unique visions of Lear's "The Owl and the Pussycat" in picture book form. Quentin Blake reinterpreted Ogden Nash and Lewis Carroll, among others, in *The Penguin Book of Nonsense Verse*. Many, many versions of "A Visit from St. Nicholas," often known as "The Night

Before Christmas," are available from a variety of illustrators and retellers. Kids Can Press has recently initiated their graphic Visions in Poetry series, "classic verse through the eyes of outstanding contemporary artists in handsomely bound collectable hardcover editions," beginning with *Jabberwocky*, illustrated by Stéphane Jorisch.

As much as I enjoy many classic works, I admit that I do not usually choose them first when I introduce poetry to children. It may seem counterintuitive since we usually begin with what we are familiar with, but I have found that children respond more immediately to the humor and relevance of contemporary poetry. I find that once I lay the groundwork with poems about school, homework, siblings, and the like, the door is open to a greater and greater variety of poetic styles, formats, and voices.

## Anthologists

Knowing which individual poets to look for is very helpful, but in this genre, anthologies are also essential, particularly for showcasing the work of new, up-and-coming poets whose work may not yet be published individually. Poetry anthologies have long been a staple of libraries, enabling us to use a single resource for a variety of purposes. In the past, anthologies were often large collections of three hundred pages or more, full of poems in small print, with few or no illustrations. They were often intended for adults to read out loud to children and not for children themselves. That has changed. Most poetry anthologies published today are slimmer volumes gathered around topics of particular interest to children and are richly illustrated.

Several anthologists have established excellent reputations for compiling numerous high-quality collections of poetry for children. Most have also published volumes of their own poetry and are known as both poets and anthologists. The popular Jack Prelutsky has compiled several anthologies in addition to volumes of his own work, including the very successful *Random House Collection of Poetry*. The NCTE Poetry Award winner Myra Cohn Livingston has many published works of her own as well as poetry anthologies and resource guides for adults on the art of poetry. *Knock at a Star*, a combination poetry anthology and instructional guide by husband-and-wife team X. J. and Dorothy Kennedy, is considered a standard. Former English teacher Paul Janeczko has created many anthologies particularly for teens as well as several excellent guidebooks for aspiring poets, such as *Seeing the Blue Between*. Lee Bennett Hopkins may be the most prolific anthologist of all, with a variety of collections gathered on topics interesting to kids (e.g., *Dinosaurs*) and friendly to teachers (e.g., *Marvelous Math*). And for many humorous collections, you can rely on the anthologies of Bruce Lansky or William Cole. Even multicultural and international poetry anthologies are available, compiled by such stellar names as Arnold Adoff, Joseph Bruchac, Ashley Bryan, Naomi Shihab Nye, Neil Philip, and Michael Rosen. Each of these anthologists has created several outstanding poetry collections full of the work of many different poets. Such books provide a helpful assortment of many poems in one spot and can lead to more in-depth study of individual books by individual poets.

### *Poetry Anthologists: A Baker's Dozen*

| | |
|---|---|
| Arnold Adoff | Bruce Lansky |
| Joseph Bruchac | Myra Cohn Livingston |
| Ashley Bryan | Naomi Shihab Nye |
| William Cole | Neil Philip |
| Lee Bennett Hopkins | Michael Rosen |
| Paul Janeczko | Charles Sullivan |
| X. J. and Dorothy Kennedy | |

## Poets from Many Cultures

In the United States today, more poetry is being published for young people by a larger variety of poets than at any time in the past. Not only is poetry experiencing a publishing renaissance, but also the field's openness to new voices has encouraged multicultural poetry to flourish. A quick survey of recent poetry titles will turn up at least thirty-five notable poets of color writing for children today, representing most of the main micro-cultures within the United States. And more and more international poetry is finding its way into libraries and classrooms in the United States as well.

The diverse viewpoints reflected in the poetry of parallel cultures enable us to show children firsthand both the sameness and the differences that make the human landscape so dynamic and fascinating. Poets of color are using the language, experiences, and images of their cultures in ways that are fresh and powerful (Vardell 2005). In addition, the special succinctness of poetry provides young people with an appealing introduction to other cultures. Powerful points about prejudice, identity, and cultural conflict can sometimes be made in a very few words. Consider Janet Wong's poem "Speak Up," from *Good Luck*

*Gold*, whose language and structure suggest the playground taunting of a child who appears different. In addition, we can often rediscover our universality in the words and feelings of poems that cross cultural boundaries. Langston Hughes's poems in *The Dreamkeeper* show human emotions and experiences that are real and vivid, no matter what color a person's skin is. I have found that young people of all colors enjoy the writing of poets from many parallel cultures. That is to say, poets do not speak only to readers from their own cultures. Asian American readers have understood "I, Too," by Langston Hughes, an African American poet, and Native American readers have related to "Speak Up," by Janet Wong, an Asian American poet. The fact that cultural heritage and the distinctiveness of language are addressed through poetry is interesting and important to all young people. Fortunately, more and more excellent examples of multicultural poetry are available for sharing.

## African American Poetry for Young People

Although rarely anthologized in the past, African American poets like Langston Hughes, Lucille Clifton, Countee Cullen, Paul Laurence Dunbar, Nikki Giovanni, Gwendolyn Brooks, Marilyn Nelson, and others are regularly featured in collections of American poetry for young people today. And anthologies of African American poetry are now available for children and young adults, including *My Black Me: A Beginning Book of Black Poetry*, compiled by Arnold Adoff; *Ashley Bryan's ABC of African American Poetry*; *Pass It On: African American Poetry for Children*, compiled by Wade Hudson; and *I, Too, Sing America: Three Centuries of African American Poetry*, compiled by Catherine Clinton.

More and more African American poets are gaining widespread recognition and praise. Eloise Greenfield won the National Council of Teachers of English Poetry Award for her lifetime contribution to poetry for children, including the popular collection *Honey, I Love*. Nikki Grimes creates an unforgettable modern heroine in *Meet Danitra Brown*. Walter Dean Myers combines antique photographs with original descriptive verses, as in *Brown Angels*. These poets speak of their lives, of their color, of their humanity, of their humor. Some write in dialect, some use rhyme, some focus on racial pride, some share emotional universals. Children of all cultural backgrounds deserve to know their names and hear their words.

## Latino and Latina Poetry for Young People

Poems, rhymes, songs, and chants are also an important part of Hispanic American or Latino (Latina) children's literature. There are also more and more published collections of Latino poetry for children from which to share. Gary Soto, for example, has several collections of poetry suitable for children and teens, such as *Canto Familiar*. His work may already be familiar to children who have read his picture books and novels. In addition, many Latino poets tackle powerful social themes about identity, language, and culture, as in *Here Is My Kingdom*, compiled by Charles Sullivan, or *The Tree Is Older Than You Are*, compiled by Naomi Shihab Nye. There are also several bilingual and interlingual (with Spanish words interspersed) collections of poetry available by poets such as Francisco Alarcón (e.g., *Poems to Dream Together / Poemas para Sonar Juntos*), Lori Carlson (*Red Hot Salsa*), Lulu Delacre (*Arrorro Mi Nino: Latino Lullabies and Gentle Games*), and Pat Mora (*Confetti*). Each of these poets has authored several works worth noting. If you are a Spanish speaker or work with Spanish-speaking children, reading poems aloud in both Spanish and English can be very inviting and empowering. Several collections of children's nursery rhymes and songs in English and Spanish are available

---

### PRACTITIONER PERSPECTIVE

I think that out of all the varieties of multicultural poetry, Hispanic and Latin American poetry have to be my favorites. I do not know if it is the poetry's language, or its take on life, but it is so vibrant! I also think that it is vital to use bilingual poetry in our classrooms—whether you teach Spanish speakers or not. The two-way writing in Spanish and English that is available in most Spanish poetry books is a great way either to introduce something new and different to English-only speakers or to help ease an otherwise rocky transition for Spanish speakers. Many teachers I know hesitate to read the Spanish versions aloud for fear that they will mess up. However, when I taught in a bilingual classroom (and no, my Spanish is not proficient), I loved trying to read Spanish the best I could. The kids would very willingly help me out with words I could not pronounce. Then we would switch roles and I would help them get through the English translation. So, if you are slightly leery of bilingual books and poetry or do not think that you have a place in your class or library curriculum for them— take a chance! If you yourself are uncomfortable reading Spanish poetry aloud, invite fluent Spanish speakers, whether they are older kids, parents, or friends, into the classroom or library as guest readers. Everyone will benefit!

Lauren Yarbrough
Reading Specialist
Calvin Bledsoe Elementary School
Frisco, Texas

for sharing with young children. They include *¡Pio peep! Traditional Spanish Nursery Rhymes*, by Alma Flor Ada and Isabel Campoy, and *Diez Deditos: Ten Little Fingers, and Other Play Rhymes and Action Songs from Latin America*, by José-Luis Orozco. The verses in those two books incorporate music and movement that invite children to participate. What an opportunity to introduce poetry, language, and culture at the same time.

## Asian Pacific American Poetry for Young People

When it comes to sharing poetry by Asian Pacific American writers, there are also several choices. Asian and Asian American poets express a deep appreciation for nature in much of their poetry for young people. Other poems explore the tensions between traditional and modern ways. Family traditions and beliefs are also the focus of many poems by contemporary Asian American writers. For example, Janet Wong's recent collection *Knock on Wood* looks at superstitions across cultures, including in her own Korean and Chinese heritage. Minfong Ho shares ancient Chinese poetry in the beautifully illustrated collection *Maples in the Mist: Poems for Children from the Tang Dynasty*, which is also available in a bilingual edition. And for bilingual Japanes/English poetry, look for the lovely collections by Michio Mado, *The Animals* and *The Magic Pocket*, both illustrated with traditional paper cuts. Or for an interesting twist, share *Cool Melons Turn to Frogs: The Life and Poems of Issa*, by Matthew Gollub, a picture book that is half biography and half haiku. Although most of these particular Asian and Asian American poems are not rhyming, children are still drawn to their simplicity and clarity.

## Native American Poetry for Young People

In many Native American or American Indian cultures, the rituals and traditions, stories and songs of everyday life are often expressed poetically. Many contemporary Native American poets consider their poetry a continuation of the oral narrative tradition of their people and heritage. This can be seen in many Native American poems about the seasons, historical events, and the like. Joseph Bruchac, for example, has published several poem collections that capture elements of land, animals, and nature, such as *The Earth under Sky Bear's Feet* and *Thirteen Moons on Turtle's Back*. Bruchac tries to incorporate Native words (from the poem's root culture) within the translated poems to provide some of the music and rhythm of the original language for the non-Native speaker. Bruchac often performs these poems aloud to the beat of a drum—a powerful auditory experience. Native poetry can include a variety of poetic forms, including rhymes, free verse, chants, charms, prayers, blessings, lullabies, warnings, eulogies, wishes, prophecies, healings, war chants, songs, night songs, medicine songs, mother/child poems, and more. John Bierhorst has compiled several collections of Native poetry, including *On the Road of Stars: Native American Night Poems and Sleep Charms*. Other examples of authentic voices can be found in Hettie Jones's collection *The Tree Stands Shining: Poetry of the North American Indian* and Virginia Driving Hawk Sneve's *Dancing Teepees: Poems of American Indian Youth*. A resource of contemporary Native poetry is *Rising Voices: Writings of Young Native Americans*. Just a reminder: some Native poetry may be presented in translations filtered through a non-Native perspective, so seek out works by Native poets whenever possible.

## International Poetry for Young People

Translation is also an issue in international poetry for young people. More and more international poets are now being published in the United States and translated into English. Remember, however, that poems that may have rhymed in German, for example, may no longer rhyme in their translated English versions. Or the translator may have opted to create rhyming patterns in English that affect the meaning in the original language. Thus, translated poems may not be as rhythmic and musical as the rhyming English poems children are used to. For more strongly rhythmic poetry, start with our neighbors to the north and south. There are several collections of poems from the Caribbean available by poets such as Monica Gunning, Lynn Joseph, John Agard, and Grace Nichols (e.g., *A Caribbean Dozen*) that are very appealing. The humorous work of Canadian poet Dennis Lee (e.g., *The Ice Cream Store*) is often compared to that of Shel Silverstein. Looking farther abroad, one finds that Michael Rosen has compiled many collections of British and other verse from a variety of countries (e.g., *The Kingfisher Book of Children's Poetry*). And Naomi Shihab Nye has gathered anthologies of international poetry with English translations, such as *This Same Sky: A Collection of Poems from Around the World* or *The Space between Our Footsteps: Poems and Paintings from the Middle East*. Sharing poems from around the world can help bring us all a little closer together.

Multicultural poetry, much like all forms of literature, is written as an individual response to personal, social, economic, or environmental conditions. It reflects a distinct point of view as well as a specific time and place. And, from a personal perspective, multicultural poetry offers each of us the opportunity to connect: to connect to the poem, to connect with the poet, and to connect with each other as readers. The best approach is to infuse all our poetry sharing with multicultural and international poets whenever and wherever the theme, subject, style, form, or topic suggests a connection. Multicultural poems are not just for cultural history months or special occasions but speak to every possible moment.

## Meet the Poets: Fifty Names to Know

In survey after survey, we find nearly every library holds multiple copies of Shel Silverstein's poetry collections. His work is a staple of children's poetry and has now been enjoyed by several decades of children. Jack Prelutsky follows as a close second in most library collections. His zany humor and musical rhythms continue to engage children. But that is where the list often stops. In my research on the poetry holdings of school and public libraries, I have found that poetry collection development is often spotty and inconsistent. Many people are unfamiliar with poetry awards, with contemporary poets writing for children today, and with multicultural poets in particular. What follows is a brief introduction to fifty poets whose work for children is worth buying, reading, collecting, and sharing. Just a bit of background information is shared along with a sampling of their work. Most of these poets have personal websites, and more poets' sites are added regularly. And of course new poets are emerging all the time. Once your radar is tuned to poetry, you will find wonderful poetry books and poets popping up in many places.

### Arnold Adoff
http://www.arnoldadoff.com

Arnold Adoff became the eighth winner of the NCTE Award for Excellence in Poetry for Children in 1988 and is recognized as one of the champions of multiculturalism in American literature for children. His poems are marked by the innovative use of shape, playfulness with the mechanics of language, and frequently strong social conscience, as seen in his groundbreaking anthology *My Black Me: A Beginning Book of Black Poetry* and his own recent work, such as *Touch the Poem* or *Love Letters*.

### Francisco X. Alarcón

Francisco X. Alarcón is probably best known for his four season-based picture book anthologies in Spanish and English: *Laughing Tomatoes, and Other Spring Poems / Jitomates risuenos y otros poemas de primavera*, *From the Belly-button of the Moon, and Other Summer Poems / Del ombligo de la luna y otros poemas de verano*, *Angels Ride Bikes, and Other Fall Poems / Los angeles andan en bicicleta y otros poemas de otoño*, and *Iguanas in the Snow, and*

*Other Winter Poems / Iguanas en la nieve y otros poemas de invierno*. His meta-phorical poetry captures personal memories as well as childhood experiences.

## Kathi Appelt
http://www.kathiappelt.com

For a unique poetic format, look for Kathi Appelt's book *My Father's Summers: A Daughter's Memoirs*. These sensitive prose poems depict a young girl's experience in a divided family through a scrapbook of photos and poetic vignettes. Her *Poems from Homeroom: A Writer's Place to Start* is also a unique resource for young people who want to know how poets work.

## Brod Bagert
http://www.brodbagert.com

Brod Bagert is the author of several collections written specifically for children to perform, including *Let Me Be . . . the Boss: Poems for Kids to Perform*, *The Gooch*

---

### PRACTITIONER PERSPECTIVE

We have several books by Francisco X. Alarcón in our classroom. His books have been exciting to have because aside from being so beautifully illustrated, they have wonderful poems written in both Spanish and English. I have five students who are learning English. Two of them speak almost no English. Just like the rest of my students, these two boys love to sign up for poetry breaks. For the first several months of school, they could choose a buddy and share a poem in Spanish and then have their buddy read the same poem in English. Now they are familiar enough with the poems that they can read them in English, too. All of the other children in the class enjoy practicing and reading poems in Spanish. Alarcón has a terrific imagination that has been especially appealing to my second and third graders. He writes about tomatoes laughing, chiles that explode, and tortillas that applaud the sun. He also writes about his grandmother's songs, pets that he has owned, and children who have worked in the fields. He honors his mother in many of his poems and shares that she is the one who taught him that with hard work and education his dreams would come true. He is definitely one of the favorite poets to read in our classroom!

Nicki Blake
Grades 2 / 3 Multiage Teacher
Tapteal Elementary School
West Richland, Washington

*Machine: Poems for Children to Perform*, and *Chicken Socks, and Other Contagious Poems*. His outrageous humor and shout-out rhymes are nearly irresistible.

### Calef Brown
http://www.calefbrown.com

Both author and illustrator, Calef Brown's picture book poem collections are billed as stories and have been compared to the nonsensical narratives of Edward Lear. Look for *Polkabats and Octopus Slacks: 14 Stories* and *Dutch Sneakers and Flea Keepers: 14 More Stories*.

### Joseph Bruchac
http://www.josephbruchac.com

Of Abenaki descent, Joseph Bruchac is a storyteller, editor, educator, publisher, and writer of many genres, including poetry for young people. Most notable are *The Earth under Sky Bear's Feet*, *Thirteen Moons on Turtle's Back*, and *The Circle of Thanks*, all richly illustrated picture books with a strong, serious tone.

### John Ciardi

John Ciardi became the sixth winner of the NCTE Award for Excellence in Poetry for Children in 1982. His many intelligent and witty poetry books for children include *You Know Who*, *The Monster Den*, and *Someone Could Win a Polar Bear*, each illustrated by Edward Gorey. In studies of children's poetry preferences, Ciardi's poem "Mummy Slept Late and Daddy Cooked Breakfast," from *You Read to Me, I'll Read to You*, is often listed as the favorite.

### Kalli Dakos
http://www.kallidakos.com

The subject of school is the central focus of Kalli Dakos's poetry, and children find the topic equal parts painful and hilarious through her work. In addition, Dakos employs a great variety of poetic forms and voices that lend themselves to varied choral performance techniques. See, for example, *If You're Not Here, Please Raise Your Hand: Poems about School* or her more recent work, *Put Your Eyes up Here, and Other School Poems*.

### Rebecca Kai Dotlich

Rebecca Kai Dotlich's gentle and lyrical collections include *Lemonade Sun, and Other Summer Poems*, *When Riddles Come Rumbling: Poems to Ponder*, *In the*

*Spin of Things: Poetry of Motion*, and *Over in the Pink House: New Jump-Rope Rhymes*. Her use of personification, in particular, is fresh and compelling and expressed exactly in terms children understand.

## Barbara Esbensen

Barbara Esbensen became the tenth winner of the NCTE Award for Excellence in Poetry for Children in 1994. Her poetry collections incorporate strong imagery, fresh perspectives, and deft use of language. Her focus on animals and nature is particularly appealing in such books as *Echoes for the Eye: Poems to Celebrate Patterns in Nature*, *Who Shrank My Grandmother's House? Poems of Discovery*, and *Words with Wrinkled Knees*.

## Aileen Fisher

Aileen Fisher became the second winner of the NCTE Award for Excellence in Poetry for Children in 1978. For a recent compilation of some of Fisher's most popular poems, look for *I Heard a Bluebird Sing*. This volume features forty-one Fisher poems chosen by children along with excerpts of interviews with and articles by Fisher about her life and work. Her simplicity and directness shine through her poems, which often reflect a childlike point of view about the natural world.

## Paul Fleischman
http://www.paulfleischman.net

Paul Fleischman is one of the few writers to win a Newbery Medal for a work of poetry, *Joyful Noise: Poems for Two Voices*. This distinctive format was preceded by another collection, *I Am Phoenix: Poems for Two Voices*. Fleischman followed these with a collection of poems for more voices, *Big Talk: Poems for Four Voices*.

## Ralph Fletcher
http://www.ralphfletcher.com

Ralph Fletcher's recent work, *A Writing Kind of Day: Poems for Young Poets*, offers advice poems for young people who want to express themselves through poetry writing. Pair this with his nonfiction work for young writers, *Poetry Matters: Writing a Poem from the Inside Out*.

## Douglas Florian
http://www.douglasflorian.com

The poems of artist and poet Douglas Florian often focus on the animal world, as in *Insectlopedia* or *Mammaliabilia*. However, his longer collections, such as in *Bing, Bang, Boing* or *Laugheteria*, include a variety of topics from the simple to the sublime. He uses large doses of humor for his descriptive poetry as well as very clever wordplay and puns. His growing body of work also includes lovely collections reflecting on the seasons, as in *Winter Eyes* and *Summersaults*.

## Kristine O'Connell George
http://www.kristinegeorge.com

Kristine O'Connell George burst onto the poetry scene by winning the Lee Bennett Hopkins Promising Poet Award for her first book, *The Great Frog Race, and Other Poems*. She continued to explore the natural world in fresh and playful imagery and rhymes in subsequent works: *Old Elm Speaks: Tree Poems*, *Toasting Marshmallows: Camping Poems*, and *Hummingbird Nest: A Journal of Poems*. A recent work, *Fold Me a Poem*, pairs crystallized descriptions of animals with their images in origami, the Japanese art of paper folding.

## Nikki Giovanni
http://nikki-giovanni.com

Nikki Giovanni is a poet who has established a notable reputation as a writer for adults, but several of her works are also embraced by young people. Among those books are *Spin a Soft Black Song*, *Vacation Time: Poems for Children*, and *The Sun Is So Quiet*, each of which addresses issues of race and culture in equal measure with experiences and observations of childhood and family life.

## Joan Bransfield Graham
http://www.joangraham.com

Joan Bransfield Graham's poetry books are wonderful examples of shape, or concrete, poetry, in which the words of a poem are laid out on the page to suggest the poem's subject. In both *Flicker Flash* and *Splish Splash*, the graphic illustrations combine with the verbal descriptions of water or light in their many, varied forms.

## Eloise Greenfield

Eloise Greenfield became the eleventh winner of the NCTE Award for Excellence in Poetry for Children in 1997. Her first book of poetry, *Honey, I Love*, has become a modern-day classic. Her poetry reflects the cultural experience of growing up African American, but her themes reach out to all children, as in *Nathaniel Talking* and *Night on Neighborhood Street*.

## Nikki Grimes
http://www.nikkigrimes.com

Born and raised in New York City, Nikki Grimes is the creator of picture book poetry collections featuring the proud and spunky character Danitra Brown: *Meet Danitra Brown*, *Danitra Brown Leaves Town*, and *Danitra Brown, Class Clown*. Grimes has won Coretta Scott King honors multiple times and has also received recognition for works such as *Hopscotch Love*, *My Man Blue*, and *Shoe Magic*, among others.

## Georgia Heard

A frequent speaker and visiting poet in schools around the world, Georgia Heard writes both insightful professional resources for adults, such as *For the Good of the Earth and Sun: Teaching Poetry* and *Awakening the Heart: Exploring Poetry in Elementary and Middle School*, and beautiful, serious poetry for young people, such as *Creatures of Earth, Sea, and Sky*. Her work includes original nature poems, many for two voices, and *This Place I Know: Poems of Comfort*, an anthology created to commemorate the attacks on the United States on September 11, 2001.

## Mary Ann Hoberman
http://www.maryannhoberman.com

In 2003 Mary Ann Hoberman became the thirteenth winner of the NCTE Award for Excellence in Poetry for Children. Hoberman's poetry often targets our youngest audience with rhythm and repetition and is usually published in picture book form or as read-aloud rhyming stories such as in *You Read to Me, I'll Read to You: Very Short Fairy Tales to Read Together*. Other inviting collections include *Fathers, Mothers, Sisters, Brothers: A Collection of Family Poems* and *My Song Is Beautiful: Poems and Pictures in Many Voices*.

## Sara Holbrook
http://www.saraholbrook.com

Few poets address the emotional roller coaster of the tween years better than Sara Holbrook. Her collection *By Definition: Poems of Feelings* pulls from several earlier works. In addition, she offers advice to young poem performers in *Wham! It's a Poetry Jam: Discovering Performance Poetry*.

## Lee Bennett Hopkins

Lee Bennett Hopkins has over one hundred books of poetry and books about poetry to his credit as a writer and anthologist. Hopkins has also nurtured many new talents in poetry, commissioning up-and-coming poets to write poems for anthologies he compiles. A few of his recent titles include *Good Books, Good Times*; *Spectacular Science: A Book of Poems*; *Opening Days: Sports Poems*; *My America: A Poetry Atlas of the United States*; and *Days to Celebrate: A Full Year of Poetry, People, Holidays, History, Fascinating Facts, and More.*

## Paul Janeczko
http://www.pauljaneczko.com

Besides his several guides for aspiring poetry writers, such as *Poetry from A to Z: A Guide to Young Writers*, Paul Janeczko has created or compiled many innovative poetry collections, including *A Poke in the I: A Collection of Concrete Poems*, *A Kick in the Head: An Everyday Guide to Poetic Forms*, and *Stone Bench in an Empty Park.*

## X. J. Kennedy
http://www.xjanddorothymkennedy.com

X. J. Kennedy became the twelfth winner of the NCTE Award for Excellence in Poetry for Children in 2000. Kennedy, known for his cagey sense of humor and witty wordplay, writes poems that are fun to read out loud to eager audiences. His collection *Exploding Gravy: Poems to Make You Laugh* is a compilation of a quarter century of some of his most humorous poems. He and his wife, Dorothy, compiled a child's guide to poetry, *Knock at a Star*, which presents an engaging introduction to the elements of poetry as well as nearly two hundred poems.

## Karla Kuskin
http://www.karlakuskin.com

In 1979 Karla Kuskin became the third winner of the NCTE Award for Excellence in Poetry for Children. Her pictures and poetry are brimming over with the experiences of children growing up in a big city. For a wonderful compilation of poems from several previous works as well as new poems, look for *Moon, Have You Met My Mother? The Collected Poems of Karla Kuskin.* And if you have a copy of *Dogs and Dragons, Trees and Dreams*, you will see that Kuskin often provides a brief note before a poem to explain where she got her inspiration for writing it.

## J. Patrick Lewis
http://www.jpatricklewis.com

With over fifty books of poetry in print or coming out soon, J. Patrick Lewis is a prolific specialist in thematic collections in picture book form. His narrative poems have strong rhythm and clever wordplay. Just a few popular examples include *Ridicholas Nicholas: More Animal Poems*, *The Bookworm's Feast: A Potluck of Poems*, *A World of Wonders: Geographic Travels in Verse and Rhyme*, and *Please Bury Me in the Library*.

## Myra Cohn Livingston

Myra Cohn Livingston became the fourth winner of the NCTE Award for Excellence in Poetry for Children in 1980. She was a giant in the field of children's poetry who authored many works about poetry writing (e.g., *Poem-Making: Ways to Begin Writing Poetry*) and inspired and taught many of today's emerging poets. Her nurturing of children's sensitivity and awareness of the world around them is apparent in such works as *A Circle of Seasons*, *Celebrations*, *Festivals*, and *Space Songs*.

## David McCord

David McCord was the winner of the first NCTE Award for Excellence in Poetry for Children in 1977. He was noted for his creative, rhythmic, and often whimsical poems. He invented a new style, symmetrics, a five-line verse form attributed to him by the *American Heritage Dictionary*. He wrote more than five hundred poems and was the author or editor of more than fifty books, such as *Every Time I Climb a Tree*, which contains many of his most popular poems for children, including "The Pickety Fence."

## Eve Merriam

Eve Merriam was the winner of the fifth NCTE Award for Excellence in Poetry for Children in 1981. Her work is playful and lively and explores language through word origins. Check your library shelves for two of her classic collections, *It Doesn't Always Have to Rhyme* and *There Is No Rhyme for Silver*, as well as more contemporary collections, such as *You Be Good and I'll Be Night*, and many rhyming picture books.

## Lilian Moore

Lilian Moore was the winner of the seventh NCTE Award for Excellence in Poetry for Children in 1985. She was a teacher, a reading specialist, and the editor at Scholastic who established the Arrow Book Club. Her accessible poetic work encourages children to wonder and imagine, as in *I'm Small, and Other Verses* and *Sunflakes: Poems for Children*.

## Pat Mora
http://www.patmora.com

Pat Mora is an award-winning author of poetry, nonfiction, and children's picture books. Many of her works are written in two languages (English interwoven with Spanish words and phrases) and draw on themes from her life experience as a bilingual, bicultural woman from the Southwestern desert. She has received critical acclaim for such works as *Uno Dos Tres / One, Two, Three*; *Confetti: Poems for Children*; and the compilation *Love to Mama: A Tribute to Mothers*.

## Walter Dean Myers

You may not know that award-winning author Walter Dean Myers is a collector of antique photographs, which led to his first poetry collections: *Brown Angels: An Album of Pictures and Verse*, *Glorious Angels*, and *Angel to Angel*. More recently he has collaborated with his illustrator son on the vivid collage poem picture books *Harlem* and *Blues Journey*.

## Naomi Shihab Nye

Naomi Shihab Nye has a gift for bringing together poets from many paths. She has compiled several distinctive anthologies that include poetry from around the world, such as *This Same Sky: A Collection of Poems from Around the World*, *The Tree Is Older Than You Are: A Bilingual Gathering of Poems and Stories from Mexico*, and *The Space between Our Footsteps: Poems and Paintings from the Middle East*. Her own work is also quite powerful and respectful of children's appetite for both light and serious themes, as in *Come with Me: Poems for a Journey*.

## Susan Pearson

Susan Pearson compiled her first anthology of bedtime poetry, *The Drowsy Hours*, after twenty years of fiction writing and editing. She loved working with poetry so much that she went on to write her own collection titled *Squeal and Squawk: Barnyard Talk*. New works include *Grimericks* and *Who Swallowed Harold? and Other Poems about Pets*.

## Jack Prelutsky

Jack Prelutsky is a prolific writer who has many collections of poetry to his credit, including anthologies of other poets' works, such as *The Random House Book of Poetry for Children*, *Read-Aloud Rhymes for the Very Young*, and *The 20th-Century Children's Poetry Treasury*. Do not miss his comprehensive poem collections, *The New Kid on the Block*, *Something Big Has Been Here*, and *A Pizza the Size of the Sun*, in addition to his many topical collections, such as *Tyrannosaurus Was a Beast: Dinosaur Poems*.

— POET PROFILE —

## Jack Prelutsky

### *In his own words:*

I get letters from kids that say, "Hi, Jack." They don't say "Mr. Prelutsky," they say, "You must have been writing about my brother," or "How did you know I did this?" I write about what's real to them. When I was a kid, I was subjected to poems about hills and daffodils, which is fine, and there's a place for that, but I was not interested in that sort of thing. I wanted to hear poems about other kids like me and about sports, monsters, dinosaurs, outer space, and weird people—silly things. That's what I write about. I really try to stay in touch with the child I used to be. In all of us are those children that we were, and hopefully remain, in some ways.

It's tough being a kid. People are telling you what to do. Grown-ups are always bossing you around. Life is very earnest and difficult. Bigger kids pick on you. Teachers tell you what to do; you have homework, you have tests. You need a friend to help you see the funny side of all the things that are happening to you. So the humor comes from real experiences. Sometimes I get completely silly and talk about a teacher that's covered with mashed potatoes or something. There's a place for that, too.

Sometimes when I visit the kids and see lights go on in heads, that's a reward. But, it's also that feeling of self-worth, knowing that I'm doing

"In his own words" excerpted from S. M. Vardell, "An Interview with Poet Jack Prelutsky," *New Advocate* 4, no. 2 (1991): 101–11. Used with permission from the author and from Christopher Gordon, Inc.

something that makes a difference, that may change the way some kids will grow up. It's getting to meet so many thousands and thousands of people, many of them children, who tell me they love my poems. And it's also a certain feeling knowing that those wonderful nonsensical things that have always run around in my brain actually have some value in the real world! I think I'm very lucky in that I'm able to make a reasonable living doing exactly what I want to do, what I love to do, and don't have to compromise. There are a lot of rewards—there's the reward of walking into almost any library or bookstore in America and seeing my books. Of all these things though, I think it's knowing that you're bringing these values home, and that what you do makes a difference. It can make a difference for a long time; someday somebody not yet born may do something incredible because they read your poems.

### Bleezer's Ice Cream
#### by Jack Prelutsky

I am Ebenezer Bleezer,
I run BLEEZER'S ICE CREAM STORE,
there are flavors in my freezer
you have never seen before,
twenty-eight divine creations
too delicious to resist,
why not do yourself a favor,
try the flavors on my list:

COCOA MOCHA MACARONI
TAPIOCA SMOKED BALONEY
CHECKERBERRY CHEDDAR CHEW
CHICKEN CHERRY HONEYDEW
TUTTI-FRUTTI STEWED TOMATO
TUNA TACO BAKED POTATO
LOBSTER LITCHI LIMA BEAN

MOZZARELLA MANGOSTEEN
ALMOND HAM MERINGUE SALAMI
YAM ANCHOVY PRUNE PASTRAMI
SASSAFRAS SOUVLAKI HASH
SUKIYAKI SUCCOTASH
BUTTER BRICKLE PEPPER PICKLE
POMEGRANATE PUMPERNICKEL
PEACH PIMENTO PIZZA PLUM
PEANUT PUMPKIN BUBBLEGUM
BROCCOLI BANANA BLUSTER
CHOCOLATE CHOP SUEY CLUSTER
AVOCADO BRUSSELS SPROUT
PERIWINKLE SAUERKRAUT
COTTON CANDY CARROT CUSTARD
CAULIFLOWER COLA MUSTARD
ONION DUMPLING DOUBLE DIP
TURNIP TRUFFLE TRIPLE FLIP
GARLIC GUMBO GRAVY GUAVA
LENTIL LEMON LIVER LAVA
ORANGE OLIVE BAGEL BEET
WATERMELON WAFFLE WHEAT

I am Ebenezer Bleezer,
I run BLEEZER'S ICE CREAM STORE,
taste a flavor from my freezer,
you will surely ask for more.

*"Bleezer's Ice Cream" is fun to read aloud (and is read aloud by Prelutsky on his CD of* The New Kid on the Block*) with a leader/narrator reading the beginning and ending stanzas, and individual or pairs of children each taking one of the crazy ice cream flavor lines. To follow up, make two-dimensional paper ice cream cones, pile them high with multicolored scoops of ice cream, and label the scoops with new wacky flavors that the children themselves invent.*

## Alice Schertle

Alice Schertle is both wickedly smart and wryly funny, as you will see in her picture books and collections such as *How Now, Brown Cow?* poems from a cow's perspective; *A Lucky Thing*, partly about barn life and partly about poetry writing; and *Advice for a Frog*, an introduction to exotic or endangered animals.

## Carol Diggory Shields

Carol Diggory Shields's poetry collections are full of her views on kids and classrooms. She looks at the funny side of life and learning in works such as *Lunch Money, and Other Poems about School* and its sequel, *Almost Late to School, and More School Poems*. Two recent collections are ideal for pairing with the school curriculum: *BrainJuice: American History, Fresh Squeezed!* and *BrainJuice: Science, Fresh Squeezed!*

## Joyce Sidman
http://www.joycesidman.com

Joyce Sidman is a new poet whose writing has a lovely focus on the natural world. Her most recent collections include *The World according to Dog: Poems and Teen Voices* and *Song of the Water Boatman, and Other Pond Poems*, sensitive depictions of animal life in verse.

## Shel Silverstein
http://www.shelsilverstein.com

Surveys of children's preferences as well as bookselling statistics confirm that

---

**PRACTITIONER PERSPECTIVE**

I am very disappointed that I did not introduce poetry earlier in the year. Now it is so exciting to see the students wanting to go to the library to get poetry books. We do sustained silent reading (SSR) every day after lunch, and my students are so absorbed in their poetry books. Wow! Because they wanted to share poems each day, I made them anthology journals so they could write their favorites and share them later. I have one student who began reading Shel Silverstein's *Where the Sidewalk Ends* about a week ago and reads it only here at school but is already on page 123 out of 164 pages. . . . I learned a good lesson—to introduce poetry in the beginning of the year and use it throughout the whole year.

Kay Hardy
Third-Grade Teacher
Pasco School District
Pasco, Washington

kids of all ages really respond to the poetry of Shel Silverstein. He wrote about everyday events and childhood experiences, often with an outrageous sense of the absurd. His pen-and-ink cartoon illustrations add another layer of originality and appeal. His most notable collections of poetry are *Where the Sidewalk Ends*, *A Light in the Attic*, and *Falling Up*, the first two of which are available as audio recordings narrated in Silverstein's own gravelly voice.

## Marilyn Singer
http://www.marilynsinger.net

Marilyn Singer's work may be best characterized by its diversity, from the distinctive poetic formats found in the poems for each month in *Turtle in July* to the recent poems of *Monday on the Mississippi*, which trace the path of the Mississippi River. Her topics include animals, water, the sky, the earth, and much more.

## Sonya Sones
http://www.sonyasones.com

For one of the freshest voices in verse novels, turn to the work of Sonya Sones. Her stories and poems for tweens and older are equally bittersweet and hysterically funny, whether dealing with a family's struggle with mental illness (*Stop Pretending: What Happened When My Big Sister Went Crazy*) or capturing the wild woes of a girl in her search for the perfect boyfriend (*What My Mother Doesn't Know*).

## Gary Soto
http://www.garysoto.com

Well-known for his adult poetry, his young adult (YA) novels, and his picture books, Gary Soto has also penned several outstanding poetry collections for young people, including *Fearless Fernie: Hanging Out with Fernie and Me*, a book of friendship poems that demonstrate his usual sprinkling of Spanish words within English texts. Other worthwhile collections include *Canto Familiar*, *A Fire in My Hands*, and *Neighborhood Odes*.

## Joyce Carol Thomas
http://www.joycecarolthomas.com

Joyce Carol Thomas has penned poetry collections that capture and celebrate African American culture in ways that help all readers acknowledge their roots. Two favorites are *Brown Honey in Broomwheat Tea* and *Gingerbread Days*, both beautifully illustrated by Floyd Cooper.

## Judith Viorst

Judith Viorst is probably best known for her ground-breaking picture book *Alexander and the Terrible, Horrible, No Good, Very Bad Day*. With her poetry book *If I Were in Charge of the World, and Other Worries: Poems for Children and Their Parents*, she tackles many poignant and hilarious moments of childhood, often with list poems that don't rhyme—a form that children enjoy, much to the surprise of many adults. Check out *Sad Underwear, and Other Complications: More Poems for Children and Their Parents* too.

## April Halprin Wayland
http://www.aprilwayland.com

For a blending of art and poetry, look for April Wayland's verse novel *Girl Coming in for a Landing*. Illustrated by Elaine Clayton, this is a wonderful work for preteen readers, who can relate to the "poetry is my underwear" emotions and experiences that Wayland depicts.

## Nancy Willard

Nancy Willard's *A Visit to William Blake's Inn: Poems for Innocent and Experienced Travelers*, an homage to earlier classic works for children, was the first book of poetry to be presented a Newbery Award. Willard's many works of poetry are filled with large doses of magic and wonder.

## Janet Wong
http://www.janetwong.com

In her poetry collections Janet S. Wong, the child of a Chinese immigrant father and a Korean immigrant mother, blends cultural details with universal feelings. Her works include *A Suitcase of Seaweed*; *Good Luck Gold, and Other Poems*; *Night Garden: Poems from the World of Dreams*; and *Knock on Wood: Poems about Superstitions*.

## Valerie Worth

Valerie Worth was the winner of the ninth NCTE Award for Excellence in Poetry for Children in 1991. Her poems are vivid observations of the quiet existence of everyday objects. Worth's careful attention to rhythm and sound and the striking images and metaphors in her succinct, free-verse poems make for engaging reading. For one collection that includes all ninety-nine of her original small poems and others, look for *All the Small Poems and Fourteen More*.

# Janet Wong

## *Some Thoughts on Poetry, Sit-ups, and Pain*

*by Janet Wong*

Some people think about poetry the way I think about doing sit-ups: it's good for me, it will strengthen my core, it won't take more than a few minutes a day to be effective—but what a pain! The exercise buffs among you would say (of sit-ups): yes, but the trouble is worth it. No pain, no gain. One minute a day, and you will feel stronger! Two minutes a day, and you will stand straighter! Five minutes, and you will live a fuller life!

I say: And so, too, with poetry.

Results, in a minute a day? Maybe not with lazy sit-ups, easy ones, the kind you do with your legs stretched out flat and your arms pumping your body up. This would be like a minute a day of silly verse, which would be fun and get your blood going and maybe even inspire you to want to do more—but which, unfortunately, would not result in the truly special benefits that come as a result of discomfort and strain. Gain, in poetry and sit-ups, comes when there is tension, when we are pushed to confront our weakest, flabbiest, grunting, groaning, ugliest human selves. And the tension need not come from dissecting a poem, or discussing it (though I would hope that most serious poems would inspire some discussion). Just reading a poem is good enough, reading it aloud. For example:

## *Coin Drive*

*by Janet Wong*

There's a coin drive going on at our school
for children hurt by the hurricane.
Teacher says, "Handful of dimes is fine.
But only give if you want to share."

Momma says, "Those people should have known.
Should have done more than they did to get out."
Poppa says, "Look how those people stole.
Criminals. Animals, them. Their kind."

I saw the pictures, too, myself.

People with nothing, no cars, for sure.
Swollen old ladies could barely walk.
Crazy boys with stolen guns,
but also daddies grabbing bread.

I saw the pictures, too, myself.

So many bodies floating, dead.
Waiting, water creeping up,
up past neck, past mouth, past eyes.
How long did they wait for help?

I feel proud for the fifty cents
I put today in the coin drive jar.
I feel proud that I can say:
I saw the pictures for myself.

Reading that poem aloud took me sixty-five seconds.

If that poem made you feel any pain or compassion or pride or shame or anger, think about it: a minute a day might be all it takes for you to get serious results from poetry.

I wrote "Coin Drive" a week past Hurricane Katrina as a way of making sense of the disaster; as an expression of confusion and sorrow and anger; and in hopes of making someone else see the way I do. What this poem offers, in my view, is an invitation to question, to wonder, to examine our own feelings and ideas about this disaster and the failed response to it.

Some people will say: children are too young to have to think about such things. Perhaps we should shelter them. We should, if only we could. The fact is, though, that most families are not that careful. The TV is on, and so the children have seen the scary looting and shooting; the magazines in the supermarket have shown the dead, bloated bodies, planting nightmarish images in our children's minds. Because our children have been troubled, they now deserve an explanation. They deserve to hear the complicated and unpleasant stories behind the trouble.

Parents should lead these discussions with their children. But so, too, should we, because we know, sadly, that many parents cannot or will not do this job. We know that we are often the best-informed and most compassionate people in a child's daily life. We teachers and librarians, if we care about the kind of world we live in, need to inspire discussions about social and moral responsibility and current events. Poetry can help us do this. Of course novels and history books and newspapers can do this, too—just the same way competing in triathlons can strengthen your core—but not as quickly or effectively as poetry (and sit-ups).

Read poetry aloud. Post poems on bulletin boards, in toilet stalls. Leave a basket of typewritten pocket poems by the check-out counter. Add poetry to mandatory summer reading lists, or hide poetry in the general categories of your reading lists, in the hopes that someone might stumble on them there. Put poetry books out on the tops of shelves so they are easy to find. And don't shy away from the difficult, serious stuff. Poetry can prod our children to grapple with important and painful issues so that they can learn to question, think, understand, and see things for themselves.

∞

A final thought: after one of those challenging, exhausting, exhilarating discussions of poetry and life, throw in twenty sit-ups for fun.

*"Coin Drive" is a serious poem that an adult should probably read aloud to the children first. Then, when the children are ready to participate, individual volunteers can read the lines designated for the teacher, Momma, Poppa, and the child narrator. The group as a whole can join in on the repeated line "I saw the pictures, too, myself" and on the end line, which is a slight variation of the repeated line. Afterward, children may want to discuss the feelings and images evoked by the poem and participate in their own coin drive for a local cause.*

Jane Yolen
http://www.janeyolen.com

Jane Yolen is another example of an author who is well known for writing hundreds of wonderful children's books in other genres. However, she also has many wonderful poetry collections that are ideal for matching with the study of science or history, such as *Once upon Ice, and Other Frozen Poems* or *Sacred Places*. Younger audiences especially enjoy her dinosaur poem collections, such as *Do Dinosaurs Say Good Night?*

## Poet Websites and Biographical Resources

Most poets have personal websites with information about themselves, their work, and their availability for public appearances. Of course websites and URLs change regularly, so be sure to double-check any address provided in this book. Every effort has been made to verify all addresses and to share the most stable sites. Some poets' websites are even rich resources for children, with advice and activities built in. Kristine O'Connell George's website, for example, was chosen as an American Library Association best website for families and kids. Other poets, such as Nikki Grimes, Sonya Sones, and Janet Wong, host lively websites with tips, techniques, and more.

Many publishers regularly feature interviews with poets on their websites. For example, see the Random House "Librarians at Random" page at http://www.randomhouse.com/teachers/librarians/ or the HarperCollins Children's

---

**PRACTITIONER PERSPECTIVE**

What is so fascinating about a poem is that it can have a different meaning for each of us. Poetry that touches one person may have no effect on another. Or, two persons may come away with different impressions after reading the same poem. That is why I think it is so important to let poetry speak to children.

S. Zulema Silva Bewley
Librarian
Tom C. Gooch Elementary School
Dallas, Texas

Publishing website at http://www.harperchildrens.com/hch/author/. The Academy of American Poets also offers a massive website with a comprehensive directory of American poets, including some poets writing for children. Check out http://www.poets.org. *Speaking with Poets*, volumes 1 and 2, edited by Jeff Copeland (1993; 1995), are excellent print resources that include personal interviews and photos of nearly fifty contemporary poets writing for young people. Lee Bennett Hopkins's oft-cited books *Pass the Poetry Please* (1986) and *Pauses: Autobiographical Reflections of 101 Creators of Children's Books* (1995) offer biographical sketches of and autobiographical essays by many favorite poets. And some poets have authored autobiographical narrative works that provide interesting background for reading their poetry.

### Biographies, Autobiographies, and Memoirs of Poets: A Selected List

The following books share information about the lives of poets and how they came to write poetry.

Michael Bedard, *Emily*, illustrated by Barbara Cooney (New York: Doubleday, 1992)

Natalie S. Bober, *A Restless Spirit: The Story of Robert Frost* (New York: Henry Holt, 1991)

Robert Burleigh, *Langston's Train Ride*, illustrated by Leonard Jenkins (New York: Scholastic, 2004)

Bonnie Christensen, *Woody Guthrie: Poet of the People* (New York: Knopf, 2001)

Floyd Cooper, *Coming Home: From the Life of Langston Hughes* (New York: Philomel, 1994)

Beverly Gherman, *Robert Louis Stevenson, Teller of Tales* (New York: Atheneum, 1996)

David Harrison, *Connecting Dots: Poems of My Journey* (Honesdale, PA: Boyds Mills, 2004)

Lee Bennett Hopkins, *The Writing Bug* (Katonah, NY: R. C. Owen, 1993)

———, *Been to Yesterdays: Poems of a Life*, illustrated by Charlene Rendeiro (Honesdale, PA: Wordsong / Boyds Mills, 1995)

Judith Pinkerton Josephson, *Nikki Giovanni: Poet of the People* (Berkeley Heights, NJ: Enslow, 2000)

Barbara Kerley, *Walt Whitman: Words for America*, illustrated by Brian Selznick (New York: Scholastic, 2004)

Karla Kuskin, *Thoughts, Pictures, and Words*, photographs by Nicholas Kuskin (Katonah, NY: R. C. Owen, 1995)

Kathryn Lasky, *A Voice of Her Own: The Story of Phillis Wheatley, Slave Poet*, illustrated by Paul Lee (Cambridge, MA: Candlewick, 2003)

J. Patrick Lewis, *Freedom Like Sunlight: Praisesongs for Black Americans*, illustrated by John Thompson (Mankato, MN: Creative Editions, 2000)

Patricia C. McKissack, *Paul Laurence Dunbar: A Poet to Remember* (Chicago: Children's Press, 1984)

Milton Meltzer, *Langston Hughes: A Biography*, illustrated by Stephen Alcorn (Brookfield, CT: Millbrook, 1997)

——, *Carl Sandburg: A Biography* (Brookfield, CT: Twenty-first Century Books, 1999)

——, *Walt Whitman: A Biography* (Brookfield, CT: Twenty-first Century Books, 2002)

——, *Emily Dickinson: A Biography* (Brookfield, CT: Twenty-first Century Books, 2004)

Jim Murphy, *Across America on an Emigrant Train* (New York: Clarion, 1993)

Penelope Niven, *Carl Sandburg: Adventures of a Poet*, illustrated by Marc Nadel (New York: Harcourt Brace, 2003)

Audrey Osofsky, *Free to Dream: The Making of a Poet: Langston Hughes* (New York: Lothrop, Lee & Shepard, 1996)

Willie Perdomo, *Visiting Langston*, illustrated by Bryan Collier (New York: Henry Holt, 2002)

Catherine Reef, *Walt Whitman* (New York: Clarion, 1995)

————, *Paul Laurence Dunbar: Portrait of a Poet*
(Berkeley Heights, NJ: Enslow, 2000)

Michael R. Strickland, *African-American Poets* (Berkeley
Heights, NJ: Enslow, 1996)

Amy Strong, *Lee Bennett Hopkins: A Children's Poet*
(New York: Franklin Watts, 2003)

Jeanette Winter, *Emily Dickinson's Letters to the World*
(New York: Frances Foster Books/Farrar, Straus &
Giroux, 2002)

## Promoting Poets

Once you have expanded your poetry collection to offer a variety of popular
poets, it is important that you showcase these poets as well. "After all, the way
Prelutsky and Silverstein became household words to many readers was
through promotion by teachers and librarians" (Wilson and Kutiper 1994,
277). Just having the books on the shelves is not enough. All the usual
methods are helpful, such as shelf and tabletop displays, bookmarks and
brochures, posters and other visuals. (More ideas are shared in chapter 4.)
However, promoting the poets themselves is worthwhile too. Designate an area
for a featured poet and gather a collection of his or her books to display. Many
poets have their own websites, so you can find a few nuggets of biographical
information, quotations, photos, and booklists to display to personalize the
poet and her or his work. In fact, children themselves can help create such a
display, reading and reviewing the books of their favorite poets and looking up
interesting information. If you have the background and web space, you might
even consider rotating your featured author presentations on your library website, with direct links to the poet's website.

If your budget allows, hosting a visiting poet is a very powerful way of promoting poetry for children. There is nothing quite equal to hearing poems read
by the poet herself or himself. Meeting the poet reminds children (of all ages)
that poets are people and that poems come from all kinds of personal experiences and emotions. Although this can be an expensive enterprise (costing
from a few hundred to a few thousand dollars), it can provide powerful connections and memories for all who participate. Information about hosting a

poet can generally be found on the poet's website or through the poet's publishing company. And if schools and libraries work together to share expenses and coordinate the appearance, it can be even more doable. So often we are eager to host authors at book festivals and other occasions, but how often do we consider poets and poetry for special events?

## Conclusion

Keeping up with poetry publishing is much like keeping up with any part of the library collection: it requires some purposeful effort. One can rely on the usual review sources as selection guides, of course, but it also can be helpful to know about major awards and authors that are standards in the field of poetry for children. As mentioned earlier, the foremost awards for poetry writing for children are

- The NCTE Award for Excellence in Poetry for Children
- The Lee Bennett Hopkins Promising Poet Award
- The Lee Bennett Hopkins Award for Children's Poetry
- The Claudia Lewis Award

Whatever the resources we rely on, it is also important to become familiar with the names of the poets who have children at the heart of their writing. Once we know their names and become familiar with some of their works, we can continue to seek out new titles likely to become gems in our collections. Adding the latest Douglas Florian book, for example, will become just as important as acquiring the latest Katherine Paterson novel for young people. Among the poets to be familiar with are

- Classic poets
- Anthologists
- Poets from many cultures
- The fifty poets profiled earlier in this chapter

Knowing the major poets and awards helps make poetry a priority and helps us feel more confident in selecting and sharing quality works with children. In addition, websites and biographical resources can help us personalize our promotion of poets and poetry. Once we incorporate poetry makers into our literary repertoire, we are one step closer to making poetry an automatic part of our thinking and sharing.

*Poetry and Hums aren't things which you get,*
*they're things which get YOU.*
*And all you can do is to go where they can find you.*

—A. A. Milne, *The House at Pooh Corner* (1928)

## Chapter Three

# ⬦ What Poetry Do Children Enjoy?

*Only the rarest kind of best in anything can be good enough for the young.*

—Walter de la Mare, Poet

$\mathcal{H}$ow do we know which poetry books to choose? In this chapter, we will look at the different ways in which poetry for young people is being published today. We will identify the traditional types as well as the more creative formats available and will cite many sample titles for each. We will look at other poetry resources, too, such as websites, magazines, and audiobooks. And we will consider studies of children's poetry preferences as well as selection and evaluation guidelines to help you decide what to look for as you develop a varied and balanced poetry collection.

Poetry for young people can have many different faces, from familiar folk rhymes to sophisticated verse novels, from songs and finger plays to standard anthologies, from traditional Mother Goose rhymes to poem picture books. Having taught sixth graders, I know that the appeal of humorous poetry is very powerful. I believe that it is a good place to begin as we gradually lead children to deeper, richer, more abstract poetry.

Did you know that generally speaking in the field of children's literature, fewer poetry books are published than books in any other genre? Poetry books go out of print more quickly, too. Thus, as you learn about the different kinds of poetry books that are published and what to look for in selecting quality poetry, be aggressive about adding those gems to your collection before they go out of print. Indeed, consider purchasing multiple copies, because popular poetry books seem to disappear off the shelves. Would one copy of *Where the Sidewalk Ends* be adequate for your library? Hardly. Statistics indicate that it is one of the best-circulating titles of any genre. And as we learn new ways of promoting and sharing poetry for children, we will hope to create the same level of interest in new and up-and-coming poets and poetry books. Since only a handful of poetry is published for children each year (some fifty titles, depending on how you define the genre), acquisition is relatively simple once you make poetry a priority.

## Kinds of Poetry Books

What kinds of poetry books are available for children and young adults? Most experts recognize four general categories of poetry books for children:

- General anthologies
- Topical collections
- Compilations of works by individual poets
- Poem picture books

### *General Anthologies*

General anthologies include many different kinds of poems by many different poets. Collections like these are usually very global but may be organized by subthemes or subcategories (such as the seasons, emotions, or childhood experiences). This kind of poetry collection has probably been around the longest of all and is a practical source for a variety of poems by many different poets. Indeed, inclusion in anthologies is probably the easiest way for new poets to get their work published and their names known. Anthologies also provide an easy way to gather poems that are in the public domain.

In days gone by, anthologies tended to be comprehensive and lengthy, often two hundred to three hundred pages long, but newer anthologies are usually shorter and often richly illustrated. They are still probably most often accessed by adults who share them with children rather than by child readers themselves. And they can be a helpful beginning point for librarians or teachers who want one place to start for selecting a variety of quality poems. One of the most popular collections continues to be *The Random House Book of Poetry for Children*, compiled by poet Jack Prelutsky and illustrated by Arnold Lobel. It is a good example of the poem variety and friendly format that characterize many contemporary anthologies.

TEN ANTHOLOGIES NOT TO BE MISSED

Bernice F. Cullinan, ed., *A Jar of Tiny Stars: Poems by NCTE Award–Winning Poets*

Beatrice Schenk De Regniers et al., eds., *Sing a Song of Popcorn: Every Child's Book of Poems*

Georgia Heard, *This Place I Know: Poems of Comfort*

Lee Bennett Hopkins, comp., *Days to Celebrate: A Full Year of Poetry, People, Holidays, History, Fascinating Facts, and More*

Paul, Janeczko, comp., *Seeing the Blue Between: Advice and Inspiration for Young Poets*

X. J. Kennedy and Dorothy Kennedy, comps., *Knock at a Star: A Child's Introduction to Poetry*

Bruce Lansky, comp., *A Bad Case of the Giggles: Kids' Favorite Funny Poems*

Naomi Shihab Nye, comp., *This Same Sky: A Collection of Poems from Around the World*

Jack Prelutsky, comp., *The Random House Book of Poetry for Children*

——, comp., *The 20th-Century Children's Poetry Treasury*

## Topical Collections

The specialized anthology is becoming a very popular form with publishers and with teachers and librarians who enjoy using thematic collections to supplement the curriculum or connect with specific topics. These are collections gathered around a single topic, such as animals, holidays, or family. They still include poems by a variety of poets, so they provide a good introduction to a variety of poetic styles and voices, all selected to provide different perspectives on the unifying theme or subject.

Topical collections offer a more concentrated exposure to poems on a single topic, thus appealing to a reader's prior interest in a topic like dogs or providing an introduction to a topic unfamiliar to readers, such as outer space. These slimmer, specialized collections are usually more visually inviting and are also very popular among both adults and children. For one lovely example, look for a smaller anthology of poems about books, reading, and libraries entitled *Book Poems: Poems from National Children's Book Week, 1959–1998*, edited by Mary Perrotta Rich. This is a gathering of the poems commissioned to celebrate Book Week every November and each poem is a gem. In contrast, it's a good example of a contemporary anthology with a variety of distinguished poets in a slim, unillustrated volume. Since all the poems are similar in subject, but by different poets, this is an excellent example of a "topical collection."

TEN TOPICAL COLLECTIONS NOT TO BE MISSED

Arnold Adoff, comp., *My Black Me: A Beginning Book of Black Poetry*

Barbara Brenner, comp., *The Earth Is Painted Green: A Garden of Poems about Our Planet*

Isabel Joshlin Glaser, comp., *Dreams of Glory: Poems Starring Girls*

Lee Bennett Hopkins, comp., *Hand in Hand: An American History through Poetry*

Wade Hudson, comp., *Pass It On: African American Poetry for Children*

Pat Mora, comp., *Love to Mama: A Tribute to Mothers*

Jack Prelutsky, comp., *The Beauty of the Beast*

Mary Perrotta Rich, comp., *Book Poems: Poems from National Children's Book Week, 1959–1998*

Javaka Steptoe, comp., *In Daddy's Arms I Am Tall: African Americans Celebrating Fathers*

Laura Whipple, comp., *Eric Carle's Animals, Animals*

## Compilations of Works by Individual Poets

At some point, most poets like to publish collections featuring only their own work. And of course such works offer the best way to get a feeling for a poet's unique voice and style. These collections may also have a topical connection, such as animals or holidays or sports, but all the poems are authored by one person, the featured poet.

Single-poet collections are also very popular with both children and adults after they have had some introduction to a collection's writer. *A Light in the Attic*, for example, is one of the most circulated books of children's poetry ever because there are now several generations of Shel Silverstein fans. Readers seek out the three anthologies of Silverstein's poetry year after year. If you are not familiar with poets like John Ciardi or J. Patrick Lewis, however, you may not pick up a book of their poetry. Unless the book's topic, cover art, or interior illustrations intrigue you, you may not realize that both Ciardi and Lewis, for example, are as clever and humorous as Silverstein. As with all reader advisory work, of course, this is where the savvy librarian can really make a difference, guiding children (and adults) to collections by poets who may become new favorites.

TEN INDIVIDUAL POET COMPILATIONS NOT TO BE MISSED

This list is harder to assemble because the titles depend very much on which poets a reader likes. Here are ten books by individual poets that recently appeared among the best-selling titles of children's poetry.

> John Ciardi, *You Read to Me, I'll Read to You*
>
> Paul Fleischman, *Joyful Noise: Poems for Two Voices*
>
> Douglas Florian, *Insectlopedia: Poems and Paintings*
>
> Eloise Greenfield, *Honey, I Love, and Other Love Poems*
>
> Mary Ann Hoberman, *Fathers, Mothers, Sisters, Brothers: A Collection of Family Poems*
>
> Langston Hughes, *The Dreamkeeper, and Other Poems*
>
> J. Patrick Lewis, *Please Bury Me in the Library*
>
> Jack Prelutsky, *The New Kid on the Block*
>
> Shel Silverstein, *A Light in the Attic*
>
> Judith Viorst, *If I Were in Charge of the World, and Other Worries: Poems for Children and Their Parents*

Obviously, there are many more compilations of works by individual poets worth sharing with children. Just as with fiction, when young readers discover an interest in the works of a certain poet, they like to read more books by him

---

### PRACTITIONER PERSPECTIVE

When I read about why some readers avoid poetry, I thought of myself. Poetry has never been one of my favorite genres, though as I read more and more poetry for children, it is definitely growing on me. I just read *Insectlopedia*. Who would have thought a book about creepy, crawly critters would be entertaining? I enjoyed this collection very much. Not only were the authentic paintings full of amusement, but in addition the style of each poem was attention grabbing and appropriate for each insect or spider. I love Florian's play of syllables in "The Ticks" and "The Inchworm." "The Whirligig Beetles" poems literally took on the shapes of the subjects. I look forward to reading more fun, whimsical poems from Florian. I suppose I am just cut out for children's poems!

> Asha Patel
> Library Media Specialist
> Eladio R. Martinez Learning Center
> Dallas, Texas

or her. So, if young readers or listeners enjoy the art and clever descriptive poems in Douglas Florian's *Insectlopedia* they will very likely respond to his *Beast Feast*, *In the Swim*, and *On the Wing*, among others. Indeed, once you become familiar with specific poets, you may want to keep watch for their new publications from year to year. The slim volumes of poetry by individual poets may be the rarest treasures of all, produced in small quantities with great care, culled from a multitude of poems to share the very best with children.

## Poem Picture Books

A relatively recent trend has been to publish individual poems, often classics, spread out line by line across the pages of a standard thirty-two-page picture book. These poem picture books offer the benefit of extensive illustrations to help readers understand and interpret, or even reinterpret, each line of a poem. Robert Frost's "Stopping by Woods on a Snowy Evening," illustrated by Susan Jeffers, is one of my favorite poem picture books. The literal portrayal of the snowy path is refreshing to many of us who have been forced to analyze the poem's deeper meaning. "The Owl and the Pussycat," by Edward Lear, has been illustrated in picture book format by several artists, and Diane Siebert has taken many of the poems she published in magazines and turned them into breathtaking poem picture books. *Heartland*, *Mojave*, *Train Song*, and others are illustrated by a variety of artists and are perfect supplements to the school social studies curriculum.

Poem picture books are not to be confused with poetic or rhyming picture books, such as Dr. Seuss books, with their strong rhythms and frequent rhymes. In a poem picture book, the poem can stand alone—without the book format or the illustrations. In the usual picture book, text and illustrations work together to convey a story. In a poem picture book, the illustrations provide one vision of the poem's meaning. This can help introduce young readers to longer, narrative poems or classic works. Poem picture books can also be helpful for visually oriented older students who may be familiar with a classic poem but may not find it moving or meaningful until they see it richly illustrated. Such books can also provide a springboard for students to experiment with their own artistic expression of a poem's meaning for them. They can create personal poem picture books for their favorite poems.

One note—these books are often not cataloged or shelved in the usual 800 poetry section. More often they are viewed and handled as picture books and are placed in the E or Easy (or Everyone) section. This is fine if the books are circulating and finding an audience, but if not, it may be worth promoting them

— POET PROFILE —

## Douglas Florian

### *Sharing Poetry Out Loud and Soft*

*by Douglas Florian*

Poetry, more so than prose, is usually meant to be read out loud. It begs to be recited to an in-person audience that can laugh, cry, gasp, or groan. It has an immediacy and intensity that so often connect people, and especially children, together. Because each line, phrase, word, or semicolon is so precise and considered, it can illuminate and educate in a most entertaining and emotional way.

Whether through a recording or live, to hear a poet recite a poem adds a whole new dimension to the static letters sitting on a page. With voice the poet can scream or whisper, whine or bewitch, howl or cajole. While prose is by nature prosaic and long winded, poetry is compact and commanding. The listener must be attuned to every word and nuance or risk missing miles of meaning. A poet's voice can s t r e t c h words out or pack them together, fall or rise in tone.

No monotone works here, but rather a moving, meandering, and progressing experience as the very sounds of words can amaze. A coyote can become a howling coyooooote and shhhhhhhhheep can lull us to sleep better than mere sheep. Words may bounce off each other and echo with alliteration, as in *lizard laze* or *chameleon comedian*.

How can poets impart their intentions to the reader? We have our ways. We use *italics* to slow things down and emphasize words. **Bold** type or <u>underlining</u> can signal loudness and force. Line breaks tell where to pause; stanzas or even empty space signify a longer pause. Type fonts and sizes can convey mood or manner. A long — alerts the reader that some surprise is wending its way, so—get ready!

One who recites poetry can be an actor playing different roles, with different voices, accents, intonations, and emotions, all in the course of one poem. Reciting a poem is re-sight-ing a poem, making it more clear and exciting. Reading a poem aloud makes it come alive and springs it off the page, gives birth to it, nurtures it, and lets it stand on its own two (or even four) feet. A spoken poem is harder to ignore. It's out there in the air, tangible, delectable, not merely intellectual. It enters us through our ears, leaving our eyes free to imagine and dream of all that the poem hints at.

A poem reading can be intimate, close, and cozy, with ten children sitting near the reader, without stage or microphone. It can be communal and commanding, with an audience of hundreds listening to words booming from a powerful sound system in an auditorium. Or it can be both personal and wide-ranged, as when poetry is read out loud on the radio or in a recording.

When poetry is read aloud before people, their response becomes part of the poem. This is especially true with children, with their great spontaneity. Their laughter or tears, their gasps or titters, their groans or moans, or even their silence all play into the performance, enriching it and amending it, enhancing or detracting from it. Good responses embolden readers and bad ones enfeeble them. Poets, like comedians, need a good crowd to connect with. Laughter is contagious and humor is infectious. Grief in a poem can be sensed by the silence of the audience, and understanding and recognition can be signaled by their nods and smiles. A poem read aloud can draw in the difficult child, capture the disruptive child, and grant gifts to the gifted child. Attention spans lengthen and moods swing in positive ways in response to poetry performances. Rhyme and rhythm lend themselves to children most naturally. Alliteration and repetition are intrinsically pleasing and satisfying to a child's ear. A group of poets reciting their own work can create an even more powerful experience. Varieties of forms and voices can have wide-ranging and cumulative effects as the lyrical mixes with the comical, the terse with the florid, and the emotional with the intellectual.

In short, reading poetry aloud connects us and collects us, heals us and reveals us, unites us and delights us in the wonder of words and all they can convey.

## *A Poem Can Sing*

### *by Douglas Florian*

A poem can sing
A poem can sting
A poem can shout
Or leap about
A poem can yell
Or sink or swell

A poem can talk
Or take a walk
A poem can wail
A poem can sail
A poem can wing
A poem can sing

*With its strong rhythm and rhyme, "A Poem Can Sing" lends itself to being read aloud. Try having two groups of children read alternating lines in call-and-response style. For variety, add motions and gestures that correspond with the words. Pause briefly at the end of each line for the pantomime. Or put it all together with a small group of mimes acting out the strong verbs while the rest of the children, in two groups, alternate reading pairs of lines out loud.*

specifically as poetry or poem picture books in various creative ways—including them in poetry bibliographies and booklists, linking them with other poetry anthologies, and so forth.

TEN POEM PICTURE BOOKS NOT TO BE MISSED

Robert Frost, *Stopping by Woods on a Snowy Evening*, illustrated by Susan Jeffers

Edward Lear, *The Owl and the Pussycat*, illustrated by Jan Brett

Reeve Lindbergh, *Johnny Appleseed*, illustrated by Kathy Jakobsen

Henry Wadsworth Longfellow, *Paul Revere's Ride*, illustrated by Ted Rand

———, *The Midnight Ride of Paul Revere*, illustrated by Christopher Bing

Walter Dean Myers, *Harlem*, illustrated by Christopher Myers

Diane Siebert, *Cave*, illustrated by Wayne McLoughlin

Robert Louis Stevenson, *Block City*, illustrated by Daniel Kirk

Ernest Lawrence Thayer, *Casey at the Bat*, illustrated by Christopher Bing

Walt Whitman, *I Hear America Singing*, illustrated by Robert Sabuda

Poem picture books lend themselves particularly well to creative follow-up activities. For example,

Read the poem first without illustrations. Then, on the second reading show the illustrations and discuss the differences in the experiences, such as how the poem looks, how it makes readers feel, and how the illustrator visualized each line.

Compare multiple picture book versions of the same poem, (e.g., several different illustrators' interpretations of "The Owl and the Pussycat" or "The Night before Christmas").

Invite kids to create a homemade book of original illustrations to accompany a favorite poem or the lyrics of a favorite song, working individually, with a partner, or in a small group.

And remember to be open to children's differing interpretations of the same poem and encourage their reinterpretations of old favorites.

## POETIC PICTURE STORY BOOKS

Even simple narrative picture books can be poetic in their use of language. Generally speaking, the text for a picture book is only a page or two of writing, about fifteen hundred words. If you separate the words from the illustrations (especially for older readers), you can get a closer look at the artistry of the writer—the choice of words, the arrangement of lines, the structure of the story. Typing out the text of a favorite picture book can help you see the beauty in the story, the poetry in the language. Some picture-book texts will seem instantly poetic, others may be more expository in nature. Some are deliberately written in rhyme but do not stand alone as poetry. They depend upon the combination of text and illustration for their power. It can be a worthwhile exercise for all those who are looking closely at poetry, poetry writing, and poetry in general to consider the variety of picture books that incorporate rhyme and rhythm in their language:

- Rhyming picture story books (à la Dr. Seuss)
- Predictable books
- Easy-to-read books (controlled-vocabulary readers)
- Alphabet books
- Counting books

I would not generally consider such works poetry books because their focus is on using rhyme as a vehicle. However, whenever rhyme or poetic language is present, it is an opportunity for children to notice and comment on the words and sounds they hear and read. It is an opportunity to invite children to join in the oral reading. It is an opportunity to link picture books with poems. It is an opportunity to look for poems that piggyback on the story experience. Picture story books that contain poetic language make the point that poetry, rhyme, and verse are all around us.

## Variations of Poetry Book Formats

Although there may be four major types of poetry books (anthologies, topical collections, individual compilations, and poem picture books), one can find poetry in several other variations of those formats. For example:

- Collections of a single poetic form (e.g., solely haiku or solely concrete poetry)
- Verse novels (generally for young adults)
- Song lyrics published in book form
- Mother Goose and nursery rhymes
- Folk rhymes
- Poetry by children

### Collections Based on Poetic Forms

In recent years, we have seen the publication of many poetry books that feature one specific form of poetry, such as concrete, or shape, poetry; haiku; or riddle poems. These can be a fun way to introduce the role of form in poetry or simply to add variety to the usual poem diet. Paul Janeczko, for example, explores poetry forms for each letter of the alphabet in *Poetry from A to Z: A Guide for Young Writers* and provides a visual introduction to poetic forms for younger children with the assistance of Chris Raschka's illustrations in *A Kick in the Head: An Everyday Guide to Poetic Forms*.

Janeczko and Raschka paired up previously to create *A Poke in the I: A Collection of Concrete Poems*, an inviting introduction to concrete poetry. Many collections of concrete, or shape, poetry are available. Children typically enjoy concrete poetry and take pleasure in the poet's creative use of the physical shape of the poem to convey meaning. It is a poetic form they like imitating and experimenting with. Joan Bransfield Graham's books *Flicker Flash* and *Splish Splash* are clever and colorful examples. J. Patrick Lewis's book, *Doodle Dandies: Poems That Take Shape* and Heidi Roemer's *Come to My Party* are both appealing books of concrete poetry, too. For a slightly more off-beat collection of concrete poems ideal for the preteen reader, check out *Technically, It's Not My Fault: Concrete Poems*, by John Grandits.

Poems in riddle format can also be very appealing to children and offer opportunities for both problem solving and poetry enjoyment. J. Patrick Lewis has several riddle poem collections about animals, science, and math, beginning with *Riddle-icious*. Charles Ghigna created *Riddle Rhymes* and Rebecca Dotlich authored *When Riddles Come Rumbling*, both full of guessing-game rhymes for very young children. Brian Swann offers riddle rhymes from African traditions in *The House with No Door* and from Native American traditions in *Touching the Distance*.

Haiku is an ancient Japanese form of poetry that has been a staple of many library collections. These short, unrhymed nature poems are available in several different formats suitable for children. Matthew Gollub blends the classic haiku poetry of the famed Japanese poet Issa with biographical narrative in the picture book *Cool Melons Turn to Frogs: The Life and Poems of Issa*. Jack Prelutsky's recent collection of animal haiku is illustrated by Ted Rand in *If Not for the Cat*. And for a completely different approach suitable for older children, look for the urban haiku accompanied by black-and-white photographs in *Stone Bench in an Empty Park*.

## Verse Novels

A relatively new poetic form with roots in ancient epic poetry, the verse novel, or novel in verse, is growing in popularity, particularly with middle school readers. Indeed the majority of verse novels currently available are probably best suited to young adults. However, there are several examples that children aged nine or ten years and up may enjoy, such as *Amber Was Brave, Essie Was Smart*, by Vera Williams, or *Minn and Jake*, by Janet Wong. The Newbery Award–winning novelists Karen Hesse and Sharon Creech have also authored several interesting novels in verse, including *Out of the Dust* and *Witness* by Hesse and *Love That Dog* and *Heartbeat* by Creech. The best verse novels are built on poems that are often lovely stand-alone works of art. A narrative unfolds poem by poem, frequently with multiple points of view and in colloquial language. This format is wooing many middle grade children both to poetry and to reading in general—a promising trend.

Some authors are experimenting with even more innovative variations combining narrative and verse. For example, throughout *Locomotion* Jacqueline Woodson uses poetry as an outlet for the protagonist's feelings, and in *Bronx Masquerade* Nikki Grimes uses poems written by students who are learning to perform poetry. And for prose poems, look at Kathi Appelt's autobiographical *My*

*Father's Summers: A Daughter's Memoir*. Appelt's poems are in paragraph form, and combined with photographs from Appelt's own life, they create a scrapbook of memories that may inspire young readers to document their own lives.

## Songs in Book Form

Studying song lyrics can be a backdoor approach to inviting readers into the world of poetry. Because children's interest in music seems to increase in the teen years, older kids may be more familiar with the words to the top 40 songs than they are with the poetry of Shakespeare or even Silverstein. Writing down song lyrics (or finding them on CD liners or the Web) can help young people look closely at the use of word choice, phrasing, repetition, and figurative language in a poetic format that they might find more relevant. Then we can take the next step by matching songs with poems and examining the similarities and differences between the two forms. (One note of caution: you may have to set some ground rules about what kinds of song lyrics are acceptable in a school or library environment.)

Sharing songs in picture-book form may help younger children see the poetry in the familiar tunes and lyrics they have grown up with. For example, Bruce McMillan's contemporary *Mary Had a Little Lamb* features a modern, African American Mary in yellow overalls. Patriotic songs children learn in school may become more understandable through the illustrations in books such as *O Beautiful for Spacious Skies*, illustrated by Wayne Thiebaud. Songs they learned at summer camp are noted in *Camp Granada: Sing-along Camp Songs*, by Frane Lessac, and songs often learned at preschool can be found in *A Treasury of Children's Songs: Forty Favorites to Sing and Play*, compiled by Dan Fox. If you are comfortable introducing Bible songs and spirituals, share *All Night, All Day: A Child's First Book of African American Spirituals*, collected and beautifully illustrated by Ashley Bryan. You will find a comprehensive resource of American folksongs in Amy Cohn's *From Sea to Shining Sea: A Treasury of American Folklore and Folk Songs*. And look to the cultural traditions of your community for more examples of songs strong in rhyme and rhythm, such as Lulu Delacre's *Arrorró Mi Niño: Latino Lullabies and Gentle Games* and José-Luis Orozco's *Fiestas: A Year of Latin American Songs of Celebration*. The rhythm and repetition of songs echo the elements found in many poems.

## Mother Goose

Over the years, I have found that many children have missed the traditional exposure to Mother Goose rhymes and may know very few of them. That is not just sad, it is a handicap, because many works of adult literature that children may encounter in the future make constant reference to Mother Goose rhymes and characters (e.g., *All the King's Men*, by Robert Penn Warren). Even with older children, it can be fun to share Mother Goose rhymes and the history behind them. Consider using the *Annotated Mother Goose*, by William and Ceil Baring-Gould, which is full of the stories behind the rhymes. For example, did you know that "Ring around the Rosie" is believed to refer to the bubonic plague and that the line "ashes, ashes, we all fall down" meant we all die and turn into ashes?

There are probably hundreds of book versions of Mother Goose nursery rhymes, and many families undoubtedly have their favorites. New versions illustrated by Rosemary Wells are very popular. They include *My Very First Mother Goose* and *Here Comes Mother Goose*, both based on verses collected by children's folklore expert Iona Opie. Many individual rhymes from these collections have also been reproduced as board books for toddlers. Tomie de Paola's illustrations enliven a collection of over two hundred rhymes (also collected by Peter and Iona Opie) in *Tomie de Paola's Mother Goose*. For a fresh, contemporary look, share *Neighborhood Mother Goose*, with lively illustrations that include photographs of children in urban settings. And for a humorous twist, consider Bernard Most's *Four and Twenty Dinosaurs*, in which Mother Goose characters are all replaced by dinosaurs.

Finger plays and rhymes with motions and movement are also staples of many children's early introductions to poetry. Although the focus of this book is school-age children, five to twelve years old, participatory rhymes may also engage older children, particularly when you have multiage groups or a book

---

**PRACTITIONER PERSPECTIVE**

I was very surprised to realize how much poetry I am already using. Every week I start story time with a poem (an action rhyme), do two to three poems during the session (in the form of finger plays or flannels), and end with a poem as well (a song that we dance to). At home, I sing songs and read Mother Goose and other books to my eight-month-old. And I have read several poem novels, especially those by Mel Glenn. It is amazing what one will find when putting on poetry-tinted glasses!

Sarah Dornback
Children's Librarian
Farmers Branch Manske Library
Farmers Branch, Texas

buddies program that pairs older children with younger ones. Many wonderful collections are available, such as *Head, Shoulders, Knees, and Toes, and Other Action Rhymes*, by Zita Newcome; *Wiggle Waggle Fun: Stories and Rhymes for the Very Very Young*, by Margaret Mayo; and *Michael Foreman's Playtime Rhymes*. And of course children from non-English-speaking backgrounds also grow up with nursery rhymes, so seek such rhymes out whenever they are available to you in book form. Consider, for example, José-Luis Orozco's *Diez Deditos: Ten Little Fingers, and Other Play Rhymes and Action Songs from Latin America* or Alma Flor Ada and F. Isabel Campoy's *¡Pio Peep! Traditional Spanish Nursery Rhymes*. For children who missed Mother Goose in their preschool years, are new to nursery rhymes in English, or simply want to revisit nursery rhymes for the pleasure of the sounds and rhythms (and the memories of early childhood!), various versions of Mother Goose rhymes are well worth having in any reputable poetry collection.

## Folk Poetry

Many children—and adults—don't realize that the silly songs, rollicking rhymes, and nonsense games we learn in early childhood are indeed a form of literature. Folk poetry is the poetry you do not even realize is poetry. Rhymes on the playground like "Cinderella Dressed in Yellow" have no known author and yet are familiar to many generations of children. These rhyming verses can also be included in our poetry collections. Books of riddles, chants, tongue twisters, jump-rope rhymes, finger plays, hand-clapping games, autograph sayings, and more often contain poetry and verse. What's more, children are often intrigued to find in print the verses they have heard and known only orally and only outside of school—at home and at play. Alvin Schwartz's collection of uniquely American verse *And the Green Grass Grew All Around* is one of my favorites and has so many wonderful examples that children will enjoy. You may be surprised, for instance, to discover that there are second and third verses to poems you knew only one verse of as a child. For additional examples, look for Iona and Peter Opie's *I Saw Esau: The Schoolchild's Pocketbook* or Virginia Tashjian's *Juba This and Juba That*. Authors and collaborators Joanna Cole and Stephanie Calmenson have also created several collections of folk poetry worth knowing about, such as *Anna Banana: 101 Jump-Rope Rhymes*. And Judy Sierra has gathered a gem with *Schoolyard Rhymes: Kids' Own Rhymes for Rope Skipping, Hand Clapping, Ball Bouncing, and Just Plain Fun*. Several comprehensive collections of folk poetry are available and very appealing to young audiences of all ages. This medium helps validate children's experiences, link oral and written modes of expression, and invite active, even physical participation (Vardell and Jacko 2005). Children can collect other examples on audio- or videotape and explore neighborhood, cultural, and linguistic variations (Vardell, Hadaway, and Young 2002). They can translate their English favorites into other languages represented in their community. Older children may enjoy exploring the historical roots of childhood folklore or writing down new and unfamiliar examples.

## Poetry by Children

It can also be very meaningful to share poem collections that include works authored by children. Several poets who have worked in schools, libraries, and with other youth projects have gathered and edited collections of poetry written by children of all ages. Collections such as *Salting the Ocean*, edited by Naomi Shihab Nye, or *Ten Second Rain Showers* and *Soft Hay Will Catch You: Poems by Young People*, both edited by Sanford Lyne, are beautiful books full of unsentimental and authentic young voices. And for a more humorous look at poetry writing, consider Australian author Gary Crew's mock journal *Troy Thompson's Excellent Peotry* [sic] *Book*, which looks like a collection of very personal poems in a child's own handwriting. For children who aspire to be writers or who may find personal poetry writing a helpful release, these books are an invitation to see themselves as writers, to see children as capable of poetic expression, too.

# Poem Selection Tools

Need help in finding poetry? Choosing the right poem is much like choosing the right storybook or novel: the more poetry books you know, the easier it is to find just the right one. So immersing yourself in the best new poets and poetry books is a good first step. It can also be helpful to maintain your own log, list, or database of favorite poems or poetry books as you read. In this way you can start with a handful of favorites to share and refer to your list over and over again. You can pair poems with other favorite books and activities and continually look for new poems to build your repertoire.

For finding particular poems, there are a variety of resources to try. Several are now available as electronic databases by subscription, which makes searching even easier. The best tool specific to poetry for children is the *Index to Poetry for Children and Young People*, a title, subject, poet, and first-line index to poetry in collections for children and young people, published in installments by H. W. Wilson every three to five years. In total, this reference tool indexes more than 82,700 poems from more than 1,050 collections. This resource is now available electronically through H. W. Wilson's Biography Reference Bank Database, a subscription database available through most libraries.

The Columbia Granger's World of Poetry (http://www.columbiagrangers.org) subscription database includes thousands of poems accessible via the Web, searchable by title, poet, subject, first line, and last line. Granger's has been a definitive source in English for locating poems in anthologies on library shelves since 1904. Although the site is primarily a resource for adult poetry, there are many children's poets represented, including Shel Silverstein, Jack Prelutsky, Arnold Adoff, Janet Wong, and Pat Mora, among others. By and large, this site does not include the actual text of the poems (which are still copyrighted), but it is a helpful poem information locator resource. The Granger Index Reprint series is also helpful and includes many print resources, such as *Poems That Every Child Should Know: A Selection of the Best Poems of All Times for Young People*, among others.

Poem Finder is another web-based subscription service that indexes more than 125,000 full-text poems and 800,000 poem references collected from anthologies, periodicals, and single-author works. Some author biographies, pictures, and explanations of poetry are also available. Poem Finder is a subset of Litfinder, a Thomson / Gale resource, and even includes a "Kids' Korner" with access to poetry in appealing categories for children, such as "Fun and Games," "Animals," and "Family."

One additional electronic database is Poemhunter.com, a resource currently containing 77,956 poems from 9,061 poets as well as songs and quotations. This site includes Silverstein and Prelutsky (among their top 500 poets, no less), but few other contemporary poets who write primarily for children. Nonetheless, the site is free and easy to navigate.

These are great tools to become familiar with. Canvassing colleagues and other poetry lovers (via electronic discussion list) can also turn up poem recommendations. Sometimes you find the perfect poem by serendipity—simply by browsing through relevant anthologies and thematic collections. This is where developing your own personal anthology, log, or database can also come in handy. But having poem selection tools available can also assist you in expanding your poetry choices.

## Poetry on the Web

As we look for new places for poetry to pop up, you can be sure that the Internet will be among them. The websites below make available actual poems, often accompanied by audio recordings of the poems or biographical information about the poet. Some include teaching activities; some even welcome child participation. Each site also offers links to additional poetry resources on the Web.

## Academy of American Poets
http://www.poets.org

This site offers poet biographies, sample poems, audio archives, National Poetry Month celebrations, curriculum resources, teacher discussion forums, teaching tips, and more. Of particular interest, is a listing of success stories describing various poetry promotion activities.

## Poet's Corner
http://www.theotherpages.org/poems/

This site includes the full texts of several thousand poems published in some form or other before 1923 in the United States and thus in the public domain. The site includes a helpful author, title, and subject index for searching for poems, too. Many classic poems for children are available here.

## Poetry 180
http://www.loc.gov/poetry/180/

Billy Collins, a former U.S. poet laureate, helped create this site with the goal of making it easy for high school students to hear or read a poem on each of the 180 days of the school year. He suggests reading one poem over the public address system daily, at the end of the day's announcements. Many contemporary poems are provided and may be appropriate for middle grade children.

## Poetry Daily
http://www.poems.com

This site offers a wonderful way to enjoy a new poem every day, although the poems are not for children, per se. It is a helpful professional source of poetry that you can tap into on a regular basis to feed your own poetic muse.

## Giggle Poetry
http://www.gigglepoetry.com

This kid-friendly website offers poems to read, with new ones posted regularly, as well as opportunities for interaction. Kids can rate the poems, enter poetry-writing contests, explore fun pages for poetry reading, and the like. There are also resource activities for adults who share poetry with children.

## Internet School Library Media Center Poetry for Children
http://falcon.jmu.edu/~ramseyil/poechild.htm

This site is particularly helpful for adults, rather than children, and provides information about forms of poetry, many teaching units and activities, some e-texts and bibliographies, and children's songs and music of all kinds.

## Library of Congress Poetry and Literature Center
http://www.loc.gov/poetry/

This site may interest older children who are interested in learning about the poet laureates of the United States, national prizes in poetry, special poetry events, and in listening to the archive of recordings of over two thousand adult poets reading their own work.

---

### PRACTITIONER PERSPECTIVE

I finally checked out Shel Silverstein's *A Light in the Attic* on cassette. He is an absolute pleasure to listen to! I am amazed at his ability to read each poem with unique expression, and I enjoyed hearing the poems one after the other. He varies the pace of the poems and the volume of his voice to give each reading personality. The background music or sounds bring the poetry to life even more. I am so excited that I ordered this for my new library collection because I know the kids will enjoy it just as much as I did. My favorite reading was of the poem "Squishy Touch," like the Midas touch, except that in this case everything touched turns to Jell-O, not gold. Silverstein brought this poem to life in a way that I never could. He had great sound effects for things turning into squishy Jell-O. Who knew one person could make that many slurpy, squishy noises! (Kids would love to try this as a group reading after hearing Silverstein's version.) I certainly hope that recorded poetry will gain the popularity it deserves, because hearing an author read her or his own poems provides a different perspective for children to enjoy.

Charry Lackey
Librarian
Castle Hills Elementary School
Lewisville, Texas

# Poetry in Magazines

Many magazines and serials that are published for children regularly feature poems. In fact, magazines are often the first medium in which many new poets get their work published. The poems in magazines are often new and not yet available in books, so they can be fresh and fun to seek out and share. Several literary magazines, such as *Cricket, Spider, Ladybug*, and *Cicada*, include poetry by leading contemporary children's poets in every issue. Nature, science, and entertainment magazines also include poetry regularly. See, for example, *Ranger Rick, Your Big Backyard, Chickadee, Odyssey*, and *Highlights for Children*. Children who are avid subscribers may enjoy sharing poems from their favorite magazines.

# Audio Poetry

In an ideal world, we would have access to all children's poems read aloud by the poets who wrote them. Hearing poems read aloud by their authors is a terrific experience. As technology improves, it may get easier to record, publish, and access audio files of poetry. Meanwhile, one has to search diligently to find poetry for children in audiotape or CD form. Two major publishers of audiobooks for young people, Listening Library and Recorded Books, offer several choices, such as the work of Jack Prelutsky and Kalli Dakos. And publishers such as HarperCollins (Harper Children's Audio) and Scholastic (including Weston Woods) often publish audiobook versions of print books they produce. The Caedmon Records imprint, now a part of HarperAudio, has a long history of issuing excellent recordings of poetry, including classic works by the likes of A. A. Milne. Audio Bookshelf offers Paul Fleischman's Newbery Award–winning poetry book *Joyful Noise* as well as works by Ashley Bryan. Live Oak Media's audio poetry selections include Javaka Steptoe's anthology *In Daddy's Arms I Am Tall* as well as John Updike's *A Child's Calendar*. In recent years, many publishers have begun to offer free promotional CDs featuring poems and poets from current works. Such recordings are typically available at conferences or from the publishing company itself.

It is also possible to use the Internet to access some audio files of poetry read aloud. For example, Audible.com, a major provider of audiobooks via downloadable files, offers a handful of children's poetry books such as *Joyful Noise*. Other poetry-related websites, such as the Academy of American Poets, include audio files among their links. The PoetryMagazine.com website(http://www.poetrymagazine.com) is also rich in audio. Of particular note is this site's emphasis on providing audio recordings of many leading poets reading their own works aloud as well as interviews with and speeches by many different poets. The site does not include children's poets, but it is an inspiring example. And more and more children's poets are using their personal websites to provide audio recordings of themselves reading their own poetry. For example, Kristine O'Connell George reads over a dozen of her poems in her Poetry Aloud link at http://www.kristinegeorge.com, accessible via simple free software such as RealAudio or Windows Media Player. If equipment and access are available, such audio experiences can be powerful components in children's exposure to poetry. Audio recordings help children hear the sounds of the words, the rhythm of the lines, and the expression of the reader in ways that make poetry come alive. And although you yourself can provide some insights by reading a poem aloud, it does not compare to the unique and memorable experience of hearing

---

### PRACTITIONER PERSPECTIVE

I used an opportunity to explore poetry performance with my daughter and nieces (aged eight, ten, and twelve years) when we were outside after a swim. We used Paul Fleischman's book *Joyful Noise: Poems for Two Voices* and a collection by Hopkins called *Side by Side: Poems to Read Together*. The poems in *Joyful Noise* are mostly call-and-response, and I introduced these first. I was going to model a poem, but my daughter said, "I can do that," and joined me. Others wanted to try it, too. It really amazed me how they took to Fleischman's book. Given its vocabulary and depth, it is not an easy read, and the format is challenging and unfamiliar, with two columns of alternating lines and some lines in unison. Though the children mentioned that the poems were difficult, they kept going back to try another and another, sometimes starting over to practice the lines, helping each other with difficult words, and commenting on the content: "Oh, that's really sad," or "Butterflies make a chrysalis, but a moth has a cocoon." I was reluctant to try this book with young readers, I admit, and actually decided not to buy another book in the same format because I (mistakenly) thought that the children would not enjoy it. Now I know better. They merely need time to find out about it, play with it, and practice it on their own terms. We just need to bring as many poems to the picnic as we can and let the children decide which ones to sample.

Jean Collier
Librarian
Foster Village Elementary School
North Richland Hills, Texas

a poem read by its author. It is worth the extra effort to seek out such recordings because they are the next best thing to personal visits from the poets.

## Children's Poetry Preferences

As we gather poetry books and seek out poems we think children will enjoy, it helps to know a little about what previous studies have found about children's poetry choices. In several studies of young people's responses to poetry (Terry 1974; Fisher and Natarella 1982; Kutiper and Wilson 1993), there were fairly consistent results. Their findings:

> Narrative poems that tell a story were the most popular form of poetry.
>
> Free verse and haiku were the least popular forms of poetry.
>
> Students preferred poems with strong sound patterns, rhyme, and rhythm.
>
> Children preferred humorous poetry, poetry about familiar experiences, and animal poetry.
>
> Younger students preferred contemporary poems.

Although these are helpful guidelines for selecting poems, they are not absolutes. Children enjoy many forms of poetry, including free verse and haiku, for example, but usually after they have had some broader exposure to poetry in general. There is also no guarantee that every humorous narrative poem about animals will be a hit with every group of children. Also, most studies in the past were based on a limited exposure to poetry over a brief period of time. Thus, we can hope that as children gain greater contact with more poetry, their appetite for poetry will grow in diverse directions. For example, I might rely on the studies' findings in my initial selection of poems to share with a new group of children, but as I get to know the children better as well as deepen my own knowledge of poetry, I feel more confident as I cast about for the right poems to share.

Poet Georgia Heard encourages us to remember what it feels like to be a child, to bear in mind the importance of liking poetry, and to introduce the *joy* of poetry. She encourages natural talk, integrating the sharing of poetry into the daily routine. We should train children's ears and start with poems that guarantee success because they are easy to comprehend. Her advice for beginners includes respecting the mood of the poem, reading slowly, reading the poem multiple times, and displaying the text of the poem. She urges students to make their own anthologies of favorite poems and to study individual poets and their works in depth. Her perspective as a poet and her experiences as a poet in residence working with children in the schools are especially insightful. Although it is helpful to be familiar with studies of children's preferences and development, we can also make a difference for children by sharing our own parallel journeys with poetry with them.

## Evaluating Poetry

How do we evaluate poetry? Poetry is clearly different from prose in its form and structure. But it has poetic elements that give it additional distinctiveness: rhythm, sound, language, imagery, and emotion. As you read poems, you can probably say whether you like them or not. Saying *why* you like them can be more challenging. For example, see if you can pinpoint how a poet is using language that makes the poem special or distinctive. Is it a unique use of figurative language, such as similes and metaphors? Or is it distinctive sound qualities, such as alliteration or onomatopoeia? Naming such elements is not an essential part of sharing poetry with children, although kids often notice them even when they do not know the terminology. Instead, familiarity with poetic elements can help us understand what is hooking us as readers and listeners. And we can look for more! Does the humor in the poem come from the poem's subject? From clever wordplay or puns? Sensory images can also be a powerful draw. Through their powerful use of language, poets can help us see, smell, hear, taste, and even feel that we can touch things. We often rely on poetic elements to guide us in discussing the genre. Which seem most prominent? How does the poet use particular poetic elements to special effect?

Sometimes the best we can do is describe the poetry.

> What is it? Humorous? Abstract? Familiar? Fresh?
>
> How does it work? Through rhyming? Free verse? Shape?
>
> Is the use of language distinctive? Which words stick with you?
>
> Can you visualize the image or feel the experience? Why?

Do not forget to look at a poetry book as a whole, too. Are the poems appropriate for young people? Is there a balance and variety of poems? Is the book well organized and designed? Do the illustrations complement or overpower the poems? Does the book make you want to read more poems by its poet (or anthologist)? Consider the following guidelines, based on questions developed by Goforth (1998), which might provide assistance in evaluating individual poetry books.

## Language

Determine the quality of the poetry by considering questions such as

> Does the poetry have the potential to evoke sensory images?
>
> Does the poetry have a cadence, a beat, a definite rhythm?
>
> If the poetry is written in a rhyming format, are the rhymes natural?
>
> Are the sounds of the poetry appealing?
>
> Does the poet use language in unique, impressive ways to succinctly present ideas, descriptions, and emotions?
>
> Does the poet present fresh, imaginative ideas and feelings?

## Organization

Consider the overall organization of a book by asking questions such as

> Which poets are represented? Are they generally familiar or unfamiliar to young readers?
>
> How current are the poem selections? Does that make a difference?
>
> How are the poems grouped or organized? Is the overall length of the collection appropriate? How is the length of each section?
>
> Is there evidence of different styles and modes of expression across the collection?
>
> Do the poems stimulate a variety of thoughts and emotions?
>
> Is background information on the poets or poems provided?
>
> Is there a table of contents? Subject index? First-line index? Are they helpful?

## Layout

Review the layout of the book by considering questions such as

> Are the poems arranged according to a particular theme?
>
> Are appropriate illustrations or visuals used to enhance and supplement the poetry?
>
> Are the poems and illustrations arranged in a suitable visual design?
>
> Is there distinctive use of spacing, line breaks, and poem formatting?

## Appeal

To match poems and children appropriately, consider questions such as

> Does the poet use poetic types and forms that are naturally appealing to young people and retain their attention?
>
> Are familiar childhood experiences or interesting topics presented in the poem?
>
> Does the poem extend and enrich a child's insight or knowledge?
>
> Will the poem's language be understood by the audience yet expand their linguistic abilities?
>
> Does the poem stimulate the emotions and imagination of the intended audience?

The preceding variables can help us look critically at the poetry books we encounter. They can help us break down the process to look at a book's language, organization and layout, and appeal to children. But ultimately, some trial and error is involved, too. Perhaps more than any other genre, poetry knows no age level or bias. Although poems may appear short and simple on the surface, they may be deceptively complex. And although long narrative poems may seem off-putting to young readers, they can still be engaging when read aloud. So much depends on what we enjoy and how enthusiastically we share it. And the more poetry we know and the more ways we share it, the more likely we are to experience success. So, build the poetry collection, read regularly and widely, and expand your repertoire of poems for reading aloud and performing. That is the recipe for guiding children toward pleasure in poetry.

## Conclusion

It seems there is a renaissance in publishing poetry for young people, with more choices available than ever. Gone are the days of the three-hundred-page anthology presented in small print with no pictures. Poetry books today are short and focused, often richly illustrated. They are visually inviting, and they contain works by more new poets than ever before: poets of color, poets from around the world, and even children and young people publishing their own poetry. Look on your bookshelves. Are any of the foregoing kinds of poetry on your shelves? Are you surprised by how much poetry you may already be using? From now on you will be wearing "poetry-tinted" glasses, looking for poetry all around you.

As much as I enjoy the poetry of Silverstein and Prelutsky and appreciate how much they have done to make poetry popular with children, I think you can see why I feel it is so important to become familiar with *many* poets and seek out *many* different kinds of poetry. This variety is so much more meaningful—and bound to capture even more children. Just as with fiction, we need to seek out a range of realism, fantasy, history, mystery, and other genres to lure as many different readers as possible. The more variety we share, the more likely we are to reach more prospective poetry lovers.

As we expand the poetry holdings in our library collections, there are many different kinds of poetry books we can add. The usual categories apply of course:

- General anthologies
- Topical collections
- Individual poet compilations
- Poem picture books

But there are also many other kinds of poetry books that interest and delight children, from Mother Goose to verse novels. In addition, one can find poems on the Web, in magazines, and in audio formats to expand children's exposure to poetry. Finally, there are helpful guidelines and questions to ask as we assess the quality of the poetry books we encounter. Bottom line: the breadth of poetry available today makes it easier than ever to find poems that children will enjoy again and again.

> *Poetry teaches us the power of a few words.*
> —Ralph Waldo Emerson, Writer

*Chapter Four*
# ⌒⌒ How Do You Promote Poetry?

*Genuine poetry can communicate*
*before it is understood.*

—T. S. Eliot, Poet

ℋow do we promote poetry effectively? In this chapter, we will focus on what to do with poetry once you've found it. We will look at the physical place of poetry in the library, how to feature poetry books in unique ways, how to use displays and materials to promote poetry, and how to connect poetry in a variety of formats through an array of preexisting activities. In addition, we will consider how to connect poetry with other genres and across the school curriculum.

## The Poetry Shelf

Think about what books you have in the children's and young adult area of your library: fiction—a great and never-ending variety; nonfiction—in a multitude of categories; and poetry. These are the primary genres we recognize in literature. We hope children will experience all three as they evolve as readers, and we recognize that each reader will have individual favorites. But how likely are children to discover the poetry books in your collection? Obviously, poetry will be a smaller subset of the total library collection than fiction or nonfiction, but that does not mean it has to be tucked away on the lowest shelf in the farthest region. Are the poetry books as easy to find as the fiction and nonfiction? Are they in a child-friendly location and easily reachable? Is the area well labeled and quickly identified? Do poetry posters and book displays invite children to browse through poetry even if they are not immediately seeking it out? Are some poetry books displayed face out? Is there room on the poetry shelves for expansion? Are the poetry books on the shelf current? Are the poetry award winners represented and highlighted? Are there multiple copies of the most current and popular titles? If there is a separate area for teen or young adult poetry, is that also clearly accessible? If we are serious about helping children discover poetry and then return to it again and again, we need to make this gem of the library obvious, easily reachable, and even unavoidable.

## Creating a Poetry-Rich Environment

Creating an environment that values poetry depends partly on the physical arrangement of space and materials and partly on the emotional climate established by the library staff. Once the poetry books on the shelf are accessible and inviting, the next step is to create a space for sharing poems. Obviously, a designated area for story time can serve for poetry sharing too. But it can also be helpful to have a portable microphone for children who want to read aloud (children often read poetry with very soft voices, even when they are otherwise loud!), and projection equipment can be useful if you want to provide enlarged versions of poem texts so that children can participate in oral or choral reading and poem performance activities.

It can also be fun to involve kids in exploring the poetry environment by presenting a poetry scavenger hunt. Such an activity can be especially productive at the beginning of a year or to kick off a poetry study program. Create a

### Poetry Scavenger Hunt

Find a book of rhyming poetry.

Find a book containing non-rhyming poetry (free verse).

Find a book of bilingual poetry.

Find a book of concrete or shape poetry or haiku.

Find a book of poetry published before 1990 (not Mother Goose).

Find a collection of Mother Goose poetry.

Find a poem picture book (containing a single poem).

Find a book of poetry by an African American poet.

Find a book of poetry by Jack Prelutsky or Shel Silverstein.

Find a thematic collection of poetry (linked by subject, like Halloween poems)

simple grid or list of different kinds of poetry books you would like participants to discover—books beyond the ones they may readily know. Children can work individually or with a partner to locate specific poetry books and browse through them. You can even provide sticky notes that kids can use to mark poems to share, if they desire. This exercise will familiarize participants with the variety of poetry resources available and may lead them to further browsing and reading of poetry.

Our own modeling is another essential ingredient in creating a poetry-priority environment. Have we found poetry that we enjoy and can recommend with genuine enthusiasm? Have we familiarized ourselves with some children's favorites so that we can promote those? Do we mention poetry choices when general subject requests come up? Do we always include poetry books on our recommended reading lists and bibliographies? Do we incorporate poems into our story times and read-alouds? Do we plan special events that focus exclusively on poetry? Wilson and Kutiper (1994, 278) reported that "one elementary school library media specialist noted an increase in poetry circulation after sharing a single poem with students each week as they entered the library." Once we have upgraded our own poetry knowledge, our enthusiastic endorsement can add spice to any literary opportunity. It becomes quite natural to think in terms of poetry when we plan activities, and fitting poems in here and there becomes second nature. And you may find yourself surprised that some children who never responded before open up when you open the door to poetry.

---

### PRACTITIONER PERSPECTIVE

I use a lot of Mother Goose in my story times, and I am surprised sometimes at the number of children and parents who have never heard (what I would consider) basic rhymes—"Little Boy Blue," "Baa Baa Black Sheep," "Old King Cole." Most everyone does seem to know "Twinkle, Twinkle Little Star," though. So it is important to me to use many of these rhymes over and over again, and, if possible, to provide a story-time sheet with the words for the parents to take home if they want to. The kids seem to love the rhymes. I had one little girl who just adored the part in "Sing a Song of Sixpence" when "along came a blackbird and nipped off her nose!" Once I did a whole story time that was just Mother Goose and other traditional stories. That was a lot of fun.

Sarah Dornback
Children's Librarian
Farmers Branch Manske Library
Farmers Branch, Texas

# Occasions to Celebrate Poetry

As we design an environment where enthusiasm for poetry will flourish, we should also consider what Georgia Heard calls poetry rituals. These include a variety of activities that occur on a regular basis, from the simple (monthly posting of poetry quotations) to the more elaborate (annual audiotaping of poems for a listening center.) Such activities become poetry traditions and provide a natural way to incorporate poetry into existing routines. They give children something to look forward to and in many cases provide opportunities for children to participate. As Brountas (1995) has said, "Poetry is a lovely gift we give to children that appreciates in value and lasts throughout their lifetime." Below is a list of possible poetry rituals. Think about choosing one to add to your current literary routine.

> Place a poster-sized poem about libraries at the entrance to the children's area; rotate posters each month.
>
> Start and end each gathering with a poem. (For example, always use the same poem to gather children together, but end each session with a different poem that connects with the story, lesson, or activity.)
>
> Finish each day or week with a poem tied to current or historical events of the day or week. Share holiday poems from varied perspectives to celebrate special holidays.
>
> Invite children to perform their own poem readings on the last Friday of the month (or on another set day).
>
> Read aloud a personally relevant poem for each child's birthday (e.g., a birthday poem or a favorite of the birthday child).
>
> Have a designated area to feature new poetry book acquisitions and to highlight kids' reviews of the books.
>
> Research poets' biographies and celebrate poets' birthdays by sharing some of their poems.
>
> Combine poems with food, sharing a poem (about food) while children enjoy a snack.
>
> If audio announcements are made on a regular basis, include the oral reading of a poem (by a child volunteer) either daily or weekly.
>
> If radio or cable television time is available, include a poem about books, reading, or libraries to begin or end a segment.

If you are truly ambitious, try sharing a different poem each day of the year. There are a few resources available to assist with this gigantic effort, including older anthologies and some calendars and websites. But most of these rely, out of necessity, on classic poems in the public domain. If possible, seek out lively, contemporary poems that correspond with events and happenings of relevance to the children you serve. One excellent resource is Lee Bennett Hopkins's book *Days to Celebrate: A Full Year of Poetry, People, Holidays, History, Fascinating Facts, and More.*

## Celebrating Poets' Birthdays

| January | 6 | Carl Sandburg | August | 17 | Myra Cohn Livingston |
|---|---|---|---|---|---|
|  | 18 | A. A. Milne |  | 19 | Ogden Nash |
| February | 1 | Langston Hughes |  | 21 | X. J. Kennedy |
|  | 2 | Judith Viorst | September | 8 | Jack Prelutsky |
|  | 11 | Jane Yolen |  | 9 | Aileen Fisher |
| March | 17 | Lilian Moore |  | 25 | Harry Behn |
|  | 26 | Robert Frost | October | 20 | Nikki Grimes |
| April | 13 | Lee Bennett Hopkins |  | 27 | Lillian Morrison |
|  | 22 | William Jay Smith |  | 29 | Valerie Worth |
| May | 5 | J. Patrick Lewis | November | 13 | Robert Louis Stevenson |
|  | 12 | Edward Lear |  | 15 | David McCord |
|  | 17 | Eloise Greenfield | December | 5 | Christina Rossetti |
| June | 6 | Nancy Willard |  | 10 | Emily Dickinson |
|  | 7 | Nikki Giovanni |  |  |  |
|  | 24 | John Ciardi |  |  |  |
| July | 10 | Rebecca Kai Dotlich |  |  |  |
|  | 16 | Arnold Adoff |  |  |  |
|  | 17 | Karla Kuskin |  |  |  |
|  | 19 | Eve Merriam |  |  |  |

SOURCE: Based on Lee Bennett Hopkins, *Pass the Poetry, Please!* 3rd ed. (New York: HarperCollins, 1998), 225–27.

## National Poetry Month

Probably the biggest celebration of poetry occurs during April, now designated as National Poetry Month across the United States. There are a variety of ways to make poetry special in April. Do not wait until April, however, to share good poems with children. April is simply a good time to reach out to parents, families, caregivers, and the community at large to share what you have been discovering all year long: poetry is wonderful! In addition, the Children's Book

Council (CBC) sponsors National Young People's Poetry Week during the third week of April, in collaboration with the American Academy of Poets (sponsor of National Poetry Month) and the Center for the Book in the Library of Congress. The CBC produces promotional materials for purchase, such as posters and bookmarks, as well as suggested articles and activities for promoting Young People's Poetry Week. See their website for additional ideas, information, and promotional materials: http://www.cbcbooks.org/yppw/. Then consider how you want to participate in the next nationwide celebration of poetry. And for an autumn poetry occasion, consider celebrating Black Poetry Week every year during the third week of October. Showcase the work of classic African American poets such as Langston Hughes or Paul Laurence Dunbar or the emerging talents of Charles R. Smith Jr. or Jaime Adoff.

Any of the poetry rituals suggested above could be initiated to celebrate National Poetry Month or National Young People's Poetry Week—if they are not already in place. But even more ambitious events are possible with a little bit of creativity and organization. Potato Hill Poetry, a wonderful web resource, suggests many unusual and innovative options at http://www.potatohill.com/npm.html. It is ideal if you can involve colleagues and kids in orchestrating these special celebrations.

## *Ways to Celebrate National Poetry Month*

Start each day with a poem read aloud by a different guest reader: thirty poems for thirty days.

Set up a coffeehouse-style poetry reading in your classroom or library. (Do not forget the refreshments.)

Contact local banks and businesses to ask them to consider displaying student poetry on their walls.

Write poems on postcards or letters and mail them to friends and neighbors.

Contact radio stations about hosting a live, on-air poetry reading at either the school, the library, or the radio station.

Record a poem on your answering machine at home or school or as a cell phone message.

Make a National Poetry Month time capsule. Students can submit favorite poems or their own original writing. Put the works in the time capsule and seal it ceremoniously, not to be opened until National Poetry Month next year.

Send a poem to your state or local representative or other government official.

Make National Poetry Month buttons. Inscribe them with haiku, short poems, or favorite lines of poetry. Wear the buttons the whole month of April.

Become pen pals with another classroom or student group, locally or nationally, and pass favorite and original poems back and forth throughout the month. Make a book of your correspondence.

Plan a poetry reading for a senior center, hospital, or local business.

Experiment with developing a poetry blog where students can share favorite poems or respond to posted poems.

## Poetry Displays

We all know that a good visual display generates interest in library materials. When was the last time poetry for children was the priority in your display? Highlighting new poetry books, low-circulating poetry book gems, books by featured poets, or children's favorite poetry books will make poetry for children more visible in the library. You can use traditional shelf, tabletop, and showcase book displays or other creative approaches. Poet Janet Wong talks fondly of her poetry suitcase filled with objects that correlate with some of her poems. These physical objects (a shoe, a pomegranate) can easily be displayed to add interest to the corresponding poems. Favorite poems can be made into poem posters (please follow fair-use practice) and displayed on doors, in hallways, at entrances, and elsewhere. One enterprising teacher displays poems on the wall over the pencil sharpener or the water fountain, where children often have to stand and wait (and can read idly). Poet Georgia Heard encourages children in the schools to create a living anthology. She says, "Instead of collecting poems we love and putting them in a book, we'll make an anthology out of the walls and spaces around the school. It will be our jobs to make sure poetry is all around the building so that other students and teachers can have a chance to read some poetry" (1999, 23). This is very similar to the initiative launched by the Poetry Society of America, the Poetry in Motion project, which put poems in public transportation systems around the country. Sit on the subway in New York, and you are likely to find poems and poem excerpts to read among all the ads and graffiti.

New or favorite poems can also be displayed via mobiles and other three-dimensional displays. One librarian created a "poet-tree" by using rolled-up brown paper to create a tree trunk and branches and inviting children to write their favorite poems on green paper cut into leaf shapes that were then attached to the tree limbs—the more leaves and poems, the better. If you have access to a hallway, you might consider creating a Hall of Poets that features children's favorite or own original poems, the writing of local poets, the work of favorite or featured poets, or a combination of these. If you want to go the extra mile, create simple mats to go around each poem or frame them in inexpensive picture frames for added impact. And if you want a poetry mascot, consider using Danitra Brown (in the poetry of Nikki Grimes) or Everett Anderson (in the poem picture books of Lucille Clifton) or Fearless Fernie (in the poetry of Gary Soto). These characters appear in multiple poetry collections and thus suggest a variety of themes to explore. Other distinctive personalities emerge from children's poetry as well, such as Mother Goose characters, Anna Banana or Miss Mary Mack, the owl and the pussycat, and Casey (at the bat).

## Poems about Libraries

To celebrate National Library Week or use as an open invitation to the library at any time, you can share, read, or display any of the following poems about libraries:

Kalli Dakos, "When the Librarian Reads to Us," in *Put Your Eyes up Here, and Other School Poems*

Kristine O'Connell George, "School Librarian," in *Swimming Upstream: Middle School Poems*

Nikki Grimes, "At the Library," in *It's Raining Laughter*

J. Patrick Lewis, "Necessary Gardens," in *Please Bury Me in the Library*

Beverly McLoughland, "Surprise," in *Good Books, Good Times!* compiled by Lee Bennett Hopkins

Jane Medina, "The Library Card," in *My Name Is Jorge on Both Sides of the River: Poems*

Eve Merriam, "Reach for a Book," in *Book Poems: Poems from National Children's Book Week, 1959–1998*, edited by Mary Perrotta Rich

Naomi Shihab Nye, "Because of Libraries We Can Say These Things," in *Fuel*

Gary Soto, "Ode to My Library," in *Neighborhood Odes*

Valerie Worth, "Library," in *All the Small Poems and Fourteen More*

Finally, if you have access to a school or library website, consider adding a poetry presence to that display. Poetry quotations can easily be featured on a rotating basis. If more space is available, showcase children's original poems (with their permission), information about new poetry book acquisitions, lists of children's favorite poems or poetry books, or a featured poet of local or national stature. Once again, children themselves can assist you with taking your poetry display efforts online. They often have very creative ideas and the technology skills to translate them into reality!

## Poetry Promotion Materials

Along with creating displays, we know that promotional materials are helpful in communicating with patrons of all ages. We regularly produce or purchase timely bookmarks, booklists, book giveaways, and other materials. How often have we considered featuring poetry in those promotional efforts? Ready-made, commercially produced poetry bookmarks, posters, and the like are available for purchase from multiple sources, including ALA and the Children's Book Council. But many libraries like to create their own innovative and current materials. Of course that is a wonderful idea and enables one to target a specific audience in more meaningful ways.

One warning, however: copyright laws regarding reprinting of poems are very strict. It is not legal to reproduce a poem for mass distribution without obtaining permission from the publishing company and the poet (and often paying permission fees). Although this can be frustrating, we need to remember how few poetry books are published each year and thus how little poets earn in contrast with the J. K. Rowlings in the field of literature. It is acceptable to cite poem titles, poets' names, poetry book titles, poetry website URLs, and the like. Unless poems are in the public domain, however, we are not being poetry advocates if we reproduce them without permission. Poems are in the public domain if seventy-five years have passed since the poet's death, assuming that the poet is the copyright holder. If this is the case, you can use the poem in any way you choose. That is why the classic poems are so often used and reused. Otherwise, I recommend contacting the publisher of the poems you intend to use and asking for permission to feature the poems in your promotional efforts. If your purpose is short-term and nonprofit, you can often get permission. If you do, be sure to include the appropriate credit line in your print materials. If you do not, please respect that poet's right to safeguard her or his artistic creation. Other alternatives are to create your own original verse, or use quotes or slogans, or recruit local poets to write for you (they still deserve compensation but are usually less expensive or willing to volunteer their poems), or invite children to share their original work (and secure permission from them and their families). Developing original poetry promotion materials can be challenging, but if we focus on getting patrons to "think poetry" as a first step, then we can lead them to the actual poems and poetry books on the library shelves.

## When to Share Poetry

Too often, poems are tacked on as an afterthought. We share them occasionally because we think we should. Sometimes we don't even have time to get to poetry. But poetry should be infused throughout our interactions with children. One teacher, Tonya Rodriguez, tried a project she called Three Minutes a Day Can Make a Difference. It was her contention that she could share a poem effectively and even invite the children to participate or respond to it in just three minutes. So for about a month, she took three minutes a day to do just that. Within a week, children were reminding her when she had forgotten their three-minute poetry break. By the end of the month, they were asking to hear favorite poems over again. Three minutes a day *had* made a difference. It had shown these students that poetry was enjoyable, even memorable.

Caroline Feller Bauer takes a similar approach with her book *The Poetry Break* (1995). She proposes a wandering poetry presenter who drops in to share a poem with classes throughout the school throughout the day. Her book is an excellent resource for creative ways to present poetry. The poetry break is an outstanding way to infuse poems throughout a school or library program. Whether a poem is used for beginning the day, starting off the hour, making the transition to lunch or a break, or wrapping things up, the idea of breaking for poetry is very practical. Of course, that does not mean that a more in-depth study of poetry is not a good idea. It is. But for the average teacher, librarian, day care provider, or parent, sharing a three-minute poem break is a good way to begin.

Poetry sharing should probably begin with an intentional plan to incorporate one new strategy into your existing routine. However, once you experience success—and children's enthusiastic responses—you will begin to look for other ways to include poetry, perhaps via poetry rituals or celebrations, or just by being ready for serendipity and the teachable moment. The more poetry you know, the more poetry you try with kids, and the more poetry kids encounter, the more opportunities will present themselves.

## Maximizing Alternative Media

As we consider various ways to present and promote poetry, it can be helpful to consider alternative media as well. Adding variety to our presentation methods provides a leaven that both adults and children enjoy. In particular, remember that many poems are available in audio form, often read by the poet herself or himself. That is a powerful experience and worth sharing. *Poetry Explained*, by Karla Kuskin, is an audiotape produced by Weston Woods that includes Kuskin reading her own poetry as well as talking about poetry in general. *The Words of True Poems*, featuring Georgia Heard reading her poetry along with brief introductory commentary, is produced by Heinemann. Although now out of print, it is still an excellent resource worth tracking down. Many examples of poetry in audio form, in magazines, and on the Web are detailed in chapter 3. One additional resource worth mentioning is Antelope Publishing, a producer of e-books on CD-ROM, among other things. Their Ongoing Tales website at http://www.ongoing-tales.com/SERIALS/oldtime/ POETRY/contains many classic poems in the public domain that have been enhanced with audio. As a poem is displayed, the reader has the option of playing accompanying music, some classical, some folk. It is quite an experience to read the poem "Falling Snow," for example, with classical piano music playing. All the poems are also illustrated in effective ways, which makes this site even more inviting.

The Ongoing Tales site can also provide a model of how to incorporate visuals, background music, and sound effects while reading a poem out loud. For the truly ambitious, reading poems aloud while projecting slides accompanied by sound effects and appropriate music can be very meaningful. For example, imagine the effects of reading nature poems aloud while projecting photos of a forest stream accompanied by the sounds of rushing water, singing birds, and soft, contemporary piano music. Older children can participate in assembling such a poetry show and may enjoy presenting it (prerecorded or live) at a special meeting or an open house. With minimal technology resources, they can create their own simple poem presentations, or video or digital films, and take poem sharing to a whole new level.

## Conducting Spoken Word Events

In "Poetry at the Crossroads of America," Sam White writes about his experiences while standing on the sidewalk in front of the MTV studios at Broadway and Forty-fifth Street in New York City and reading ten of his favorite poems to passersby: "I suspected reading a poem in Times Square would be like throwing an ice cube into a forest fire. I didn't know what place poetry—to my mind the quietest art form—would have." But it worked. People stopped. People listened. People doubled back to get a copy of the homemade anthology White had created. He says, "I believe they stopped at first because these are odd words to hear seemingly out of nowhere, but they took an anthology or stayed to hear the poem read because it's poetry . . . and it made them feel human. Stopping in the middle of the busiest intersection in the country to listen to a poem is a radical act in a hyperactive age. . . . You need only slow and listen" (http://www.pw.org/mag/0301/newswhite.htm).

This is an impressive example of the power of the spoken word as an art form. It is an experience children of all ages respond to—the immediacy of storytelling along with the music of language. For most children aged five to

---

### PRACTITIONER PERSPECTIVE

When I taught sixth-grade English, we did the required kinds of poetry and the lessons we were supposed to do, but then we decided to do something fun. I told the students that we were going to transform the room into a 1950s beatnik coffeehouse. They looked at me as if I had three heads, so I showed them a clip from the movie *Funny Face*, with Fred Astaire and Audrey Hepburn, and they were fascinated. The kids wrote their own poetry—any kind they wanted, on any subject they wanted. They brought pillows from home, and we all dressed in black. My student teacher and I brought hot chocolate (in place of coffee) and cups. We got a spotlight from the Drama Department, moved all the furniture next to the walls, and turned out the lights. I put a stool at the front of the room and announced that the kids could volunteer or not. When someone got up to recite, we snapped our fingers and said, "Oh, yeah, baby, I feel your vibes!" and "Go, man, go!" and turned the spotlight on them. We drummed on the floor and clicked for applause as we exclaimed, "Oh, that is so deep, man!" The readers laughed at us, and we laughed with them. Eventually, everybody participated. Someone on my team got the principal to come down to the room, and she thought it was a blast. The kids had a great time, learned a little cultural history, wrote some very nice poetry, and ended up thinking poetry was fun!

Bonnie Boyd McCormick
Librarian
Crownover Middle School
Denton, Texas

twelve years, however, it is not generally a performance experience they initiate, at least as soloists. In chapter 5, we present a variety of techniques for involving children in spoken word performance, but we take a gentle approach that asks kids to participate in groups of various sizes. It usually requires a bit of maturity, confidence, and experience to prepare poetry for formal, public performance, although there are amazing exceptions, of course. Spoken word events, poetry slams, open mic readings, def poetry, and the like usually target an adult or young adult audience.

For elementary school children, I prefer to emphasize choral reading, readers theater, poetry jams, poetry café readings, puppets and poetry, and the like à la Sara Holbrook's approach in *Wham! It's a Poetry Jam: Discovering Performance Poetry*. Such spoken word events allow children to participate with the support of a partner or group and help them gain confidence as they share poetry with an audience. For example, poetry jams usually begin with one volunteer choosing a favorite poem to share. Then another child can choose a word or image from the poem and find another poem on that topic to share. Other children continue the connection with additional poems. For example, Rose Rauter's "Peach" might connect to Constance Levy's "Moon Peach" or Eve Merriam's "Sunset." This creates a synergy of poetry sharing that is fast paced and inviting. Children look at poems in more open-ended ways, seeking connections and ready to share them in an almost gamelike fashion.

Invite guests to read poetry aloud, particularly professional actors in your area who can offer a polished delivery of poetry and bilingual members of your community who can read poems both in English and in other languages. For younger children, try using puppets to share poems aloud. One children's librarian enjoys creating her own finger puppets out of felt to use with the poem "My Shadow," by Robert Louis Stevenson, for example. She made a person-shaped finger puppet using a die cut and felt and then made an identical black one to represent the shadow. The kindergarteners found it fascinating. Another librarian involved all the sixth graders on her campus in conducting a Poet's Day as a culminating activity for their unit on poetry. Each kid selected a favorite poem and then researched the poet. Each decided how to perform his or her poem, whether to memorize the poem, whether to use props, and so forth. On the actual day, the kids were scattered all over the building. They stood frozen until touched and then performed their poems and shared some quick biographical information about the poets. The rest of the school loved hearing the poems that the sixth graders performed.

Another teacher formed a poetry troupe and worked with volunteers to perform their favorite poems at school and library events (such as open houses and PTA/PTO meetings). And one other colleague allowed her older students to select some of their favorite poems to perform for younger students. They chose to come in costumes and use props. Some worked in pairs; all were successful. And with older students, verse novels can often be adapted for readers theater performance, with excerpts being shared by multiple voices reading different parts. See chapter 3 for examples of verse novels appropriate for nine- to twelve-year-olds.

All children should have the opportunity to enjoy poetry as an event, to see the power of spoken word performance. Volunteers who are eager for the limelight can even work with a coach or mentor to prepare readings and performances for a public audience. We should support their efforts, suggest creative alternatives, provide comfortable venues for practice, and never pressure children who prefer to follow rather than lead.

## Featuring the Poets

One final feature of an environment that encourages a love of poetry is the celebration and study of the poets themselves. From featuring a poet of the month to hosting a visiting poet, there are many ways to showcase the people behind the poems we love. Highlighting a variety of poets on a rotating basis will provide more depth of exposure to their poems and poetry writing. Start with the award-winning poets and other contemporary poets whose works children enjoy (see chapter 2). And look for poets who may live and work in your immediate vicinity.

> Collect the poet's works and make them available.
>
> Create a bulletin board, poster, or display featuring the poet. Include a photo, a printout of his or her website home page, and a few fun facts about his or her life.
>
> Read the poet's works aloud often.
>
> Look up biographical information about the poet and share it with children.
>
> Look for poet-related autobiographies, video and audio interviews, and websites to share.
>
> Investigate setting up an online chat with or even a guest appearance by a poet. Be sure to prepare the children beforehand with extensive reading.
>
> If funds allow, see about setting up a poet-in-residence program, inviting a poet to work with children on an ongoing basis for a short period of time.

## Lee Bennett Hopkins

### *In his own words:*

The main reason I compile theme-oriented collections of poetry such as *Marvelous Math* is due to my being an elementary school teacher. I compile the kinds of poetry books I wish I had had while I was teaching. And why not combine poetry with mathematics? Why not combine poetry with every area of the curriculum? My philosophy is that poetry must be shared every day in every way possible.

Sometimes the subject I am working on sparks me to write a verse of my own, one which I might never have thought about doing before.

I love the sky, particularly at night. Wherever I am I look out the window at the sky's vastness, its mystery, thinking how the moon and stars are above *me* yet also above people miles and miles away.

The sky and math seem to go together. Taking terms like *decimal points, fractions, percentages, multiply, finite* seemed a natural link to create a metaphor between mathematics and the wonders of sky. The sky is indeed "mathematic-filled" isn't it?

Find time to share poetry with our children. Enhance story hours by combining a poem with a picture book. For example, when sharing a classic such as *The Snowy Day*, by Ezra Jack Keats (Viking, 1962), finish the session with Gwendolyn Brooks's "Cynthia in the Snow," from her must-have volume *Bronzeville Boys and Girls*. Within a few minutes children will hear the text of a Caldecott Award–winning volume and also hear words by a Pulitzer Prize–winning poet.

Give children poetry. It is one of the best gifts you can give them . . . a gift to last a lifetime.

### *Sky*

#### *by Lee Bennett Hopkins*

Decimal point
meteors
streak
through the night—

Fractions
of moonbeams
gleam
white-bright—

Percentages
of stars
seem
to multiply—

in the finite
dramatic
mathematic-filled
sky.

*After reading "Sky" out loud once, turn out the lights and invite the children to read it with you by flashlight in four groups, one group per stanza.*

New York City teacher Richard Cappuccio models a new way to use a visiting writer, whether flesh and blood or virtual, in his curriculum unit "Influences, Poems, Product: A Model for Using the Visiting Writer." Through a series of seven lesson plans, Cappuccio and a visiting poet draw students into a dialogue that explores both the poems that have influenced the writer and the poems she or he has written. After examining each group of poems, students have the opportunity to respond by posing questions to the author via e-mail and during classroom visits. The curriculum unit is at http://www.onlinepoetry classroom.org/how/LessonPlan.cfm?prmLessonPlanID=16.

We often feature popular fiction writers with displays and book talks in our daily work. But have we considered giving poets this same publicity? Creating time and space for featured poets helps introduce their work and encourage children to read more poetry. In addition, it can be inspiring for your would-be poets to see that there are successful adults who have made poetry writing their career.

## Pairing Poetry

One way to begin incorporating poetry is to inject poems into the genres and disciplines that are already a part of your schedule. If you regularly read a picture book out loud, try following up with a poem that has a similar subject or theme. If you enjoy reading aloud excerpts or installments of novels, try sharing a related poem to set the stage. If you regularly field questions about classic poems, suggest contemporary poems as bridges to understanding the older works. If you regularly provide support for science or social studies units, try connecting thematic poetry collections with those topics. No matter what we are already doing, poetry can help supplement, support, and enrich it.

Start with a story or book you share often and look for a matching poem. But do not be surprised if you start to work in the opposite direction, falling in love with a poem and seeking out a novel or picture book to pair it with. For example, the classic Grimm folktale "Hansel and Gretel" is available in many picture book versions. Did you know it is also the backdrop for Jane Yolen's mysterious poem "The Magic House," in *Halloween Poems*, compiled by Myra Cohn Livingston? Follow the storybook reading with the Yolen poem and prepare for a rich discussion. Or share Judith Viorst's now-classic picture book *Alexander and the Terrible, Horrible, No Good, Very Bad Day* and follow it with Karla Kuskin's poem listing the same kind of bad-day woes, "I Woke Up This Morning," in *Dogs and Dragons, Trees and Dreams*. If you introduce novels to young readers in book talks or through reading aloud in installments, consider sharing a poem to whet their appetites for the story that follows. For example, Langston Hughes's famous poem "Dreams" can help introduce Linda Sue Park's Newbery Award–winning *A Single Shard*, and Eloise Greenfield's poem "Education," from *Nathaniel Talking*, can set the stage for Louis Sachar's Newbery Award book *Holes*. And, of course, there are many different ways to match a poem with a work of fiction. You may choose a poem that is similar in subject or suggests the same emotions or feelings. And once you make such connections, do not be surprised if children come to you with poems they feel match stories they are reading or books you are sharing. Making connections can be contagious.

## *Pairing Fiction and Poetry: A Sampler*

Some suggested pairings of fiction and poems are

■ Judi Barrett, *Animals Should Definitely Not Wear Clothing* (New York: Aladdin, 1988)
   *Paired with*
   Douglas Florian, "Elephant Pants," in *Bing Bang Boing*

■ Judy Blume, *Superfudge* (New York: Puffin, 2002)
  *Paired with*
  Judith Viorst, "I Love Love Love My Brand-New Baby Sister," in *Sad Underwear, and Other Complications: More Poems for Children and Their Parents*

■ Christopher Paul Curtis, *Bud, Not Buddy* (New York: Delacorte, 1999)
  *Paired with*
  Sara Holbrook, "Blueprints?" in *Am I Naturally This Crazy?*

■ Jacob and Wilhelm Grimm, *Hansel and Gretel*, illustrated by James Marshall (New York: Puffin, 1994)
  *Paired with*
  Jane Yolen, "The Magic House," in *Halloween Poems*, compiled by Myra Cohn Livingston

■ Kevin Henkes, *Kitten's First Full Moon* (New York: Greenwillow, 2004)
  *Paired with*
  Karla Kuskin, "Moon, Have You Met My Mother?" in *Moon, Have You Met My Mother? The Collected Poems of Karla Kuskin*

■ Lois Lowry, *Number the Stars* (Boston: Houghton Mifflin, 1989)
  *Paired with*
  "Birdsong," in *I Never Saw Another Butterfly: Children's Drawings and Poems from Terezin Concentration Camp, 1942–1944*, edited by Hana Volavkova

■ Linda Sue Park, *A Single Shard* (Boston: Clarion, 2001)
  *Paired with*
  Langston Hughes, "Dreams," in *The Dreamkeeper, and Other Poems*

■ Louis Sachar, *Holes* (New York: Farrar, Straus & Giroux, 1998)
  *Paired with*
  Eloise Greenfield, "Education," in *Nathaniel Talking*

■ Chris Van Allsburg, *The Sweetest Fig* (Boston: Houghton Mifflin, 1993)
  *Paired with*
  Mary Ann Hoberman, "Changing," in *The Random House Book of Poetry for Children*, compiled by Jack Prelutsky

■ Judith Viorst, *Alexander and the Terrible, Horrible, No Good, Very Bad Day* (New York: Atheneum, 1972)

*Paired with*

Karla Kuskin, "I Woke up This Morning" in *Dogs and Dragons, Trees and Dreams*

Pairing one poem with another can also be an enjoyable activity. In fact, once you find two poems that seem similar, you will often find yourself hunting for more and more and more similar poems, until you build your own topical collection. Of course, any two poems on the same subject can be matched, compared, and discussed. And poems can be about the same topic but reflect very different points of view, style, or tone. For example, one might be humorous and the other serious. Or you can select two poems that are similar in form—two ballads or two haiku—and talk about the choices each poet made in creating her or his poem just that way. You do not have to be an English teacher with a master's degree to guide this experience. When you share poems on a regular basis and are open to children's individual comments and responses, you may be surprised at what kids notice. Their spontaneous observations are the first steps in literary analysis. They may not always notice what you notice or what you think they should notice, but they notice plenty and will share that with you, if you are receptive.

---

### PRACTITIONER PERSPECTIVE

At the end of the day one Monday I decided on the spur of the moment to read aloud Shel Silverstein's poem "Smart." I read it a couple times, first for the students just to listen, then for them to decide if the kid in the poem is really smart. We finished off with a little bit of math: How much money had he gotten in each trade? Today I read another Silverstein poem, since I am most familiar with him. Again we talked about the poem and what it meant. This discussion was very lighthearted—no analyzing—just why we could not see the kid (he is invisible) and then, because my kids are bilingual, what the word *invisible* means. I have discovered that poetry is missing in my classroom, and now that I have realized it, I will not restrict the sharing of poems to a poetry unit or to National Poetry Month. I will make a wholehearted effort to get poetry where it belongs—in the hands, eyes, ears, and mouths of my students.

> Mary Wegher
> Third-Grade Bilingual Teacher
> Woodrow Wilson Elementary School
> Denton, Texas

As you experiment with pairing poems, it can be helpful to have a handy list of contemporary poems that parallel some of the classic poems kids may encounter in school or in more formal poetry experiences. Sometimes a contemporary poem can offer a bridge to understanding an older, classic poem. Or for students who are already familiar with the classic poems, pairing them with contemporary poems can provide a basis for comparison and discussion. Encourage children who particularly enjoy this exercise to seek additional poems to pair with classics and to share them. It may also be worthwhile to collaborate with YA librarians or high school teachers, who may use classic poetry more often.

## Pairing Classic and Contemporary Poems: A Sampler

Some suggested pairings of classic poems and contemporary poems are

- William Blake, "The Tyger"
  *Paired with*
  Valerie Worth, "Tiger," in *The 20th-Century Children's Poetry Treasury*, compiled by Jack Prelutsky

- Robert Frost, "Stopping by Woods"
  *Paired with*
  Douglas Florian, "Winter Night," in *Winter Eyes*

- Langston Hughes, "Dreams"
  *Paired with*
  Tzu Yeh, "The Frost," in *Leaf by Leaf*, compiled by Barbara Rogasky

- Henry Wadsworth Longfellow, "Paul Revere's Ride"
  *Paired with*
  Gary Crew, "The Ballad of Sergeant Thompson," in *Troy Thompson's Excellent Peotry* [sic] *Book*

- Edna St. Vincent Millay, "Afternoon on a Hill"
  *Paired with*
  Wendy Cooling, "There Is Joy," in *Come to the Great World*

- Ogden Nash, "The Tale of Custard the Dragon"
  *Paired with*
  Shel Silverstein, "Sarah Cynthia Sylvia Stout Would Not Take the Garbage Out," in *Where the Sidewalk Ends*

- Laura E. Richards, "Eletelephony"
  *Paired with*
  Calef Brown, "Kansas City Octopus," in *Polkabats and Octopus Slacks: Fourteen Stories*

- Carl Sandburg, "Fog"
  *Paired with*
  Valerie Worth, "Frost," in *All the Small Poems and Fourteen More*

- Robert Louis Stevenson, "My Shadow"
  *Paired with*
  Joan Bransfield Graham, "Light," in *Flicker Flash*

- Ernest Thayer, "Casey at the Bat"
  *Paired with*
  Charles R. Smith Jr., "The Amazing Jason Williams," in *Hoop Kings*

Pairing nonfiction and poetry may seem to be an unlikely partnership at first, but these two different genres can complement one another by showing children how writers approach the same topic in very different and distinctive ways. In addition, children will see that they can learn a lot of information from both a poem and a work of nonfiction. Poetry has an advantage over nonfiction in that it typically consists of many fewer words. Poems can be read and reread in very little time. Each rereading can be approached in a slightly different way, for example, through choral reading or poetry performance. Poems can also serve to initiate a topic or to enrich and extend it. Their length is less intimidating to children who may be overwhelmed by longer prose and streams of new vocabulary. Although poetry may also present new words and concepts, its shorter appearance provides a motivating advantage. Poems and nonfiction books can be linked by topic to provide multiple perspectives on the same topic. Look for poetry anthologies organized by subject matter, when possible, since they help make the content connection obvious.

## Pairing Nonfiction and Poetry: A Sampler

Some suggested pairings of nonfiction books and topical poem collections are

- Jennifer Armstrong, *Shipwreck at the Bottom of the World: The Extraordinary True Story of Shackleton and the Endurance* (New York: Crown, 1998)
  *Paired with*
  Jane Yolen, *Once upon Ice, and Other Frozen Poems*

■ Rudy Bridges and Margo Lundell, *Through My Eyes* (New York: Scholastic, 1999)
   *Paired with*
   Wade Hudson, comp., *Pass It On: African American Poetry for Children* (New York: Scholastic, 1993)

■ Robert Burleigh and Mike Wimmer, *Flight: The Journey of Charles Lindbergh* (New York: Philomel, 1991)
   *Paired with*
   Constance Levy, *A Crack in the Clouds*

■ Steve Jenkins, *Actual Size* (Boston: Houghton Mifflin, 2004)
   *Paired with*
   Jack Prelutsky, comp., *The Beauty of the Beast: Poems from the Animal Kingdom*

■ Barbara Kerley, *The Dinosaurs of Waterhouse Hawkins* (New York: Scholastic, 2001)
   *Paired with*
   Jack Prelutsky, *Tyrannosaurus Was a Beast: Dinosaur Poems*

■ Kathryn Lasky, *The Man Who Made Time Travel* (New York: Farrar, Straus & Giroux, 2003)
   *Paired with*
   Lee Bennett Hopkins, comp., *It's about Time*

■ Jacqueline Briggs Martin, *Snowflake Bentley* (Boston: Houghton Mifflin, 1998)
   *Paired with*
   Barbara Rogasky, comp., *Winter Poems*

■ Sy Montgomery, *The Tarantula Scientist* (Boston: Houghton Mifflin, 2004)
   *Paired with*
   Lee Bennett Hopkins, comp., *Spectacular Science: A Book of Poems*

■ Doreen Rappaport, *Martin's Big Words* (New York: Hyperion, 2001)
   *Paired with*
   Myra Cohn Livingston, *Let Freedom Ring: A Ballad of Martin Luther King Jr.*

■ Walter Wick, *A Drop of Water: A Book of Science and Wonder* (New York: Scholastic, 1997)
   *Paired with*
Joan Bransfield Graham, *Splish Splash*

Poetry's brevity, conceptual focus, and rich vocabulary make it a natural teaching tool for connecting with nonfiction. Like nonfiction, poetry can be informative as well as inspiring. Several additional advantages come with using poetry across the curriculum:

Poetry is accessible to a wide range of reading abilities.

The brief format of much poetry taps the essence of a subject.

Poetry can provide sensory experiences, giving children the sense of touching, feeling, smelling, hearing, and seeing.

Poetry can make a topic memorable through the use of highly charged words and vivid images.

Poetry can help children talk about issues that concern them.

## Poetry across the Curriculum

Enterprising teachers and librarians will find that poetry lends itself to integration across the curriculum, in areas such as language arts, science, mathematics, and social studies. If you offer instructional support on a regular basis, there are several ways that poems can enhance current teaching and learning in every subject area. Poetry breaks across the curriculum can serve to

- Jump-start or introduce a lesson or topic
- Present examples of terminology or concepts
- Offer a transition between activities
- Supply a stretching (poetry) break
- Provide closure
- Extend a topic further

Three rich resources full of strategies for connecting poetry with the major curricular areas (math, science, social studies) are Barbara Chatton's book *Using Poetry across the Curriculum* (1993); Bernice Cullinan, Marilyn Scala, and Virginia Schroder's collaboration, *Three Voices: An Invitation to Poetry across the Curriculum* (1995); and Poet Sara Holbrook's *Practical Poetry: A Nonstandard Approach to Meeting Content-Area Standards* (2005). But in her

— POET PROFILE —

# Nikki Grimes

## *In her own words:*

I can't overestimate the value of poetry performance. I get letters and e-mails from K–12 teachers from all over the country, and from as far away as New Zealand, all commenting on the excitement their students are experiencing as open-mic poetry readings and slams are making their way into the classroom. Kids who were falling asleep are suddenly lit up with enthusiasm. This is one bandwagon we all need to jump on!

The form of poetry performance may differ from elementary school to middle school to high school, variously incorporating call-and-response, oral interpretation, readers theater, choreographed poetry, and poetry slams. In general, though, performance is a tool in confidence building and in nurturing a love of, and respect for, language. Some of the back story on *Bronx Masquerade* demonstrates what I mean.

For several years, I'd had the idea to write a book in which I'd follow a group of high schoolers over the course of a year, exploring their lives in poetry and prose. I'd sketched out the characters and their issues and began writing their monologues and poems. What I didn't have was an overall plot.

Enter Drew Ward, a local poet and high school teacher. Drew was teaching a section on the Harlem Renaissance and wanted his students to meet a living poet from Harlem who'd been influenced by the poets of that era. I obliged with a school visit. What I didn't know was that Drew had started an open-mic series in his classes earlier in that year, and by the time of my visit, a poetry movement was in full sway. Students from other classes frequently got passes to visit his homeroom so that they could observe, and even participate in, these readings.

How did this come about? In teaching students about the Harlem Renaissance with an emphasis on poetry, Drew brought in poetry to read, including his own. The students liked what they heard, and after Drew read one of his pieces, a student raised his hand and said, "I have a poem. Can I read mine?" Drew said yes. Immediately, other hands went up around the room. There were, he discovered, closet poets in each of his classes, and so he scheduled regular readings, eventually setting up a stage, of sorts, in the center of the room. He brought in spotlights and a video camera to document it all, and the budding poets were off and running. Those readings are still going on and they inspired the plot of *Bronx Masquerade*.

I sometimes run into that first crop of kids on the street in my community and they're still talking about that experience, four years later. They express how much they learned about themselves and one another, how their preconceived notions of other races and other cultures disintegrated. Within that experience, they formed a sense of community that none of them thought possible. All that from a series of poetry readings!

Looking for a way to get your students' attention? This is one way to do it.

### *April Ala Carte*
#### *by Nikki Grimes*

The long afternoon walk
whet my appetite.
I greedily scooped
two dollops of cloud
from the sky
drizzled them
with sunshine
and silently
said grace

*After sharing "April Ala Carte," encourage the kids to consider what their recipe for a perfect April afternoon might be. Which ingredients would they include? Clouds? Sunshine? And what might their quantities be? A teaspoon? A pinch? Work together to create a collective poem with the students' own ingredients and measurements.*

work *Give Them Poetry: A Guide for Sharing Poetry with Children K–8*, Glenna Sloan (2003) issues "a word of caution in the matter of 'using' poetry in the service of other areas of study: Poetry should be allowed to develop literacy on its own" (16). There are many possibilities for linking poetry with subject matter, but do not forget to stop and enjoy the poems for their own sake, too.

# Poems for Reading and Language Arts Study

Once you start gathering a small collection of poems related to social studies, science, or math, you may be surprised to discover how many poems you can find. But remember that poetry study deserves a place in the reading and language arts curriculum, too. We have seen how poems can be matched with novels, picture books, and nonfiction books. Poems can even serve to gently reinforce mini lessons on grammar and parts of speech. And of course poems can serve as a subject of study all their own. A unit devoted exclusively to poetry can focus on

- One favorite poem (e.g., "Paul Revere's Ride")
- A thematic collection of poems (e.g., poems about school)
- A poetic formula (e.g., concrete poems)
- A stylistic device (e.g., personification)
- One poet (e.g., Douglas Florian)

This crystallized focus of poetry can aid children as they use their word knowledge to make sense of new content. A poem's context can help the reader or listener incorporate new vocabulary. When children read a poem, hear a poem read aloud, and participate in a choral reading of a poem, they have had multiple modes of reinforcement for meaningful language learning. Poetry also contains elements of predictability, such as rhyme, rhythm, and repetition, which make reading easier. Cullinan, Scala, and Schroder (1995) provide a multitude of strategies that can be used with poetry across the curriculum. Some of the most intriguing and innovative options are labeled

- Art, Music, and Poetry
- Biography and Poetry
- Poetry and History in Songs
- Poetry Maps
- Science Riddles
- Science Sentence Poems
- Think Like a Scientist
- Time, Poetry, and Problem Solving

### Poetry about School: A Thematic Collection

Children particularly enjoy poetry about school since most of their daily lives are spent there. The ups and downs of class-room life make fine grist for both humorous and serious poetry. Share the following poems as a school year begins, for special school events, and even with homeschooling families.

> Kalli Dakos, *If You're Not Here, Please Raise Your Hand: Poems about School*
>
> ———, *Don't Read This Book, Whatever You Do! More Poems about School*
>
> ———, *Put Your Eyes up Here, and Other School Poems*
>
> David L. Harrison, *Somebody Catch My Homework*
>
> Florence Parry Heide and Roxanne Heide Pierce, *Oh, Grow Up! Poems to Help You Survive Parents, Chores, School, and Other Afflictions*
>
> Lee Bennett Hopkins, ed., *School Supplies: A Book of Poems*
>
> Dorothy M. Kennedy, ed., *I Thought I'd Take My Rat to School: Poems for September to June*
>
> Betty Paraskevas, *Gracie Graves and the Kids from Room 402*
>
> Carol Diggory Shields, *Lunch Money, and Other Poems about School*
>
> ———, *Almost Late to School, and More School Poems*

## Poetry and the Social Studies

We have long recognized the value of children's literature for teaching social studies with the annual publication of "Notable Children's Trade Books in the Field of Social Studies." But poetry can also be a valuable tool in this area. "Curriculum Standards for Social Studies: Expectations of Excellence," formu-lated by the National Council for the Social Studies, identifies ten strands of

### Poems for Social Studies Standards

Below is a sample poem for each of the curriculum standards for social studies established by the National Council for the Social Studies.

1. Culture: "Speak Up," by Janet Wong, in *Good Luck Gold*
2. History: "Harriet Tubman," by Eloise Greenfield, in *Honey, I Love*
3. Geography: "Someday Someone Will Bet That You Can't Name All Fifty States," by Judith Viorst, in *Sad Underwear, and Other Complications*
4. Identity: "So I'm Proud," by Jean Little, in *Hey World! Here I Am!*
5. Institutions: "If Kids Were Put in Charge of Schools," by Kalli Dakos, in *Don't Read This Book, Whatever You Do!*
6. Government: "When I Am President," by Felice Holman, in *The Song in My Head*
7. Economics: "How Things Work," by Gary Soto, in *A Fire in My Hands*
8. Technology: "Plugging In," by Shel Silverstein, in *Falling Up*
9. Global connections: "Wars," by Jean Little, in *Hey World! Here I Am!*
10. Citizenship: "Pledge," by Carol Diggory Shields, in *Lunch Money*

Source: Based on "In Search of a Scope and Sequence for Social Studies," *Social Education* 53, no. 6 (October 1989): 376–85.

study within the discipline. Poetry can be linked with each of those standards and subject areas (Vardell 2003).

Pile up the poetry books, bring together teachers and librarians, or challenge the children with a social studies plus poetry scavenger hunt. Many examples of social studies–related poems can be found in various anthologies and poetry books. Those poems can be used to introduce the topic of a lesson, to supplement the content, or to extend the themes studied. Such poetry nuggets can give children a hook for incorporating new information. When integrated into traditional social studies lessons, they also provide motivation and variety.

## Ten Poetry Collections for Social Studies Not to Be Missed

Susan Altman and Susan Lechner, eds., *Followers of the North Star: Rhymes about African American Heroes, Heroines, and Historical Times*

Catherine Clinton, ed., *I, Too, Sing America: Three Centuries of African American Poetry*

Amy L. Cohn, ed., *From Sea to Shining Sea: A Treasury of American Folklore and Folk Songs*

Lee Bennett Hopkins, ed., *Hand in Hand: An American History through Poetry*

---

### PRACTITIONER PERSPECTIVE

I teach zoo school in the summer. I usually work with the third and fourth graders for a week to teach them about the different animals found in the zoo and then take them on tours. When we spent an entire day on snakes last week I decided to include Shel Silverstein's poem "Boa Constrictor" and see what movement the kids could incorporate into it. I got all the kids on the floor for the lesson and spent about ten minutes talking about the boa and the characteristics the snake has. We discussed how snakes can unhinge their jaws and swallow their prey whole. Then I got out the Silverstein book and the kids got very excited: "I have that book!" "My teacher read that to us!" and so on. I told the kids to listen to the poem once with their eyes closed. They all had smiles on their faces. Then we spread out and I read it again as they acted it out with whatever movements they wanted. It was very funny watching them, and I barely made it through the poem without laughing. The best thing was that some of them had memorized the poem, and they quoted it along with me. After we finished they begged me to read some more and were even willing to trade their zoo visit for a chance to hear more poems! I told them we could do some more later, and they made sure I kept my promise.

Lindsey Mendrop
Librarian
Weatherford Ninth-Grade Center
Weatherford, Texas

———, ed., *My America: A Poetry Atlas of the United States*

J. Patrick Lewis, *A World of Wonders: Geographic Travels in Verse and Rhyme*

Nora Panzer, ed., *Celebrate America in Poetry and Art*

Neil Philip, ed., *Singing America: Poems That Define a Nation*

Charles Sullivan, ed., *Here Is My Kingdom: Hispanic-American Literature and Art for Young People*

Hana Volavkova, ed., *I Never Saw Another Butterfly: Children's Drawings and Poems from Terezin Concentration Camp, 1942–1944*

## Poetry and Science

The list "Notable Children's Trade Books in the Field of Science" appears every spring in the journal *Science and Children*. It reminds us that trade books have a great deal of potential for supporting science learning, too. Poetry, in particular, offers the special language, imagery, and conciseness that helps introduce or reinforce important science concepts. A brief consideration of a handful of poetry books will quickly reveal many poems that connect with the sciences. In fact, there are many thematic poetry collections devoted to science-related subjects, such as animals, weather, seasons, space, dinosaurs, and geography, to name a few.

### *Ten Poetry Collections for Science Not to Be Missed*

Barbara Brenner, ed., *This Earth Is Painted Green: A Garden of Poems about Our Planet*

Paul Fleischman, *Joyful Noise: Poems for Two Voices*

Douglas Florian, *Insectlopedia*

———, *Mammalabilia*

Georgia Heard, *Creatures of Earth, Sea, and Sky*

Lee Bennett Hopkins, *Spectacular Science: A Book of Poems*

Myra Cohn Livingston, *Space Songs*

Jeff Moss, *Bone Poems*

Jack Prelutsky, comp., *The Beauty of the Beast: Poems from the Animal Kingdom*

Jane Yolen, *Once upon Ice, and Other Frozen Poems*

# Poetry and Mathematics

Again, in the area of mathematics teaching and learning, poetry has a great deal of potential. Indeed, because much of mathematics deals with numbers, theories, and calculations, the language and imagery of poetry may help children visualize abstract concepts and operations. Hunting for math poems, however, is a bit challenging. A handful of poetry anthologies are devoted exclusively to math topics, but many more math-related poems can be found in general anthologies.

## Ten Poetry Collections for Mathematics Not to Be Missed

Barbara Juster Esbensen, *Echoes for the Eye: Poems to Celebrate Patterns in Nature*

Betsy Franco, *Counting Caterpillars, and Other Math Poems*

———, *Mathematickles!*

Lee Bennett Hopkins, comp., *It's about Time*

———, comp., *Marvelous Math: A Book of Poems*

J. Patrick Lewis, *Arithme-Tickle: An Even Number of Odd Riddle-Rhymes*

Richard Michelson, *Ten Times Better*

Mary O'Neill, *Take a Number*

Nikki Siegen-Smith, *First Morning: Poems about Time*

Harriet Ziefert, *Mother Goose Math*

Interdisciplinary or thematic teaching is one popular way to bring the curricular areas together for maximum learning. According to Barbara Chatton (1993), including poetry in thematic units that seek to integrate subject areas offers multiple opportunities for extending instruction.

- Poetry can provide cognitive transfer from concept to concept.
- Poetry deepens comprehension by providing another example of a concept.
- Poetry provides more personal connections.

The more connections we can provide between what children are learning in various areas of study, the deeper their learning will be. If poetry can be that vehicle for connecting books, skills, concepts, and information across the curriculum, we owe it to children to infuse poetry wherever we can.

## Conclusion

Once we are well versed in children's poetry, recognize popular titles, and know major poets, how do we present poetry effectively? We can begin by conducting a quick assessment of our facilities and activities, checking the poetry shelves, and looking at our programming calendars. Are there poetry events and celebrations in the works? What poetry-related visual aids and promotional materials are visible (or in the files)? Is poetry part of future planned displays?

Then, as we incorporate poetry into our routines, we only need three minutes to begin to make a difference. Whether we use poetry breaks or another approach, poems can quickly be incorporated into existing activities. In addition, we can add novelty by incorporating a variety of media alongside the poetry we select. As we build on that base, we can also create spoken word events that help children enjoy the oral qualities of poetry. One additional way for promoting poetry is to highlight the poets themselves.

Finally, as we inject poetry into our plans, we can pair poetry with other genres, such as fiction and nonfiction, or couple related classic poems and contemporary poems. Or if we consider the school curriculum of language arts, social studies, science, and mathematics, we can find many relevant poems. A quick list to guide a poetry checkup might include the following:

Check the children's poetry shelves for ease of access and appeal.

Look for signage that highlights children's poetry.

Create promotional materials and displays that include children's poetry.

Plan for National Poetry Month and Young People's Poetry Week.

Consider establishing poetry rituals as part of your routine.

Start sharing children's poetry in as little as three minutes' time.

Emphasize aural (spoken word) qualities of children's poetry.

Feature children's poets in displays, materials, and book talks.

Pair children's poetry with picture books, novels, and nonfiction.

Inject children's poetry into instruction in language arts, social studies, science, and mathematics.

   With these building blocks in place, poetry can have a well-established place in any library. What's next? Strategies for sharing poetry and inviting children to read along are helpful in making poems come alive. Once we have invited children into the world of poetry, our next step is to engage their active participation in that world.

> *Instead of building a fence of formality around poetry,*
> *I want to emphasize its accessibility, the sound, rhythm,*
> *humor, the inherent simplicity. Poetry can be as natural*
> *and effective a form of self-expression as singing or*
> *shouting.*
>
> —Karla Kuskin, Poet

## Chapter Five

# ⌒⌒ How Do You Present Poetry to Children?

*A child's first encounter with
poetry happens only once.*

—Brod Bagert, Poet

𝓗ow do we introduce poems to children? What strategies are engaging and effective for young audiences? In this chapter, we will consider basic guidelines that can assist adults when they read poems aloud. We will look at how to set the stage for children to participate and consider in detail ten key strategies for enabling their active participation. Finally, we will examine creative alternatives that add variety to poetry-sharing activities.

## Why Share Poetry Out Loud?

The first step in inviting children into the oral world of poetry is very simply to read poems aloud. Hearing poems read out loud helps children attend both to the sounds of the words and lines and to their meaning. It sets the stage for children's participation in the read-aloud process. It familiarizes them with what the words of the poem should sound like and engages their listening comprehension in making sense of the poem's meaning. In addition, there is an affective benefit in that a reader can communicate to children his or her personal pleasure in poetry, in the sounds of words, in the rhythm of the lines. Also, through our willingness to share poems out loud, we subtly extend an invitation to children to follow our lead in trying on poetry.

Poetry is meant to be read aloud. Meaning is more clearly communicated when a poem is both read and heard. As poet Brod Bagert (1992) has said, exactly as songs are not just sheet music, poetry is not just text. The rhythm or rhyme of poetry can help children begin to get a sense of the sound of artful yet natural language. When children participate in reading aloud, they have the opportunity to develop their own oral fluency. Experimenting with various approaches to reading poetry aloud can help children express themselves and build confidence.

## Guidelines for Oral Reading of Poetry

So how do you begin? As I experimented with sharing poetry with children of different ages, I found specific steps for leading children to become comfortable with performing poetry out loud. I always begin by choosing poems that I enjoy. That may seem obvious, but so often we choose poems that we think we should choose or that we think children may enjoy. Over the years, I have found it is hard to sell a poem that does not speak to me personally. And there are so many poems available nowadays that it is easier than ever to find poems you connect with. Of course each person may choose completely different poems. I enjoy sharing humorous poems and find that most children respond readily to humor, but there are many other possibilities, too.

Next, I practice reading the poem aloud to myself a few times to get comfortable with the words, lines, pauses, and rhythm. Poet Eve Merriam advocates reading out loud, even when you are by yourself. And Chatton (1993) suggests avoiding the tendency to read in a singsong voice and instead paying attention to the line breaks for read-aloud cues.

On his Poetry180 website former Poet Laureate Billy Collins writes about reading a poem:

> Reading a poem slowly is the best way to ensure that the poem will
> be read clearly and understood by its listeners. Learning to read a

---

**PRACTITIONER PERSPECTIVE**

It is interesting that the idea of reading poetry with the right expressions and voice seems new and exciting, but we read prose stories out loud to children in this manner all the time. What is it about poetry that causes us to think we need to read in a different way? I know that not all picture books or even all novels make good read-alouds, but poetry is meant to be heard. It seems, then, that it would not be too difficult to use poetry during read-aloud times. But we just don't think about it much.

Jackie Chetzron
Librarian
Lake Highlands Junior High
Richardson, Texas

poem slowly will not just make the poem easier to hear; it will under-score the importance in poetry of each and every word. A poem cannot be read too slowly, and a good way for a reader to set an easy pace is to pause for a few seconds between the title and the poem's first line. . . . Read in a normal, relaxed tone of voice. It is not neces-sary to give any of these poems a dramatic reading as if from a stage.

I prepare a brief introduction to cue the children to listen to a poem rather than to a story or other genre. For example, I might say, "I have a few poems here I'd like to share with you. They are short and funny and you may have heard them before. If not, you're in for a treat. I'll read the poem out loud and you can follow along." I always read the title of the poem, then the poet's name, then the poem itself. I follow this pattern every time so that listeners become fa-miliar with the routine and learn where the reading begins and ends. As I intro-duce successive participation activities, it helps to have this routine in place.

Poet and anthologist Lee Bennett Hopkins suggests the following strategies for reading a poem aloud:

> Choose a poem you like that you think the audience will enjoy too. Familiarize yourself with the poem by reading it aloud to yourself several times. Get the feel of the words and rhythm. Mark words and phrases you want to emphasize. Read to the group in a natural style. Follow the rhythm of the poem. Note how the physical appearance of

---

**PRACTITIONER PERSPECTIVE**

I think line breaks and negative space are useful in engaging the reluctant reader. I have seen so many students flip through a book with an interesting title to check for word density or chapter length, only to put the book back on the shelf when it looks overwhelming. In poetry, line breaks and negative space make the page airy and manageable. The reluctant reader can take big or little bites as he or she desires.

I gave my daughter a verse novel to read last night. She opened it, flipped through, returned to page one, and read the first fifty pages without pause. I am convinced that the white space on the page and the small commitment required to read one page at a time set the hook.

Clarice Howe-Johnson
Associate School Library Media
Specialist
Harding Elementary School
Kenilworth, New Jersey

### Understanding Line Breaks and White Space in Poems

Poet Georgia Heard (1999) teaches us about line breaks and white space as cues that can enhance our effectiveness when reading poems aloud. In fact, she lists what she calls line-break fundamentals:

- Line breaks are there on purpose to help us pause.
- Like breaks affect a poem's rhythm (short lines are more choppy).
- Each poem line is a unit of meaning.

Heard also talks about the use of white space and the creation of stanzas. She tells us that poets use white space to

- Slow a poem down
- Encourage the reader to stop and think
- Set off the final line and give it more impact
- Single out a line

If we study the way a poem is presented on the page, we can use the poet's cues to guide our oral reading.

the poem on the page dictates the rhythm and mood. Stop for a moment at times when it pleases you and when it fits with the content and mood of the poem. Use your normal voice, as if describing a daily event. Be sincere. Stay quiet at the end of the reading (http://www.rif .org/educators/rifexchange/programdescriptions/QA_show205.mspx).

Cullinan, Scala, and Schroder (1995) recommend that we read a poem at least twice, although children may often ask to hear it even more. Poet and teacher Georgia Heard says that we should make sure there is a lot of silence around a first reading (1999). Try mentally counting to five if you are initially uncomfortable with the quiet. Give children a few moments to absorb the words and meaning of the poem.

## Using Body Language Effectively

It is also helpful to consider your nonverbal presentation of poetry, including the hand gestures and facial expressions you are using. In his article "Act It

Out: Making Poetry Come Alive," Bagert (1992) encourages us to become aware of how we can use our faces, voices, and bodies to perform poetry effectively. With modeling and practice each nonverbal variable can be more consciously manipulated. He recommends the following exercise:

> Make a sad face. Droop your eyes, pout your bottom lip, tilt your head to the side and say, "I am not very happy." You will find that voice, body, and timing tend to follow your expression. Now try to defy nature. Make the same sad expression and try to say "I am very happy" in a cheerful voice. You will find that it is very hard to sound happy when your face is sad. Conduct the search for what a poem means and how to perform it by asking a single question: What face should I make when I say these words? Then make the face and say the words.

Be aware of how you can use your face and gestures to enhance your poem delivery. Audiotape or videotape yourself occasionally to assess your delivery. You may be surprised at the difference between how you think you are coming

---

## PRACTITIONER PERSPECTIVE

I think an important aspect to remember when reading poetry is that despite what others try to teach us, there are really no rules on how to read it. I typically read a poem a few times. One time I may read it the way the punctuation flows and next I might read it pausing only at line breaks, but usually I like a poem best when I combine punctuation and line breaks to make it sound right to me. Not only that, but I might read the poem an entirely different way the next time to get a different effect.

When I was a dancer many years ago, my coach always told us that even when we did not feel like dancing our hearts out or putting forth any energy at all, we should just smile as big as we could. She said that if we showed energy on our faces, it would translate into our actions—and it did. I think this is an excellent way to teach kids how to read poetry dramatically. Have them decide which face goes with the poem they are reading, and if you have written the poem on chart paper—draw a picture of the face on the side to remind everyone. Often when kids are making the right face, their voices will reflect the right feeling and intonation.

Lauren Yarbrough
Reading Specialist
Calvin Bledsoe Elementary School
Frisco, Texas

across and how you are actually coming across. Experience with book reading and storytelling is helpful too, of course, but poetry reading is even slower and filled with more pauses than prose reading. Fortunately, children are generally very forgiving and ready to engage in whatever we prepare and share.

## Getting Children Involved

Reading the poem out loud oneself, however, is only the first part of sharing poems with children. Although it can be enjoyable for them to listen repeatedly to an enthusiastic and knowledgeable adult share appealing poems out loud, the idea is to invite children into the pleasures of poetry through participating in the experience more actively. Thus, the rest of this chapter will focus on ways to invite children into the read-aloud performance of poetry. In the past, this was often called *choral reading* of poetry. This label is fine, but it suggests a chorus style of reading poetry in groups. I have found that there are many ways to involve children in large groups, small groups, and as single volunteers. Others use the term *poetry performance* for reading poems aloud. This label is also fine but often suggests a more formal, polished performance based on knowing the poem by heart or poetry created on the spot for an audience. Although some children enjoy poetry so much that memorizing a poem or performing it in front of an audience is a treat, I look for ways to involve kids of all kinds in experiencing poetry in more informal, spontaneous ways. Poet Sara Holbrook reminds us to "show the world that poetry was never meant to simply lie quietly on the page, any more than kids were meant to sit quietly in their seats to read it" (2002, 54).

What about shy children? I have visited many libraries and classrooms of all levels to lead poetry performances and often find that there are a few children who do not participate, even after several visits. And that is perfectly fine. My goal is to invite children into poetry—as far as they want to go. Over time, I generally find that kids warm up and jump in—but not all. Even if I were their classroom teacher, I would still not *require* all children to perform in front of the whole class. There are many other smaller steps they can take to get comfortable expressing themselves orally. I was one of those shy children who are mortified to be required to speak in front of a group. I still have vivid memories of standing up by the teacher's desk in sixth grade to recite a Longfellow poem. Not a fun and happy moment. Yes, it is true that we get more confident with practice and experience, but we should also be able to build that confidence in safe and supportive surroundings. Educator Regie Routman (2000) has found that children proudly read aloud their favorite poems in group environments when they are supported and comfortable.

**Poetry Break Pointers**

Caroline Feller Bauer's book *The Poetry Break* (1995) is an excellent resource for additional ideas on sharing poems with children. Here are some of her pointers:

Be sure to give the title and author of the poem.

If possible, show the book the poem comes from.

Feel free to reread the poem immediately.

Be sure you distinctly enunciate each word (and check uncertain pronunciations and meanings beforehand).

Be careful of singsong delivery of rhyming verses.

Use commas and periods as signals to pause in your reading.

Dramatize miniconversations in poems.

Glance at your audience occasionally.

Try sharing the poem read on tape by the poet.

Add variety by setting the stage with a flashlight or music.

Invite a guest presenter to share a poem (including in multiple languages).

A favorite puppet can present the poem.

A portable microphone can add to the effect.

Poem introductions can include

- a sign announcing Poetry Break
- information about the poet
- information about the topic of the poem
- how you felt when you first read the poem or how it affected you
- why you chose that poem (or chose that particular day to read the poem)
- a prop that fits the poem
- a "This reminds me of" connection to another poem, book, or song.

## Ten Strategies for Sharing Poetry Out Loud

Through research and reading as well as trial and error in classrooms and libraries, I have identified ten general strategies for involving children in reading poems out loud. This is not rocket science. You may have heard of all these or tried them yourself in the past. However, I have ordered them in a way that eases children into participating in comfortable ways, provides the adult leader with a helpful framework, and suggests specific poems for each approach. In addition, the diversity of the approaches adds spice to the practice of reading poetry aloud. Just trying the different strategies and incorporating them into your read-aloud repertoire will add a variety of tools that will come in handy again and again.

The ten strategies I have found most successful are presented in order of general difficulty. They begin with recommending that the adult take the lead, but they gradually invite greater and greater child participation. This helps children get their feet wet at participating in the oral reading of poetry in groups so that they gain confidence and get comfortable with volunteering to read solo lines, poems for two voices, and so forth. As the strategies get more complicated, they take more explaining and preparation, but the results can be very rewarding for everyone involved. The strategies are

1. *Modeling*: The adult reads the poem aloud.
2. *Unison*: Everyone reads the poem together at the same time.
3. *Refrain*: Children join in on a repeated line, stanza, or word.
4. *Movement*: Children read in unison using motions or gestures.
5. *Call-and-Response*: Two groups read alternating (not simultaneous) lines or stanzas.
6. *Groups*: Multiple groups read various lines or stanzas.
7. *Solos*: Individual children read individual lines.
8. *Two Voices*: Two people read two parts, sometimes with simultaneous but differing lines.
9. *Canon*: Two groups read the same poem, with one group delaying its start until the other reaches a predetermined point.
10. *Singing*: Children sing poems set to familiar tunes.

Once you are familiar with these strategies, you can combine them in a variety of ways. Once children gain some experience, they themselves will often spontaneously suggest performance possibilities. And of course every poem performance should be celebrated and acknowledged with soft applause (the golf clap), a silent cheer, pats on the back (each person patting herself or himself on the back), or even finger snapping, just as they do at coffee-house poetry readings.

# J. Patrick Lewis

## *In his own words:*

Poetry is the singular literary genre that begs to be read out loud, even if you are in a room all by yourself. As I tell children at school visits, you want your ears to have as much fun as your mouth is having. Among its many charms, poetry's sheer musicality is undeniable.

Having said that, I hasten to add that there is the reading of a poem and then there is the droning on. Ask third, fourth, and fifth graders to read poetry in front of the class, and you will not want for volunteers. Yet almost invariably, the young reader does a disservice to the verse. With most child readings, a good poem is made bad; a bad poem is made worse. The child reader buries his or her face in the page, mumbles to the first row of listeners (at best), and reads in a monotone with the rapidity of tracer bullets—da-dum, da-dum, da-dum, da-dum / da-dum, da-dum, da-dum, da-dum. (The final *da-dum* usually falls off—da-dum—like the last poor petal on a dead flower.)

Even though the English language is heavily iambic (da-DUM, da-DUM, as in, for example, "HelLO, is ANyBOdy THERE?"), reading in a singsongy style is far from natural. If this is not the way people actually speak, then why should it be the way they recite poetry?

But at the end of a mediocre presentation, the child is rewarded with a hearty round of applause from both teacher and class, thereby, unfortunately, confirming in his or her mind that this was a bravura performance.

I don't want to explore here the reasons why poor poetry reading among schoolchildren is the norm. Is it due to the influence of TV? The way children hear poetry that is read to them? Perhaps it's the pernicious view that all poetry must rhyme. Whatever the causes, children can do better, can become accomplished poetry readers/reciters themselves, if they are given the best models, namely teachers and librarians who care deeply about the written word.

One does not have to speak in the stentorian voice of, say, Dylan Thomas, to be a mesmerizing, or simply an effective, poetry reader. The words sing themselves. What would help inordinately, however, is *pre*reading. Teachers or librarians owe it to their young audiences to read with the feeling the poet intended, to read with the right pauses (at the caesuras, to be technical, or at the line breaks, unless they are enjambed), to slow it down and make each word count. And to do this, one must have read the poem, practiced the poem (out loud, all alone), *before* dispensing such a verbal gift to the young.

Reading deserves the same kind of close attention as writing. Reading in a stumbling, half-hearted way is akin to writing with slipshod spelling and indifference to grammar.

But the prereader is always ready to take their breath away. Pull the emotion out of the poem, let it rest in the palm of your hand. Tell them, *Look. Look at what you have just heard.* Then be quiet. Let the words sing.

### Button-down Bill

*by J. Patrick Lewis*

Button-down Bill
Had buttons a-plenty.
He buttoned his buttons
Where he didn't have any.
He buttoned his shoes,
His pants and coat,
He buttoned his buttons
Till he buttoned his throat.
He buttoned his lips,
His ears and nose,
He buttoned his head
Like he buttoned his clothes!
He buttoned his kids
And he buttoned his wife.
"Button up!" said Bill,
All his button-down life.
So if you should hear
A buttoned-up shout,
That's button-downed Bill . . .
*Pllzzzz! Lt me ouutt!*

*Bring a jar of buttons and pass them out so that each child holds one. Read "Button-down Bill" and encourage the children to raise their buttons each time they hear the word* button. *Then on a second reading, invite them to join in and say the word* button *as they raise their buttons high. If time allows, have them create illustrations of Button-down Bill and glue their buttons on their pictures in an appropriate button-y place. Post the pictures along with the poem.*

## Strategy 1: Modeling

In strategy 1, the adult reads the poem aloud. It is best to begin by choosing poems you enjoy personally and sharing them with expression and enthusiasm. Try to avoid the common tendency to read lines, especially rhyming lines, in a singsong voice. Chatton (1993) recommends studying the line breaks to determine how the poem should be read. Do not rush the lines. Look around the room as you read the poem, if you can. If possible, display the words of the poem on a poster or chalkboard or with an overhead or digital projector. Seeing the words while hearing them provides additional reinforcement for children learning to read or learning English (Hadway, Vardell, and Young 2002). I always begin by reading every poem aloud. It is an important way to ensure that the vocabulary and pronunciation will not be stumbling blocks for any child. As you choose poems to share with children, begin with those that strike your fancy. Obviously, *any* poem can be read aloud by a fluent adult reader. However, because it is hard to manufacture enthusiasm, choose poems you enjoy so that your enjoyment shows in your voice and face. Read the poem aloud slowly and with expression. Be prepared to read it several times—children generally want and need multiple oral readings.

I often choose poems with seasonal relevance. For example, in October I often read "Trick-or-Treating at Age Eight," by Liz Rosenberg, and "The Magic House," by Jane Yolen. In November I might start with "Our Daily Bread," by Janet Wong. Each poem offers a slightly different point of view on the familiar celebrations of Halloween and Thanksgiving. Or, if you want to begin with humorous poems on families and housework, try "Mummy Slept Late and Daddy Fixed Breakfast," by John Ciardi, or "Sarah Cynthia Sylvia Stout Would Not Take the Garbage Out," by Shel Silverstein. Both are longer narrative poems with fun surprise endings. Feeling brave? Try free verse poems, which often surprise children with their lack of rhyme. I have enjoyed sharing an untitled poem by Karla Kuskin that begins with some rhyme—"Three wishes/Three./The first/A tree,"—and then goes on to itemize three wishes for a happy afternoon: a tree, a chair, and a book. For greatest effect, read this poem out loud while seated in a chair near a window with a view of a tree. Then invite the children to find their own wished-for books. Or, try Gary Soto's "Ode to Family Photographs," a wry look at the common experience of taking photos in which people's heads are inadvertently cut off. If you have such a family photo yourself, share it. I did this and the kids really enjoyed seeing a crooked photo of my family—without their heads!

## Strategy 2: Unison

In strategy 2, everyone reads the poem together at the same time. Once I have set the stage for hearing poems out loud, I invite children to join in for unison read-aloud. I choose a shorter poem with a strong rhythm and first read the poem out loud as a model. Even nonreaders can participate in reading aloud when their voices need not carry the whole poem. Of course you have to provide the words of the poem in some format that is visible to the group. And remind the children of the protocol: you read the title of the poem and the name of the poet, and then the kids join in. One poem that has been irresistible to first through fourth graders is "My Monster," by Douglas Florian, a poem that humorously compares teachers to monsters. On a more serious note, Langston Hughes's classic poem "Dreams," in eight short, straightforward lines, expresses a powerful message regarding dreaming about the future. Eloise Greenfield's "Education" is a short, potent poem about getting involved in a fight. And on a lighter note, share Karla Kuskin's "I Woke up This Morning" by beginning with soft voices and gradually getting louder as the poem builds momentum. It is the perfect follow-up to a read-aloud of Judith Viorst's classic picture book *Alexander and the Terrible, Horrible, No Good, Very Bad Day.*

## Strategy 3: Refrain

In strategy 3, invite group participation by encouraging children to join in on a repeated line, stanza, or word. This strategy for choral reading requires that children learn about timing and jump in only when their lines come up. However, they still participate as a whole group, with no pressure to perform individually. As always, you read the poem out loud first. Then in repeated readings, invite the children to join in on a line or refrain that pops up repeatedly in the poem. This time, you can enable participation by putting the repeated stanza, line, or word on a large strip of paper or a display board rather than displaying the text for the entire poem. Doing so makes this strategy even easier to carry out with large groups of kids. However, if it is possible to show the whole poem, that is always ideal. Children are even more likely to learn the poem if they can both hear it and see it.

    Many poems are particularly effective for the refrain performance strategy. Once you begin gathering poems to read aloud, you may be surprised by just how many have a repeated stanza, line, or word. Probably the most successful such poem I have tried is "Homework! Oh, Homework!" by Jack Prelutsky. This popular lament on the woes of homework touches a responsive chord among children. They enjoy saying the repeated line "Homework! Oh, homework!" with a great deal of anguish. Another poem with a repeated line is "Things," by Eloise Greenfield. In this commentary on the lasting value of poems versus other, more fleeting pleasures, the repeated line "Ain't got it no more" allows the kids to use slang that would usually lead to their being corrected. There are so many examples of poems with repeated lines that children enjoy performing. Among them are "Look in a Book," by Ivy O. Eastwick, about the power of reading a book; "If My Hand Didn't Get So Tired," by Kalli Dakos, about the possibilities in writing; and "The Boa," by Douglas Florian, a pithy portrait of the snake.

Once the children get the hang of simple refrains, a more challenging variation involves reading poems with a repeated word that appears in differing places. The repeated word may not be at the beginning of a line but rather in the middle or at the end, which motivates children to pay closer attention and to practice the reading more than once. Another Prelutsky poem that is very effective with this strategy is "Louder," in which the repetition of the word *louder* describes the snoring of the narrator's father! The word *louder* begins many, but not all, of the lines of the poem, so alert the children to that variation ahead of time. Two additional examples use repetition in creative depictions of winter. Frank Asch's poem "Sunflakes" imagines snowy traditions in sunny weather with cleverly coined words such as *sunman* and *sunball*. Karla Kuskin's poem "Snow" portrays a more traditional picture of winter's snowy moments. But remember, the repeated word *snow* occurs in various places in the lines of the poem, sometimes as part of a compound word. The read-aloud can be somewhat chaotic at first but is lots of fun.

One other possibility for spontaneous group participation is to find poems that include counting or days of the week. Most children are well versed in counting from one to ten or reciting the days of the week, so when poems incorporate these elements, they invite impromptu involvement. For example, Prelutsky's poem "Countdown" begins "There are ten ghosts in the pantry," which encourages the children to shout out the decreasing numbers, starting with *ten*. Or in Florian's poem "Weather It," each line begins with a day of the week that the children can anticipate and announce. Such techniques not only simplify participation but also reinforce the learning of basics, especially for younger children or children learning English.

## Strategy 4: Movement

Strategy 4 combines unison reading with appropriate motions or gestures. This is a bit more challenging because it involves listening for cues and integrating physical movement. However, children often have had experiences pantomiming motions to songs like "I'm a Little Teapot" in preschool, so strategy 4's kinesthetic approach incorporates many familiar gestures. Lots of poems include descriptions of movement that are natural for children to act out, such as the explicit movements in "Boa Constrictor," by Shel Silverstein, or "The Bully," by Douglas Florian. Others have a topic or even a rhythm that lends itself to pantomime or movement. Motions can be as simple as alternating standing and sitting, clapping at key intervals, or gesturing with hands. In Rebecca Kai Dotlich's "A Circle of Sun," the words suggest possible movements such as leaping, skipping, and swinging. You might want to perform Prelutsky's poem "I Am Running in a Circle" outdoors so that kids can actually run in a circle. And with the poem "August Heat" (anonymous), children can perform the repeated line "and sit" from their chairs. Try assigning four different groups to sit at different intervals as the line "and sit" is repeated four times. It is also possible to incorporate basic American Sign Language into poetry readings.

## Strategy 5: Call-and-Response

In the fifth strategy, two groups read alternating (not simultaneous) lines or stanzas of a poem. Once children are familiar with poems that are read aloud in parts, try dividing the group in half to practice call-and-response. The best poems for this performance strategy are those with lines that are structured in a back-and-forth way. In "Copycat," by Sara Holbrook, for example, the lines sound just like two groups of children mimicking each other, each repeating

---

### PRACTITIONER PERSPECTIVE

As a kindergarten teacher, I try to incorporate a variety of poems into my curriculum. I am always amazed by how quickly my students are able to connect to poems. They are always creating movements to accompany the poems or coming up with more rhythmic ways to perform them. Even at an early age, children are able to connect with poems. The rhythmic quality is especially attractive to young students. It is exciting to see kids bring poetry to life.

Ashley Stephenson
Kindergarten Teacher
Hamilton Park Pacesetter Magnet
School
Dallas, Texas

what members of the other group say. It is the perfect poem to read out loud antiphonally. Another great example for two groups is "Clock-Watching," by Carol Diggory Shields, which features the interplay of one child's daydreaming and working through the school day. Shel Silverstein's "The Meehoo with an Exactlywatt," a poem based on the knock-knock joke formula, is ideal for two groups to read by alternating lines. The same format will work for Jack Prelutsky's Thanksgiving poem "I'm Thankful," which, in alternating lines, juxtaposes two points of view on thankfulness. Janet Wong uses spacing to indicate the two parts in her poem "Speak Up." Here many voices could read the left side of the poem, which represents a group of questioning children, while a solo voice (perhaps the adult) responds by reading the right side of the poem, which expresses an immigrant child's point of view. One other poem that reveals cultural bias is "Two Plus Two, or Why Indians Flunk," edited by Beverly Slapin and Doris Seale, which juxtaposes the voice of an ill-informed teacher with the voice of an innocent Native girl. Finding poems for call-and-response is a bit more challenging because it requires a tension in the back-and-forth of the lines that does not occur in many poems. Nonetheless, this approach provides an inviting way for children to participate in groups and demonstrates the added emphasis that many voices can provide.

## Strategy 6: Groups

If you have tried all the variations in strategy 5, the children are probably eager to try even more challenging choral reading methods. Strategy 6, using multiple small groups, is the next step in bringing poems to life through oral presentation. Reading in multiple groups puts the focus on fewer children and thus may take more practice. But when children have participated in unison and large-group read-alouds, practicing is not usually a problem. Take "Face It," by Janet Wong, for example. This poem has three stanzas that reflect the writer's musings on her nose, her eyes, and her mouth and how each represents a different part of her identity. Three groups could each read a different stanza, using motions to point to each body part in turn. Or try "The Question," by Karla Kuskin, a poem that poses multiple answers to the question, "What do you want to be when you grow up?" Different groups can each pipe in with a different answer. In Shel Silverstein's poem "Smart," each stanza reveals a bit more about a child's misunderstanding about the value of a dollar bill and various coins. This structure makes it easy for each group to read a different stanza. In "And the Answer Is . . . ?" by Carol Diggory Shields, there are two major stanzas, one reflecting the point of view of a student who is anxious that the teacher might call on him or her and the other presenting the perspective of a student who is eager to be called on. Typically, each group reads a different stanza. Ask for volunteers, or invite children to participate in the groups suggested by their seating arrangements. One other quick and effective method is to use a deck of cards. Give each child a card, and use color (red and black) to form two groups or suits (clubs, hearts, diamonds, spades) to form four groups.

## *Strategy 7: Solos*

Some poems are listlike in their structure and work well for what is sometimes called line-around choral reading, in which individual voices read individual lines. After children have participated in group variations, most are usually eager to volunteer to read a line solo. However, be sure that children are familiar with the poem before they volunteer for individual lines, and allow children to volunteer rather than be called upon. Children who are particularly shy or who are struggling with learning English can feel especially vulnerable about mispronouncing words or making mistakes in timing. With practice, the interplay of group voices and individual ones can be very powerful for bringing a poem to life. Try "Whatif?" by Shel Silverstein, with each what-if worry line read by a different voice. Or try reading Carol Diggory Shields's mock recitation of the Pledge of Allegiance, "Pledge," with individual voices alternating with the whole class. (Be sure to clarify in advance what the correct Pledge of Allegiance should sound like.)

Other poems that incorporate a linear format that lends itself to line-around reading include "April Fool," by Myra Cohn Livingston, a humorous list of April Fools' jokes; "By Myself," by Eloise Greenfield, a listing of personal qualities; "What Is Black?" by Mary O'Neill, a series of images of things that are black in color or feeling; and "Rules," by Karla Kuskin, a listing of rules such as "Do not jump on ancient uncles."

Most of the preceding examples begin and end with a line or lines that could be led by a narrator, with the intervening lines read aloud one by one by individual volunteers. Begin by reading the entire poem aloud as the leader, then seek volunteer readers and allow them a moment to practice their lines. They may turn to a buddy nearby to read their line aloud softly or to double-check a pronunciation. Then cue the oral reading as usual with the title of the poem followed by the name of the poet. It will be important to provide the text of the poem in a readable format—via a projector, a poster, or even a Power-Point slide.

## *Strategy 8: Two Voices*

Probably the most difficult form of choral reading is poetry written for two voices, which requires that two people read two parts, sometimes with simultaneous but differing lines. It requires the performers to synchronize their reading and get used to hearing two completely different lines being read at the same time. Paul Fleischman may have written the best-known examples of poems for two voices: the Newbery Award–winning *Joyful Noise*, a collection of poems about insects, and *I Am Phoenix*, a collection of poems about birds. These are excellent beginning points for children in the middle grades. Two of my favorites are "Honeybees" and "Book Lice," both popular with older children and adults.

Other poems, not necessarily written for two voices, can be adapted for performance by two voices through the arrangement or rearrangement of lines. Some lines can be identified for Voice 1 or Voice 2, with key lines designated for both voices. Although they take practice, poems for two voices are almost magical when read aloud. Paul Fleischman has even created what he calls spoken quartets, or poems written for four simultaneous voices, in his book *Big Talk*.

Another poet who has written poems expressly for two voices is Georgia Heard. Her poem "Fishes" is one of many in the two-voice format in *Creatures*

---

**PRACTITIONER PERSPECTIVE**

I have been using poetry with the students I am working with in summer school, and one of their favorite things is to do choral readings of the selected poems each day. This activity did not start with enthusiasm. As a matter of fact, I got the typical groans and grumbles when I said we were going to explore poetry every day during summer school (and these are second graders, so they should not be grumbling yet). Because poetry has been accompanied by low-pressure and fun activities in my center, which is the writing center, the children's attitudes have definitely shifted. I introduced choral reading with all the students as one group and myself as the other, and we alternated lines. Then we split the group in two and each group read specific lines. We have also done boy/girl, tall/short, tennis shoes/sandals, and other choral combinations that the students have proposed.

Kirsten Murphy
Librarian
Coder Elementary School
Aledo, Texas

*of Earth, Sea, and Sky*. And if you hunt, you can find poems that may not be intended for two voices but may be very effective delivered that way. For example, Jennifer Clement's poem "Arbol de Limon / Lemon Tree" appears in both Spanish and English (translated by Consuelo de Aerenlund) in Naomi Shihab Nye's collection *The Tree Is Older Than You Are*. If you are a Spanish speaker, you can read the poem in Spanish, followed by a reading in English. Or you can ask a Spanish-speaking volunteer from the audience to read the Spanish version. Once the readers have taken turns presenting their versions of the poem, *both* read their versions simultaneously. Just be sure to encourage the readers to pause at the end of each line and to start the next line together. The effect is quite stunning.

## Strategy 9: Canon

In a canon, two groups read the same poem, but one group delays its start until the other reaches a predetermined point. Reading poems in a canon is one other strategy that involves timing and overlapping lines and can be challenging for children. In addition, not many poems lend themselves to reading in a round. They must have a very regular beat or meter and some repetition. But when you find a suitable poem and try this technique with children, you will find it is fun and challenging, just like singing "Row, Row, Row, Your Boat" in a canon. For variety, try "No," by Judith Viorst, or "I'm Much Too Tired to Play Tonight," by Jack Prelutsky. These usually take practice, but they can be very appealing, like chanting or cheering at a sports event. Asking the children to clap the rhythm of the poem can also help them with reading a poem canon-style.

## Strategy 10: Singing

The final strategy for performing poetry is to sing poems by setting them to familiar tunes. This is not a particularly complex method, although it can require extra preparation, and it is irresistibly fun. I have tried this approach with nearly every age level, and children of all ages love the connection of music and poem. Basically, you match poems and song tunes that contain the same meter in their first lines, often with an equal number of strong stresses. Count the beats in the first line or two of the poem, and then count the beats in the first line or two of the song to see if they match. This strategy seems to be most effective with nonsensical or humorous poems and with tunes that have a strong, rhythmic beat, such as "Row, Row, Row Your Boat" or "Mary Had a Little Lamb." One of the children's all-time favorites has been "School Cafeteria," by Douglas Florian, a hilarious poem about cafeteria food that can be sung to the tune of "Ninety-nine Bottles of Pop." And "The Dog Ate My Homework," by Sara Holbrook, is fun to sing to the tune of "On Top of Old Smoky." The appeal of music is undeniable, and connecting music with poetry makes the poems especially memorable. Setting poems to music is one of my favorite poem-sharing strategies because kids *always* love it. And you may be surprised by how many poems have strong enough rhythm and structure to be effective when sung. Many of Jack Prelutsky's poems, in particular, match song tunes, which may not be surprising given that he was a singer and musician before turning to poetry. Try singing "Allosaurus," his poem describing the ferocious qualities of a dinosaur, to the tune of "Row, Row, Row Your Boat." It is a hilarious juxtaposition of lyrics and tune. Or use the same melody to accompany Judith Viorst's poem, "Someday Someone Will Bet That You Can't Name All Fifty States," which leaves one state off the list. See if the children can guess which one.

Matching poems and songs has been a fun trial-and-error exercise for me. I made a list of my favorite childhood song tunes (you may have a very different list), counted the beats in the first lines of each tune, and started hunting for poems with the same number of beats. Then I tried singing the poems myself. Sometimes the beats fit, but the tune just did not match the poem, so I kept looking. Once you introduce this strategy, you may be surprised by how much the children enjoy it and how eager they are to join the search. What good practice this provides for the children's study of poetic meter, which they will encounter later in their school careers.

## SELECTED TUNES FOR MATCHING WITH POEMS

"She'll Be Coming 'round the Mountain" (11 beats in the first line)

"Battle Hymn of the Republic" (11 beats)

"Ninety-nine Bottles of Pop" (10 beats)

"When Johnny Comes Marching Home" (9 beats)

"Are You Sleeping?" (8 beats)

"I've Been Working on the Railroad" (8 beats)

"If You're Happy and You Know It" (8 beats)

"Oh Tannenbaum" (8 beats)

"Bingo" (8 beats)

"Clementine" (8 beats)

"Twinkle, Twinkle Little Star" (7 beats)

"Mary Had a Little Lamb" (7 beats)

"Old MacDonald" (7 beats)

"Yankee Doodle" (7 beats)

"London Bridge" (7 beats)

"On Top of Old Smoky" (6 beats)

"Ring around the Rosy" (6 beats)

"Three Blind Mice" (6 beats)

"The Farmer in the Dell" (6 beats)

"Hot Cross Buns" (6 beats)

"Home on the Range" (5 beats)

"Row, Row, Row Your Boat" (5 beats)

"Turkey in the Straw" (5 beats)

— POET PROFILE —

## Brod Bagert

### *Beyond Self-Expression*

#### *by Brod Bagert*

Writing poetry usually begins as an act of self-expression, but too often it ends there. Self-expression is a wonderful thing, but it's only a first step in the development of a poet. It's what Virginia Woolf alluded to when she wrote that "the impulse toward autobiography" being spent, the writer begins "to use writing as an art, not as a method of self-expression" (*A Room of One's Own*, 1929).

While this concept is a little tricky to grasp in the context of poetry, it becomes almost self-evident in the context of the novel. Novelists have always written in the voice of characters, a practice which I think accounts in part for the novel's popularity. So the question is, what would happen if poetry took a lesson from the novel? I asked myself that question some years ago, and the answer has driven my work ever since.

As a young poet I loved to hear the sound of my own voice, but after writing five or six hundred self-expressive poems I began to get a little bored with it. So instead of continuing to peer into the inner world of self, I began to look outward to the world of others and discovered a chorus of voices longing for expression. I began to write in those voices and immediately my poetry began to change. I discovered that writing in the voice of others forced me into a more consistent use of common dramatic elements, things like setting, action, conflict, even dialogue. Here's an example of such a poem:

### Aunt Aurora's Promise

*by Brod Bagert*
*in the Voice of Shayna Potts*

I don't think Daddy likes her,
He says she's really wild,
Just because she dresses
With her own Aurora-style.

She never ever wears her hair
The way my daddy likes,
She uses lots of gooey stuff
And shapes it into spikes.

Her lips are painted purple
And her nails are painted black,
So Aunt Aurora looks as though
She's ready to attack.

So daddy's feeling nervous,
He's feeling full of stress,
Cause Aunt Aurora promised me
She'd teach me how to dress.

Brod Bagert, "Aunt Aurora's Promise," in *Hormone Jungle: Coming of Age in Middle School* (Gainesville, FL: Maupin House, 2006). Used with permission.

This poem is in the voice of a sixth-grade girl and is driven by a classic three-way dramatic conflict between the girl, her father, and her free-spirited aunt. Though I'm the author of the poem, it's not about me, it's not my voice, and it's not an expression of my internal feelings, which for my readers is a very good thing. My feelings would be just a bit boring to the middle school readers for whom this poem is intended. A poem about me would drive them away from poetry; this poem draws them toward it, and I never would have written it if I had limited my writing to self-expression.

So permit me a sweeping overgeneralization: when poets go beyond self-expression and write in a voice other than their own, their poetry becomes more dramatic, resulting in better poems, a broader audience for poetry, and eventually more poets in print.

It's perfectly okay to encourage young writers to use poetry as a vehicle for self-expression, but you can also encourage them to reach beyond self-expression to the idea of writing as art. It's not a path for everybody, but the few who reach it will be on their way to writing some very entertaining poetry.

*Children may enjoy drawing their own picture of Aunt Aurora or creating their own flamboyant Aunt Aurora doll or figurine. Of course "Aunt Aurora's Promise" also begs to be read while dressed up like Aunt Aurora—for the truly fearless!*

## Combining Strategies

As you experiment with using each of these ten strategies for sharing poems with children, it will quickly become obvious that the strategies can be combined and overlapped. For example, there are many poems that have both a repeated line or refrain suited to whole-group participation and a linear list format that invites individual volunteers. For example, "Delicious Wishes," by Douglas Florian, repeats the words *I wish* many times within a series of lines expressing multiple wishes. The words *I wish* can be read by the whole group while individual volunteers read individual "wish" lines. The poem "It's a Wonderful World, but They Made a Few Mistakes," by Judith Viorst, begins and ends with the titular line but also contains a variety of individual lines ideal for solo voices.

In some poems, we can juxtapose lines that lend themselves to whole-group reading with stanzas or lines that are suited to small-group reading. For example, the poem "I Rise, I Rise," about a young man's first buffalo hunt, repeats the phrase "I rise, I rise," which the whole group can recite. In between are lines from the buffalo's point of view, which for contrast can be read aloud by small groups or pairs of children. Another example is "Napoleon," a poem by Miroslav Holub of the Czech Republic, which appears in translation in *This Same Sky*, selected by Naomi Shihab Nye. This poem describes a classroom moment from the perspectives of a teacher-narrator, the class as a whole, and an individual student named Frankie. Many poems offer similar combinations of whole-group, small-group, individual, and other read-aloud configurations. Often a poem will show you how to perform it if you study the lines and their arrangement on the page. Once you begin inviting children's participation in poem performance, you will find that they themselves will have ideas about how to try a poem this way or that way. Follow their lead!

## Seeking Out Audio Poetry

Enthusiastically sharing poems out loud with students for the pleasure of the words, sounds, rhymes, and meaning is our primary responsibility. Steinbergh (1994) recommends having a listening center or audiobook adaptations to highlight oral poetry as well. Poems on tape, along with their corresponding written forms, make excellent additions to the library. They provide further practice in listening and reading; more models of effective reading aloud, pronunciation, and expression; and other samples of writing. Many recordings of poets reading their own poems are available, and there is nothing quite like them. Shel Silverstein's gravelly voice, Jack Prelutsky's outrageous singing,

---

**PRACTITIONER PERSPECTIVE**

I have had great success with the middle school students I work with. The key? Just do exactly what you are asking them to do. Want them to wear costumes? Make sure you wear one too! They have to see you doing it before they will even think about trying it. You have to be passionate and encouraging. Have fun! Let them know it is OK to laugh at yourself. I think kids take themselves too seriously and miss a lot. Want them to read dramatically? Make sure you do the same! Use different voices, make different faces, and use dramatic hand gestures. They will laugh and, you can hope, be tempted to try doing the same thing. You will not get results overnight, but the kids will slowly come around. They have to trust you first, and they will have to watch you perform a few times to understand how cool it really is. Try it all with the middle school kids. They will love you for it!

Wendy Watson Fox
Media Specialist
St. John Catholic School
Panama City, Florida

and Ashley Bryan's mellifluous delivery are all perfect on audiobooks and compact discs. And when children become comfortable with reading poetry aloud, they may want to tape record themselves reading a favorite poem aloud, copy the poem in their best handwriting, illustrate it, and present their poem performance as a gift to a loved one. Such an activity can be a source of pride in addition to providing language practice. Several Internet sites offer audio versions of poems, including new kinds of experimental poetry. Check out the following:

> Electronic Poetry Center
> All kinds of experimental poetry
> http://wings.buffalo.edu/epc/

> Poets and Writers, Inc.
> Audio files of some poems, poem trivia
> http://www.pw.org

> PoetryMagazine.com
> Audio clips of individual poems
> http://www.poetrymagazine.com

> Favorite Poem Project
> Former Poet Laureate Robert Pinsky's project
> to have average citizens audiotape their
> favorite poems
> http://www.favoritepoem.org

## Other Creative Alternatives

Once the invitation to share poems chorally has been extended, children can generate their own creative alternatives or combine some of the strategies above. For instance, Georgia Heard reported that "one first-grade class performed a poem using silent movements, and the rest of the class guessed which poem they were performing" (1999, 13). Barbara Chatton (1993) challenges us to consider adding pantomime, sound effects, and background music to our read-alouds and inviting children to translate their favorite poems from English into their native language or American Sign Language. Caroline Feller Bauer (1995) encourages us to experiment with using special effects, varying voice volume and pitch, adding sound effects, or reading poems to carefully selected music. Children may want to adapt their favorite poems to rap, chants, or yells, and accompany them with puppets, props, gestures, or clapping. Poet Sara Holbrook, in her children's book *Wham! It's a Poetry Jam: Discovering Performance Poetry*, provides helpful guidelines for staging poems in a variety of ways, including hosting contests and competitions.

Alma Flor Ada and her co-authors of the poetry program *A Chorus of Cultures: Developing Literacy through Multicultural Poetry* (1993, 32) suggest that "physical involvement puts children at ease and encourages listening comprehension" and that "representing the actions of a poem, the feelings in the poem, allowing even for silent participation, especially for children acquiring English," is essential to language learning. Invite the children to create their own poetry performance techniques. Acting out a poem enables children to better understand the poem's meaning, its events or scenes, and the sounds and rhythm of its language. However, the emphasis of a poetry performance should be on the process of discovering a poem's meaning, not on executing a polished product, so props and costumes should be minimal.

As a traveling company of professional actors who present "verse as theater," the Poetry Alive organization shows us how poems can be shared in lively, personal ways. They suggest a sequence that consists of adult reading of poems, guiding children in choosing poems, establishing poetry teams, scripting the chosen poem into a kind of play, scoring the motion and emotion of the poem with gesture or pantomime, and then performing the poem. When Poetry Alive members perform a poem they have memorized it. They give performance points for having a confident stance, facing the audience, using an outside voice, filling the space, and using big gestures. They even insist on taking a bow! Oral reading demonstrates for children the ways to use the voice to express thoughts, feelings, and moods. Thus it is important to establish a respectful sense of audience for poetry performances. Poetry performance can help teach children to listen attentively, respectfully, and responsively. Some children may discover a real affinity for expressing themselves through poetry performance. This may even lead to establishing a poetry troupe and having students perform poems at other libraries or on the morning announcements at school or during poetry month. Some children may want to investigate participating in University Interscholastic League or other organized events that still hold competitive recitations of poetry.

As poet Brod Bagert (1992) says about encouraging children's involvement in poetry, we can "awaken inside them the power of their own presence, and breathe life into young spirits." As the poets themselves have said, poetry is meant to be heard and savored person-to-person. Emily Dickinson wrote

A word is dead
When it is said,
Some say.
I say it just
Begins to live
That day.

## Conclusion

As we move into sharing poetry out loud with kids, we need to make sure that we will be comfortable and confident in taking the lead. That includes, for example, getting comfortable with quiet moments, understanding how to interpret line breaks, using appropriate facial expressions, and planning effective introductions. And we can experiment with ten different strategies that involve children in the oral reading of poetry. To review, make yourself a checklist of poetry performance strategies and challenge yourself to try each one—eventually!

Begin with the leader reading aloud and modeling.

Read poetry aloud in unison.

Invite group participation with repeated refrains.

Use movement with poems.

Organize call-and-response read-alouds.

Use multiple groups.

Lead line-around and solo line readings.

Orchestrate poems for two voices.

Lead two groups in reading a poem as a canon.

Set poems to familiar tunes and sing them.

And as you become comfortable with these approaches, try creative alternatives and combinations, including sign language, puppetry, and the like.

*Don't just make poetry available,*
*make it unavoidable.*

—Bernice Cullinan, Scholar and Editor

## Poems Cited in "Ten Strategies for Sharing Poetry Out Loud"

Full publication information for the following resources can be found in appendix B.

### 1. MODELING: THE ADULT READS THE POEM ALOUD

Liz Rosenberg, "Trick-or-Treating at Age Eight," in *Halloween Poems*, compiled by Myra Cohn Livingston

Jane Yolen, "The Magic House," in *Halloween Poems*, compiled by Myra Cohn Livingston

Janet Wong, "Our Daily Bread," in *A Suitcase of Seaweed*

John Ciardi, "Mummy Slept Late and Daddy Fixed Breakfast," in *You Read to Me, I'll Read to You!*

Shel Silverstein, "Sarah Cynthia Sylvia Stout Would Not Take the Garbage Out," in *Where the Sidewalk Ends*

Karla Kuskin, "Untitled" (begins "Three Wishes"), in *Near the Window Tree*

Gary Soto, "Ode to Family Photographs," in *Neighborhood Odes*

### 2. UNISON: EVERYONE READS THE POEM TOGETHER AT THE SAME TIME

Douglas Florian, "My Monster," in *Bing Bang Boing*

Langston Hughes, "Dreams," in *The Dreamkeeper*

Eloise Greenfield, "Education," in *Nathaniel Talking*

Karla Kuskin, "I Woke Up This Morning," in *Dogs and Dragons, Trees and Dreams*

### 3. REFRAIN: CHILDREN JOIN IN ON A REPEATED LINE, STANZA, OR WORD

Jack Prelutsky, "Homework, Oh Homework," in *The New Kid on the Block*

Eloise Greenfield, "Things," in *Honey, I Love, and Other Poems*

Ivy O. Eastwick, "Look in a Book," in *I Like It Here at School*, compiled by Jack Prelutsky

Kalli Dakos, "If My Hand Didn't Get So Tired," in *Don't Read This Book, Whatever You Do!*

Douglas Florian, "The Boa," in *Beast Feast*

Jack Prelutsky, "Louder Than a Clap of Thunder!" in *The New Kid on the Block*

Frank Asch, "Sunflakes," in *Ring out, Wild Bells: Poems about Holidays and Seasons*, collected by Lee Bennett Hopkins

Karla Kuskin, "Snow," in *Snowy Day: Stories and Poems*, edited by Caroline Feller Bauer

Jack Prelutsky, "Countdown," in *It's Halloween*

Douglas Florian, "Weather It," in *Bing Bang Boing*

## 4. MOVEMENT: CHILDREN READ IN UNISON USING MOTIONS OR GESTURES

Shel Silverstein, "Boa Constrictor," in *Where the Sidewalk Ends*

Douglas Florian, "The Bully," in *Bing Bang Boing*

Rebecca Kai Dotlich, "A Circle of Sun," in *The 20th-Century Children's Poetry Treasury*, selected by Jack Prelutsky

Jack Prelutsky, "I Am Running in a Circle," in *The New Kid on the Block*

Anonymous, "August Heat," in *The Sky Is Full of Song*, selected by Lee Bennett Hopkins

## 5. CALL-AND-RESPONSE: TWO GROUPS READ ALTERNATING (NOT SIMULTANEOUS) LINES OR STANZAS

Sara Holbrook, "Copycat," in *Which Way to the Dragon! Poems for the Coming-on-Strong*

Carol Diggory Shields, "Clock-Watching," in *Lunch Money, and Other Poems about School*

Shel Silverstein, "The Meehoo with an Exactlywatt," in *A Light in the Attic*

Jack Prelutsky, "I'm Thankful," in *The New Kid on the Block*

Janet Wong, "Speak Up," in *Good Luck Gold*

"Two Plus Two, or Why Indians Flunk," in *Through Indian Eyes: The Native American Experience in Books for Children*, edited by Beverly Slapin and Doris Seale

## 6. GROUPS: MULTIPLE GROUPS READ VARIOUS LINES OR STANZAS

Janet Wong, "Face It," in *A Suitcase of Seaweed*

Karla Kuskin, "The Question," in *Dogs and Dragons, Trees and Dreams*

Shel Silverstein, "Smart," in *Where the Sidewalk Ends*

Carol Diggory Shields, "And the Answer Is . . . ?" in *Lunch Money, and Other Poems about School*

## 7. SOLOS: INDIVIDUAL CHILDREN READ INDIVIDUAL LINES

Shel Silverstein, "Whatif?" in *A Light in the Attic*

Carol Diggory Shields, "Pledge," in *Lunch Money, and Other Poems about School*

Myra Cohn Livingston, "April Fool," in *Celebrations*

Eloise Greenfield, "By Myself," in *Honey, I Love, and Other Poems*

Mary O'Neill, in "What Is Black?" *Hailstones and Halibut Bones*

Karla Kuskin, "Rules," in *Dogs and Dragons, Trees and Dreams*

## 8. TWO VOICES: TWO PEOPLE READ TWO PARTS, SOMETIMES WITH SIMULTANEOUS BUT DIFFERING LINES

Paul Fleischman, "Honeybees" and "Book Lice," in *Joyful Noise: Poems for Two Voices*

——, *I Am Phoenix: Poems for Two Voices*

——, *Big Talk: Poems for Four Voices*

Georgia Heard, "Fishes," in *Creatures of Earth, Sea, and Sky*

Jennifer Clement, "Arbol de Limon / Lemon Tree," translated by Consuelo de Aerenlund, in *The Tree Is Older Than You Are: A Bilingual Gathering of Poems and Stories from Mexico*, edited by Naomi Shihab Nye

## 9. CANON: TWO GROUPS READ THE SAME POEM, WITH ONE GROUP DELAYING ITS START UNTIL THE OTHER REACHES A PREDETERMINED POINT

Judith Viorst, "No," in *If I Were in Charge of the World*

Jack Prelutsky, "I'm Much Too Tired to Play Tonight," in *Something BIG Has Been Here*

## 10. SINGING: CHILDREN SING POEMS SET TO FAMILIAR TUNES

Douglas Florian, "School Cafeteria," in *Bing Bang Boing*

Sara Holbrook, "The Dog Ate My Homework," in *The Dog Ate My Homework*

Jack Prelutsky, "Allosaurus," in *Tyrannosaurus Was a Beast: Dinosaur Poems*

Judith Viorst, "Someday Someone Will Bet That You Can't Name All Fifty States," in *Sad Underwear, and Other Complications: More Poems for Children and Their Parents*

COMBINING STRATEGIES

Douglas Florian, "Delicious Wishes," in *Bing Bang Boing*

Judith Viorst, "It's a Wonderful World, but They Made a Few Mistakes," in *Sad Underwear, and Other Complications: More Poems for Children and Their Parents*

"I Rise, I Rise," from an Osage prayer before a young man's first buffalo hunt, in *Dancing Teepees: Poems of American Indian Youth*, collected by Virginia Driving Hawk Sneve

Miroslav Holub, "Napoleon," translated by Kaca Polackova, in *This Same Sky: A Collection of Poems from Around the World,* selected by Naomi Shihab Nye

## Chapter Six

# ☞ What Happens after You Share the Poem?

*Poetry begins in delight and ends in wisdom.*
—Robert Frost, Poet

*W*hat happens after you share poetry with children? What kinds of questions are appropriate to ask? How do you lead a discussion gently? In this chapter, we will consider how to encourage children's responses to poetry through drama, music, art, and other activities. We will also briefly examine how best to nurture budding poets and how to share children's responses in meaningful ways.

## Asking Questions

When we read aloud a poem to children, we are often hesitant about what to do next. We need to give a few moments for the poem to sink in, but the silence sometimes seems uncomfortable. And we would like to know what kids are thinking. Did they enjoy the poem? Understand it? Want to hear it again? How do we ask them without being too pushy or ruining the magic of the moment? Following up on poetry reading is not a lockstep process: Read poem—Ask questions—Done. It is more intuitive, following the lead of the children, the poem, the moment. And this becomes clearer and more natural the more often you share poems with children. Nonetheless, there are a few guidelines that can help establish some basics.

In her work in the schools, Amy McClure (1990) found that the children seemed unsure of what was expected and were more concerned about offering correct answers than exploring alternative possibilities. How do we avoid this trap, this conditioning from our own past? McClure suggests using one or two of these facilitating questions:

What did you think?

What did you like about this poem?

Does this remind you of anything you know about?

What is the poet saying here?

Any comments about that?

Let's discuss what is going on here.

Pulitzer-winner Jorie Graham (2005) explores the value of poetry in the education of our children in a thought-provoking essay in which she comments:

> When you give a child poems (remembering, once the silence closes back over the end of the poem, not to ask "what does this mean?" but rather, "what did you feel?" or "what did you see?"), you are opening up different parts of his or her reading apparatus than fiction or drama or journalism open up.

### Poetry Follow-up Discussion Questions

Here are ten questions to help guide discussion with children after sharing poetry aloud. They are based on Patrick Groff's poetry talk questions (cited in Booth and Moore 2003, 64–65).

1. Why is this a poem? How is it like or unlike a story?
2. Why did this poet write this poem?
3. How are the people in this poem like people you know? Or not like people you know?
4. Would you like to go to the place pictured in this poem? Why or why not?
5. Did the things in this poem ever happen to you? Where or when?
6. What things are there in this poem to see? Have you seen them before? Where?
7. What things are described in this poem?
8. Is this poem honest or true? Do you believe what it says? Why or why not?
9. What things happen in this poem that you would like to happen to you? Or not happen to you?
10. Are there any words or lines that you think are interesting? Why?

Our questions need to be as open-ended as possible, and we need to be open to all kinds of responses from children. They may not give us the answers we expect to hear, but their answers will help us understand how they see the poem and perhaps help us see the poem itself in new ways.

A colleague at the University of Arizona South, June Harris, writes about sharing poetry with her students:

> What I learned . . . is that when we give students a "translation" of a poem, they stop thinking about it. They take our word, give those words back to us, and don't bother thinking or discussing any more. I've found it much more effective to let THEM come up with ideas, only correcting or intervening when they make inferences NOT supported by the words in the poem. As long as they can support their statements, I've found it more worthwhile to let them do the interpreting.

We can follow up our questions by probing gently to help children articulate their reasons for their responses—often a challenge for young children. It

---

**PRACTITIONER PERSPECTIVE**

Poetry is so personal on so many levels. It seems to get right to the point of what the writer is feeling in his or her soul, yet other times poetry creates more questions than answers. Poetry is so different from fiction. It is not trying to create a story with a plot to follow, it is simply stating feelings and experiences. It is just amazing how so much can come from so few words. To share this with students, I think you definitely need to let them know you care about them and care about their feelings—whether they are reading poetry or writing poetry. That a teacher or librarian cares to ask what they think of something, and for there not to be a wrong answer, is a big deal. Some kids today do not have anyone to ask them what they think or how they feel. What a great opportunity this affords kids, especially high-risk kids! If we start out with some poetry and let children know right off the bat that what they think is important, we just might get them hooked for the year for the other classroom tasks and hooked for life as poetry readers and writers! It just seems that poetry can be such a catalyst for building a supportive, nurturing, trusting classroom or library environment.

Rhonda Brockett
Librarian
Ponder Elementary School
Ponder, Texas

is an interactive dynamic that involves a give-and-take, not a "guess what the grown-up is thinking" game.

Georgia Heard says:

> To read and understand the meaning of a poem takes patience. . . . Reading a difficult poem challenges us to read in a different way. We must learn to read a poem multiple times, and even then keep returning to it. It's a very different kind of reading than what most of our world demands—quick, easy sound bites to get us through the day (1999, 44).

Some poems are immediately accessible, but others need more time to grow on us. Do not be surprised if children refer to a poem days or weeks after you shared it.

As Booth and Moore recommend in their book *Poems Please! Sharing Poetry with Children* (2003, 59):

> We must seek our children's views, listen to their interpretations, treat them with respect and seriousness, interact with them in consultation and conferences, allow conversation and informal discussion, and encourage the explorations of their own experiences in relation to the poems. We must not make them afraid to say the wrong thing, but enable them to voice their own ideas. . . . Open-ended, divergent thinking helps children formulate their own questions about poetry. Aesthetic learning comes from experiences provided by teachers where the poem is understood in the deepest way possible, with the mind and the heart.

In poetry sharing, the emphasis should be balanced between the poem and the response, allowing for time to read, time to think, time to talk. Not every question will generate spontaneous responses. Some trial and error is involved in finding questions that seem comfortable to you. And not every child will respond verbally. Some of the quietest children may experience the poem deeply but not ask or respond to questions in a group setting. That is OK. And none of the follow-up questions should overwhelm the poem itself. A few minutes is often enough to open the door to discussion. Just be sure that *you* are not doing most of the talking. Ask your question and wait for the response. Do not answer your own question. Do not bombard children with too many questions. Do not interrupt the poem reading with questions or explanations. One or two questions can often be enough to follow up a single poem. When this dynamic is in place time after time, children will become comfortable with follow-up questions and will often volunteer their own responses before you can ask your questions because they know you are already open to their opinions! In *Tigers, Lilies, Toadstools, and Thunderbolts: Engaging K–8 Students with Poetry*, Iris McClellan Tiedt reminds us that "children's reactions to poetry at all ages will be influenced greatly by your presentation as their interpreter of poetry, for attitudes and values are reflected in your voice as you read, in the way you introduce the poem, and in your enthusiasm" (2002, 18). Often the best way to

---

### PRACTITIONER PERSPECTIVE

I was student teaching a third-grade class in a farming community in Kyle, Texas. Suddenly, the principal announced over the intercom that we had a Kansas Alert. That was code meaning that a tornado was coming and we were to take cover immediately. One of the boys spied the storm out the window and yelled, "I see a tornado coming!" Chaos ensued. Children began panicking and crying all around me. Amazingly, I was able to stay calm and take the children to our designated safe spot, a one-person, disabled-access bathroom. Let me tell you, it was a tight squeeze! The children had to take turns standing and sitting so we would all fit. Two actually had to sit on the toilet! I had grabbed *Where the Sidewalk Ends* from the shelf as we filed into the restroom. The kids were still crying, sniffling, and hugging each other. To calm everyone down and really get their minds off of the situation, I stood crammed in the corner by the sink and began to read from the book in a very silly fashion. Little by little, the sniffling stopped and the heartbeats slowed. I began taking requests and the laughter echoed (loudly) in our small space. We just kept going and they never got tired of it.

Eventually, after over an hour (I had forgotten to pay attention to the time), the teacher from next door opened the door to the bathroom. She looked at us incredulously and said, "The all-clear came half an hour ago!" We had not been able to hear the intercom from the restroom. Upon finding we were coming out, the children groaned a chorus of "AAWWWW." "Can we do this again?" "Can we keep reading?" were the questions I heard as we made our way back to our desks. Later, as I prepared to leave, I saw that the tornado had literally ripped through the field adjacent to the school. I was shaky when I realized the seriousness of the situation. We came very close to disaster, but we had our minds on other things—poetry.

Melanie Letendre
Librarian
Pike Middle School
Northwest Independent School District
Justin, Texas

end a poetry-sharing session is to follow up a few questions and responses with a return to the poem: "Shall we read it again?"

## Leading Discussion

Asking questions is only part of what we do after sharing a poem. Opening the floor to discussion is also a critical step. Manning and Manning remind us:

> Discussing poems after they are read helps children develop critical thinking skills. By responding to poems, children make decisions about their likes and dislikes. Allowing children to select poems for oral reading also helps develop their evaluative skills. It also makes the children feel that their opinions are valued, and encourages them to participate (1997, 100–101).

Alternative grouping may be even more helpful than asking the right questions. Ask children to turn to a partner and talk with her or him about what the poet is saying. Children are often more comfortable sharing their opinions with one peer rather than with the whole group. Or small groups or poetry circles can also function well for digging deeper into a poem's meaning. One colleague, June Jacko, used art projects done in small groups to help children explore multicultural poetry. Each group had a different poem, and after all the poems had been introduced, read by the teacher, and performed by the class, each group created a minimural to illustrate their poem. Then they explained their murals to the class as a whole. This kind of response activity helps children think deeply about a poem, talk critically with classmates about the words and ideas, make connections to the lesson's content, and express themselves creatively about their own interpretations of the poem's meaning.

Poetry circles, patterned along the line of literature circles, offer a wonderful collaborative opportunity for children to share preferences, read aloud, and talk about poems. Poetry circles, like book clubs or book groups, usually allow children to bond with the same peers over time, and the small-group atmosphere establishes a safety level that encourages the sharing of more personal reactions, positive and negative. One librarian I know holds a Poetry at Lunch group. The students bring their lunches and poetry to the library and share their favorite poems and poetry books. The meetings are fairly informal and unstructured but very successful. Another colleague, Janet Hilbun, ran a Poetry and Pop-Tarts Club before the day started at her middle school. She provided the Pop-Tarts and juice drink, and kids read their favorite poems or poems they had written themselves. It was a big draw for these tweens. Notice something else? Combining poetry and food is a good way for gathering group activities.

Poet and teacher Georgia Heard is often a poet in residence in the schools. She writes:

> Rather than standing up in the front of the room and asking questions about a poem I already know the answers to, I want to put my students in the position of learning about the poem for themselves. The key to learning how to enter the door of a difficult poem is to teach our students how to unlock the door themselves, and for them to find pleasure in this process (1999, 43).

In her work with children, she recommends:

> When you give a poem to your students, center it on a clean sheet of paper with a lot of white space around it so they can write directly on the sheet. . . . They can circle important or difficult words, write questions about parts they don't understand, or just write their thoughts about the poem—making the poem more accessible and less distant (1999, 44).

If students can write-think-share, they are mustering all their language resources to try to put their thoughts into words. Although this may take a few extra minutes or may even become the focus for the session, it is time well spent as we provide opportunity for children to respond to poems they find meaningful.

---

### PRACTITIONER PERSPECTIVE

Although my first experiences with poetry were positive, I often felt inept in high school and college as we were forced to dissect, analyze, and memorize poems. Invariably, my analyses were different from those of my teachers or professors. While some instructors were flexible and open to discussion, others were dogmatic and thought that what was written in the teacher's guide was the *only* correct response. My own negative experiences with inflexible teachers have caused me to be open to all responses from students. They often think in new and creative ways that open new vistas for me.

Hilary Haygood
Librarian
San Andres Elementary School
Andrews, Texas

In their article "Talk about Poetry," Manning and Manning (1997) suggest that natural, front-porch-type discussions are the best method for enhancing children's enjoyment and understanding of poetry. They found that responses often cluster around the reader and his or her personal enjoyment of the poem and its rhyme (if the poem rhymes), the topic of the poem, or the word choice. Manning and Manning recommend using questions as a guide to encourage open discussions about poetry but advise against asking *all* of them or feeling limited to asking them in any particular order. In fact, the ideal approach may be displaying the guiding questions on a large poster and allowing children to select the question they want to address within their small-group settings. For further guidance, you can assign each member of a four-person group a distinctive role in facilitating the group dynamics. In this way, each person is sure to participate in some capacity and to feel included in the group activity. Roles in a four-person poetry circle might include the following:

> *Reader*—reads the poem out loud to the group
>
> *Writer*—writes down the group's responses
>
> *Researcher*—looks up other poems, other books, other information, as needed
>
> *Reporter*—shares the group's response with the whole class or large group

Or small groups can be used in other creative ways. For example, children could work together in small groups to introduce new poetry books, with each group examining a different book and presenting a book talk or poetry performance of it for the large group. Children could also work in small groups to consider multiple works by the same poet, with each group member examining a different title and then presenting the poet and all of his or her works to the large group. For an even more ambitious use of group discussion, try organizing a learning center, with each group participating in a different poetry experience, such as a featured poet center, an audiobook center of commercially produced poetry to listen to, a jam session center with equipment for children to record their own poem readings, and a poetic arts center where children create art to accompany designated poems. When each group has completed its center, they can report on their experiences to the larger group. After trying this approach, older children might enjoy planning similar centers for the future.

As we move from sharing poetry to encouraging children to respond to poetry, we can rely on poetry partners or small groups for a variety of other activities. As we offer options in drama, music, art, crafts, and other areas, we often find that allowing children to express themselves with a friend or small group increases their comfort level with the task at hand.

— POET PROFILE —

# Marilyn Singer

## *For Me*

*by Marilyn Singer*

Telephone call,
Not for me.
Package in the hall,
Not for me.
Card from Bombay,
Not for me.
Letter from L.A.,
Not for me.
New magazine,
Not for me.
Answering machine,
Not for me.
Mama's home—
Come and see.
She found a poem,
Just for me.

Everyone sees things differently. Everyone feels the same emotions. That contradiction tells us part of what poetry is about—the combination of fresh ways of viewing the world with feelings we all share.

In that regard, children's poetry is no different from poetry for adults—good poetry, that is. It surprises us with fresh images and genuine emotions. Of course, the way these are presented differs—and that is something I discovered when I set out to write poems for younger kids. Each word still has to count, but the words are generally simpler, and their pattern is more direct. The rhythms tend to be stronger and the feelings closer to the surface.

Does that clarity and simplicity make such poems easier to write? Nope. To create "young poems," I found that I have to *become* young. This isn't a matter of getting inside a child's brain but of summoning up my own young mind while using my grown-up craft to fashion my thoughts and feelings into poetry. How do I manage to see and feel like a child? Beats me! But I'm sure glad I can.

I wrote "For Me" when I was in that young mindset; it's part of a group of diverse pieces about nature, play, emotional states, and so forth. I recall quite well that left-out feeling when all the phone calls, letters, packages, postcards were for my mom, dad, sister, grandmother (or husband, neighbor, houseguest!). A friend of mine suggested that I like to buy things on eBay because that way I'll always get presents in the mail. He's got me pegged.

I remember, too, the times my mom would read poems to me—and my dad would sing songs—and how special that made me feel. To me, those gifts were more precious than the material ones because they shaped my life-long love of words, music, reading—and they can do the same for a contemporary kid.

Teachers and librarians can also convey those gifts. One way to do so is to read poetry aloud to students with enthusiasm. Poetry is *meant* to be read aloud. And as you read it, it's important to let your own feelings shine through. When I was a high school teacher, I wept every time I read Dylan Thomas's "Fern Hill" aloud to my classes. I couldn't help it. And I had to get beyond embarrassment to explore *why* the poem affected me so strongly. That led to important and honest discussions of which poems moved my students and why, and about the power of poetry to soothe, stir, sadden, or delight.

Another fun thing to do in the classroom is to have several kids read the same poem with emphases on different sentences or sections. How many ways can one poem be read? A duet or group reading can also elucidate the tension between individual perception and common emotion.

Above all, children are not the only ones who should *play* with poetry. Adults should, too. Keep your mind open to the wonder of words and the world around you. Come to think of it, *that's* how we grown-ups can manage to keep our child-mind alive—and how we can appreciate (and sometimes create) those special poems for each of us to treasure.

*After reading "For Me" aloud once by yourself, invite children to read the line "Not for me" in unison while you read the other lines. For extra support, create a sign with "Not for me" on it and hold it up to cue students to speak.*

# Dramatizing Poetry

What happens after you share a poem? In my experience, talking about the poem naturally occurs first. But there are also other possibilities for engaging children in activities that expand their responses to a poem they have heard or read. This includes connecting drama and poetry. Dramatic activities include a wide spectrum—from the informal and improvisational to the more planned and structured. Resources like *Creative Drama in the Classroom and Beyond*, by Nellie McCaslin (2000), provide a multitude of ideas for connecting poetry and drama, including:

- Trying physicalization (acting out motions, movements, gestures)
- Using pantomime (movement without speech)
- Creating sound and voice effects
- Planning and participating in a tableau (a moment of a poem frozen and posed as a scene)
- Role-playing (taking on the persona of a character to speak the related lines)
- Performing monologues or dialogues
- Using improvisation
- Orchestrating scripted performances

As we bring drama into poetry, we can allow children to exercise their natural wiggliness in acting out poems full of descriptions of motion and movement, such as "A Circle of Sun," by Rebecca Kai Dotlich, from *The 20th Century Children's Poetry Treasury*, compiled by Jack Prelutsky. Or we can challenge them to use mime to perform the movements suggested in a poem without speaking at all. A poem that lends itself well to mime is "Hiccup Cure," by Shel Silverstein, from *A Light in the Attic*. Add sound back into poetry reading with sound or voice effects for poems such as "The Mosquitoes," by Douglas Florian, from *Insectlopedia*. And use "I, Too," by Langston Hughes, from *Singing America: Poems that Define a Nation*, collected by Neil Philip, as a powerful poem for staging a tableau. Set a table as if for dinner and seat a guest in every chair. The poem reader stands aside, reading the poem. Photograph or film the tableau to share it more widely.

For role-playing, choose a poem with a strong point of view. For example, "Moon, Have You Met My Mother?" by Karla Kuskin, from the book of the same title, asks a question that could be addressed by a reader of any age, culture, or gender. Try using different readers to convey different perspectives on the mother-child relationship. Individual or paired readers can also be used to perform poems written in monologue or dialogue. For example, "I Brought a Worm," by Kalli Dakos, from *If You're Not Here, Please Raise Your Hand*, lends itself to a solo reading (along with a Gummi Worm prop!). For those brave enough to try it, improvisation can be a dramatic tool for poetry sharing. Children with a spontaneous and dramatic flair can have a lot of fun acting out a poem's meaning on the spot. For example, Judith Viorst's "Credit," from *Sad Underwear*, is a short poem about a child's frustration about an unidentified "it." The child actor can improvise what "it" might be. And finally, for those who want to orchestrate a full-blown dramatic interpretation, I urge you to invite children to work with you to choose and script a favorite poem for performance. Seek out a drama coach or drama teacher, incorporate local actors or children's theater companies, and help children learn the process of taking poetry public. One poem that lends itself to a full performance is "Harriet Tubman," by Eloise Greenfield, from *Honey, I Love, and Other Love Poems*. It has a strong narrative, vivid imagery, and even a refrain. In addition, it is a true story from history!

---

### PRACTITIONER PERSPECTIVE

My first exposure to poetry was in first grade. I had a teacher who asked her students to memorize a poem a week. Eager to please, I chose my favorite, which was and still is "The Night before Christmas." My teacher, knowing that I was determined and that my choice was certainly longer than the usual first-grade poem, allowed me to take longer than a week to memorize it. She was extremely supportive. To top off this experience I was chosen to recite the poem in front of the entire school during the annual Christmas assembly!! This was an exciting accomplishment for a first grader. I can still recite the poem and love to share it with the different classrooms I teach in. I am sorry to say that my memorization of poetry is limited to that one selection. However, my first-grade experience has given me lots of confidence in other areas. In the past I have had to perform several monologues for which memorization skills were an absolute necessity. My ability to memorize has also boosted my test-taking skills. As I reflect back, I am amazed at what one poem can do!

> Pam McWhorter
> Third-Grade Teacher
> Pasco School District
> Pasco, Washington

Never underestimate the possibilities drama offers for making poetry come alive. I have found that we grown-ups are often a bit shy and hesitant about hamming it up, but children usually are not. The world of pretending comes quite naturally to children, and extending that world to include poetry makes sense. So start with short, humorous poetry at first, and make it active and participatory. When kids *do* poetry, the experience is often deep and meaningful and creates a memory that lasts for a long, long time.

## Music and Poetry

Poetry and music have a strong, natural relationship, given how rhythmic much of poetry is and how poetic many song lyrics are. Children enjoy the steady beat of nursery rhymes, Mother Goose, and many light and humorous poems. They can clap or move to the beat, responding to the music of the rhyme. If you collaborate with music teachers or local musicians, it is even possible to use musical instruments to accompany poems with strong rhyme or rhythm and plan other poetry-music connections. Or try choosing music to

### Books of Poetry and Songs for Children

Lulu Delacre, comp., *Arrorró Mi Niño: Latino Lullabies and Gentle Games*

———, comp., *Arroz con Leche: Popular Songs and Rhymes from Latin America*

Dan Fox, comp., *A Treasury of Children's Songs: Forty Favorites to Sing and Play*

Frane Lessac, comp., *Camp Granada: Sing-along Camp Songs*

José-Luis Orozco, comp., *Diez Deditos: Ten Little Fingers, and Other Play Rhymes and Action Songs from Latin America*

———, comp., *De Colores, and Other Latin American Folk Songs for Children*

Alvin Schwartz, comp., *And the Green Grass Grew All Around: Folk Poetry from Everyone*

play as a backdrop for the oral reading of a special poem. And with older children, writing down song lyrics, looking at line breaks, and separating out the words and the musical notes are effectives approaches to poetry appreciation. Songs in book form can help young children see how language is used to tell a story poetically. So many songs and poems from different cultures are now available in book form. And some poems with strong meter can be put to the tune of a familiar song and sung (as described in the strategies in chapter 5). Whether we beat a poem's rhythm, sing a poem, unpack song lyrics, seek out a song poem picture book, or create a poem performance that incorporates words and music, we can help children enjoy the *sound* of poetry when we look for ways to connect poetry and music.

## Art and Poetry

Poetry and art go hand in hand, since poems are full of imagery and poetry books are often full of illustrations. As a result, there are many possibilities for using art activities following the reading of poetry. Obviously, children can draw a picture to accompany a favorite poem or use a variety of other media (clay, paint, fabric, etc.) to create art to pair with poems. They can also experiment with some of their artistic styles and media used to illustrate their favorite poetry books, such as collage, pen and ink, computer-generated art, or photography. Consult with art teachers, art students, or local artists to learn more about various techniques.

Children can also create posters, bookmarks, or book covers to promote favorite poetry books. These can be displayed alongside the usual poetry promotion materials. Homemade poetry anthologies can be richly illustrated by the children as gifts for loved ones on special occasions.

And do not forget to introduce poetry books that incorporate art explicitly. For example, the classic poetry book *Hailstones and Halibut Bones*, by Mary O'Neill, introduces primary and secondary colors through individual poems that conjure up all kinds of sensory associations for pink, black, yellow, and so forth. There are also several poetry anthologies that are illustrated by fine art. These mini art museums can help children compare how artists and poets have expressed themselves through the ages.

Look at contemporary poetry books for additional examples of distinctive art and crafts. For example, Kristine O'Connell George's book *Fold Me a Poem* links poetry with origami, the Japanese art of paper folding. Or consider the poetry collections of Douglas Florian, a recipient of both illustration and poetry awards for his unique paintings, collages, and poems. His book *Zoo's Who*

## Poetry Books That Showcase Fine Art

Jan Greenberg, comp., *Heart to Heart: New Poems Inspired by Twentieth-Century American Art*

Kenneth Koch and Kate Farrell, comps., *Talking to the Sun: An Illustrated Anthology of Poems for Young People*

Naomi Shihab Nye, comp., *The Space between Our Footsteps: Poems and Paintings from the Middle East*

——, comp., *The Tree Is Older Than You Are: A Bilingual Gathering of Poems and Stories from Mexico with Paintings by Mexican Artists*

Nora Panzer, comp., *Celebrate America in Poetry and Art*

Belinda Rochelle, comp., *Words with Wings: A Treasury of African-American Poetry and Art*

Charles Sullivan, comp., *Here Is My Kingdom: Hispanic-American Literature and Art for Young People*

——, comp., *Imaginary Gardens: American Poetry and Art for Young People*

Hana Volavkova, comp., *I Never Saw Another Butterfly: Children's Drawings and Poems from Terezin Concentration Camp, 1942–1944*

Laura Whipple, comp., *Celebrating America: A Collection of Poems and Images of the American Spirit*

even incorporates rubber stamps in its illustrations. Concrete poems also display an artistic connection since they take the shape of their subject. Seek out some of the books of concrete poetry by Joan Bransfield Graham, John Grandits, J. Patrick Lewis, or Paul Janeczko to see how poem and shape work together. Children can take other poems (or write their own) and copy them into the shapes of their subjects, illustrating in any way they choose.

Another way to reexperience a poem is by manipulating its layout. Using technology to do the manipulating offers another opportunity for children to express themselves. They can use simple audiotape recorders to tape themselves reading their favorite poems or capture the voices of friends, family members, or others reading poems, much like Robert Pinsky's Favorite Poem Project. Children may also use digital or video photography, which allows them to add more artistic elements. Children can create a short film for their favorite poem, with voice-over readings accompanying the images they choose to evoke their poem. A PowerPoint slide show can achieve a similar result using still photography and audiotape of voice, music, or sound effects. And any of these productions can be broadcast on school or community audio or cable networks or presented at special occasions, such as open houses, community meetings, or Poetry Month celebrations. Most children enjoy experimenting with technological tools, and many are very savvy about creative ways to express themselves. Using these tools to encourage children to share their responses to poetry can have powerful results.

## Magnetic Poetry

Nearly everyone has seen the low-tech but very inviting Magnetic Poetry Kits that are now sold far and wide. The simple concept began with a guy named Dave who decided to glue words to pieces of magnets and stick them to a pizza tin as he was trying to write a song. He made the first kits himself and sold them locally and since then has sold over three million poetry kits. Clearly, the idea of manipulating words to create poems from a limited repertoire is a challenge that many enjoy. And the magnetic backing makes it possible to create poetry venues on refrigerators, file cabinets, cookie sheets, and any other metallic surface. Magnetic Poetry, Inc. now has its own website (http://www.magnetic poetry.com) offering a multitude of options, including Shakespeare, haiku, and foreign language kits as well as kits designed especially for children. The company website even publishes poetry created by adult or child magnetic poets.

A public library branch in my area has a place for magnetic poetry in its teen area. The staff made their own magnets using colored paper and different fonts, and creating magnetic poetry has become very popular. And I heard of another library in the area with an entire magnetic wall in their storytime room. What fun it would be to create gigantic words for that wall! Homemade alternatives need not be expensive and can be personalized to include words and names that are locally relevant. One librarian I know found her magnetic poetry words were so popular that they kept disappearing little by little. As an alternative, she made a word bank on cards, strung clotheslines across a bulletin board, and left a bag of clothespins nearby—low tech, low budget, and it worked. The informality and spontaneity of magnetic (or nearly magnetic!) poetry makes creating poetry seem fun and easy, and can serve as an appealing bridge to writing poetry—on paper.

— POET PROFILE —

## Naomi Shihab Nye

### *In her own words:*

As a child, I started writing poems because my ears were filled with voices—the rich, musical voice of my mother, who sang us a string of wonderful lullabies every night to put us to sleep. The whimsical, graciously tender accent of my immigrant Palestinian father. The poems of Carl Sandburg on the public television station, which I still love more than thirty years later. The grave German tones of my grandparent and the mixed rhythms of all our neighbors . . .

Although the voice of my first-grade teacher did not like me very much, the voices of friends I made through children's magazine poetry pages assured me, as did my father's folktales, that there was a larger world beyond our classroom. The young writers I read were my secret friends. When I started sending poems to magazines at age seven, the act was colored with no hope of proving anything—that my writing was "good" or "original"—but simply as a reaching out to those secret friends, a kind of correspondence. Where were they living? How would it change our lives to know one another? Because I read and wrote, the borders of everywhere always felt big. My brother and I visited the library every Saturday, balancing huge skyscrapers of books. In the library, everyone was rich.

My second-grade teacher, a legend at age seventy, *did* like me—thank goodness. She liked everybody most of the time and bopped us on the heads with her bangle bracelets when we acted up. She was steeped in a deeper love of poetry and literature than any other teacher I would ever have. (This is hard, I realize later—to have the best teacher of your academic life in second grade. The rest of those years you keep hoping for someone to live up to him or her.) We memorized William Blake's "Songs of Innocence" in her class when we were seven years old. She did not worry about our not understanding Blake's mystical poems, or anything else. She said the human mind had plenty of room for mysteries. If there was something we didn't understand, we could turn it over and over with our minds, like a lemon drop or a lozenge. She had faith in us. What we didn't know we were on our way to learning. Poetry gave us doors. "Swing it open!" she said. And we were swinging.

"In her own words" is excerpted from Naomi Shihab Nye, "Texas Authors: Naomi Shihab Nye." *The State of Reading* 1, no. 2 (1994): 77–79. Used with permission from the author and from the Texas State Reading Association.

A long time later, working with students and their writing in Texas, I tried to remember all the reasons we have every day for needing to speak out on paper. Because sometimes paper listens better than people do. Because paper doesn't interrupt. Because our own stories will surprise us when we look at them like that, outside our minds. They will lead us, if we let them. One discovery will lead to more than we can imagine from any given spot.

### Because of Libraries We Can Say These Things

*by Naomi Shihab Nye*

She is holding the book close to her body,
carrying it home on the cracked sidewalk,
down the tangled hill.
If a dog runs at her again, she will use the book as a shield.

She looked hard among the long lines
of books to find this one.
When they start talking about money,
when the day contains such long and hot places,
she will go inside.
An orange bed is waiting.
Story without corners.
She will have two families.
They will eat at different hours.

She is carrying a book past the fire station
and the five-and-dime.
What this town has not given her
the book will provide; a sheep,
a wilderness of new solutions.
The book has already lived through its troubles.
The book has a calm cover, a straight spine.

When the step returns to itself
as the best place for sitting,
and the old men up and down the street
are latching their clippers,

she will not be alone.
She will have a book to open
and open and open.
Her life starts here.

"Because of Libraries We Can Say These Things" from *Fuel*, p. 19, copyright 1998, by Naomi Shihab Nye, BOA Editions, Ltd., http://www.boaeditions.org. Reprinted with permission.

*Fuel is a collection of Nye's poems published for adults. "Because of Libraries We Can Say These Things" is a lovely, serious poem about what reading can mean for children. It also reminds us that poetry can cross boundaries from adult to child and back again.*

## Writing Poetry

Children who hear poetry read aloud by an enthusiastic adult and browse through poetry books in their self-selected reading naturally turn to writing poetry when they have the chance. Poetry writing is one more type of writing that children of all ages should have the opportunity to experience. What may surprise you, however, is just how many models of poetry writing there are. What follows are several sources, forms, formulas, and activities that offer a fun introduction to poetic writing. Any of these can serve as a motivating springboard for a writing workshop. By collaborating with teachers, librarians can provide a great deal of support in promoting and developing poetry writing. But even with the sometimes limited time available for activities or instruction in the library setting, we can incorporate poetry-writing opportunities there, too.

It may be helpful to consider the advice of poets themselves when setting the stage for poetry writing. In several poetry collections for young people, each poem is accompanied by a paragraph explaining the poet's sources of inspiration.

Poet Georgia Heard (1994) reminds us how important listening is in the sharing and writing of poetry and relates specific anecdotes about children and their writing. She also suggests helpful questions to ask that guide but do not overwhelm children in *For the Good of the Earth and Sun: Teaching Poetry*

## Poetry with Commentary by Poets

In the books below, the poets provide a few lines of explanation about where the ideas for the poems came from—fascinating and insightful, especially for aspiring poets.

Barbara Brenner, comp., *Voices: Poetry and Art from Around the World*

Catherine Clinton, comp., *I, Too, Sing America: Three Centuries of African American Poetry*

Bernice E. Cullinan, comp., *A Jar of Tiny Stars: Poems By NCTE Award Winning Poets*

Aileen Fisher, *I Heard a Bluebird Sing: Children Select Their Favorite Poems*

Paul B. Janeczko, comp., *Poetspeak: In Their Work, About Their Work: A Selection*

———, comp., *The Place My Words Are Looking For: What Poets Say about and through Their Work*

———, comp., *Seeing the Blue Between: Advice and Inspiration for Young Poets*

X. J. Kennedy and D. Kennedy, comps., *Knock at a Star: A Child's Introduction to Poetry*

Karla Kuskin, *Dogs and Dragons, Trees and Dreams: A Collection of Poems*

George Ella Lyon, *Where I'm From: Where Poems Come From*

Gary Soto, *A Fire in My Hands: A Book of Poems*

Janet S. Wong, *A Suitcase of Seaweed, and Other Poems*

(1994) and *Awakening the Heart: Exploring Poetry in Elementary and Middle School* (1999). She invites us to share what we notice about poems as we invite children to do the same. As we share more and more poetry, children will begin to point out the patterns and language that are interesting to them. These are the teachable moments that enable us to insert relevant mini-lessons. We can draw ideas from the previously presented question lists and group-discussion activities to set the stage for writing—whether individual, partner-based, or group collaboration.

Working together with teachers or parents, we can provide aspiring young poets with the support and guidance they need to keep writing. We can listen and nudge, provide resources and opportunities, and offer empathy and en-

### Resources for Teaching Children to Write Poetry

Full publishing information for the titles below can be found in the list of references.

Bob Barton and David Booth, *Poetry Goes to School: From Mother Goose to Shel Silverstein*

David Booth and Bill Moore, *Poems Please! Sharing Poetry with Children*

Barbara J. Esbensen, *A Celebration of Bees: Helping Children to Write Poetry*

Mary Kenner Glover, *A Garden of Poets: Poetry Writing in the Elementary Classroom*

Georgia Heard, *Awakening the Heart: Exploring Poetry in Elementary and Middle School*

———, *For the Good of the Earth and Sun: Teaching Poetry*

Sara Holbrook, *Practical Poetry: A Nonstandard Approach to Meeting Content-Area Standards*

Lee Bennett Hopkins, *Pass the Poetry Please*

Kenneth Koch, *Wishes, Lies, and Dreams: Teaching Children to Write Poetry*

———, *Rose, Where Did You Get That Red?*

Amy McClure, *Sunrises and Songs: Reading and Writing Poetry in the Classroom*

Regie Routman, *Kids' Poems: Teaching First-Graders to Love Writing Poetry*

Judith Steinbergh, *Reading and Writing Poetry: A Guide for Teachers*

Iris McClellan Tiedt, *Tiger Lilies, Toadstools, and Thunderbolts: Engaging K–8 Students with Poetry*

couragement. But keep in mind that not every child will be a poet, as Myra Cohn Livingston eloquently reminds us in *The Child as Poet: Myth or Reality?* (1984). Each child should have the opportunity to try poetry writing and have that outlet of self-expression, but not everyone aspires to write poetry professionally by any means. And that is OK. Experimenting with poetry writing gives us a greater appreciation for the poet's art and craft when we read published poetry.

## Poetic Form

Once children are immersed in poetry, they often begin to notice poems can take many different forms. They enjoy seeing the innovative ways poets have crafted poems. Chapter 3 introduced examples of published poetry books organized by poetic form, such as haiku, concrete poetry, and riddle poems. What poetry forms and techniques can children and young people learn to use? Poems can rhyme or not, be completely free-flowing, or follow a specific form. Adults can introduce children to the various forms and techniques in context by using interesting examples from excellent poetry. Here are a few examples of the most common forms of traditional verse that we can point out or explain:

> *Couplet*—two lines that rhyme
>
> *Tercet / triplet*—three lines ending in the same rhyming sound
>
> *Quatrain*—four lines with any metrical pattern or rhyme scheme
>
> *Cinquain*—an unrhymed stanza in five lines totaling twenty-two syllables. (The first line has two syllables, each of the next three lines is longer than the previous one, and the last line returns to two syllables.)

Paul Janeczko has a helpful picture book resource for introducing poetic form in *A Kick in the Head: An Everyday Guide to Poetic Forms*. Poet Helen Frost showcases several distinctive poetic forms, such as the sestina, sonnet, pantoum, acrostic, and haiku, in her recent works *Keesha's House* and *Spinning through the Universe: A Novel in Poems from Room 214*. She includes back matter in each book that explains each poetic form as well as her reasons for choosing it.

### Poetic Forms from A to Z

The alphabet has often been used as a framework for poetry. Avis Harley has written two picture books for middle grades that include a different poem and poetic form for each letter of the alphabet. They are *Fly with Poetry: An ABC of Poetry* and *Leap into Poetry: More ABCs of Poetry*. Paul Janeczko has a wonderful resource book for children and young adults filled with both serious and wacky poetry forms: *Poetry from A to Z: A Guide for Young Writers*. This can provide the background for expanding poetic repertoires. Children may enjoy discovering unusual forms of poetry or even trying their hands at writing them. Or working as a group, children can create their own alphabet book of poetry with each child responsible for a letter to build a poem upon. Just a few of the forms introduced by Harley and Janeczko are

| | |
|---|---|
| Autograph rhyme | Haikuestion |
| Blessing / prayer poem | How-to poem |
| Cheer / chant | Letter/note/diary poem |
| Clerihew | List/litany poem |
| Crossword puzzle poem | Onelinepoem |
| Curse poem | Persona poem |
| Draw and tell poem | Question poem |
| Elevator poem | Recipe poem |
| Epitaph and elegy poems | Terse verse |
| Graffiti poem | Triangular triplet |

## Biopoems

The biopoem is a popular format for children to try because it provides a framework to ease them into poetry writing and offers an opportunity for autobiographical writing—often a good place to begin. Thus, you can use biopoem writing at the beginning of a school year as a get-acquainted activity or pair biopoems with children's photographs or artwork for posting on special occasions. Actually, a biopoem does not have to be about the writer. It can be used to describe another person or even a literary character.

### The Biopoem Formula

Line 1:   First name

Line 2:   Four traits (characteristics) that describe the person

Line 3:   Relative (such as brother, sister, husband, wife, daughter) of _____

Line 4:    Lover of _____ (three things or people the person loves)

Line 5:    Who feels _____ (three items)

Line 6:    Who needs _____ (three items )

Line 7:    Who fears _____ (three items)

Line 8:    Who gives _____ (one item fully explained)

Line 9:    Who would like to see _____ (one item)

Line 10:   Resident of _____

Line 11:   Last name

SOURCE: Adapted from http://library.thinkquest.org/11883/data/biopoem.htm.

Here is a sample biopoem I wrote about the protagonist of Natalie Babbitt's classic fantasy novel *Tuck Everlasting* (Farrar, Straus & Giroux, 1975):

**Winnie**

caring, curious, sensitive, smart

companion of Mae, Tuck, Miles, Jesse

lover of family, friends, life

who feels afraid, adventurous, ambivalent

who needs an anchor, a challenge, a choice

who fears death, danger, decisions

who gives the gift of life with love

who would like to see the future

resident of Treegap

**Foster**

## Found Poems

Another poetic form that lends itself to practical application is found poetry. Found poetry is created by taking text from other sources, such as newspaper articles, ads, and picture books, and converting it into a poem. I enjoy using newspaper articles (or news from the Web) because such material is handy and offers current information that is often interesting and relevant to young people. Mining poems for words and ideas for a found poem helps children process the information and focus on key points for discussion. This activity can be conducted with the whole group, in small groups, or individually once children are familiar with the process. It begins with choosing a news article (or other text) of interest, then reading it, discussing it, and highlighting and writing the key words and ideas that seem particularly sharp, interesting, or relevant. From that list of words and ideas, you arrange a poem, eliminating unnecessary words and phrases and inserting a few others, if needed, for sense or meaning. What emerges is often interesting news plus powerful poetry. Then post the poem along with the news article, and if time allows, a drawing or photograph that the kids choose or create.

To illustrate, we will start with a sample news report from the Web:

Peace One Day Commitments 2004

As one way of observing the Day, many peace-based NGOs and individuals representing a wide variety of religious and spiritual traditions are observing "International Day of Peace Vigils" with the following objective: "To encourage worldwide, 24-hour spiritual observations for peace and nonviolence on the International Day of Peace, 21 September 2004 in every house of worship and place of spiritual practice, by all religious and spiritually based groups and individuals and by all men, women and children who seek peace in the world." These global 24-hour observations for peace are meant to demonstrate the power of prayer and other spiritual observations in promoting peace and preventing violent conflict. They will also help raise public awareness of the International Day of Peace and can directly support the establishment of a global ceasefire. You can personally support this worldwide initiative by committing to conduct a spiritual observation and promulgating the Vigil idea among religious and peace-based groups in your community (http://www.peaceoneday .org/bin/venda.plex?ex=co_disp-view&bsref=peaceoneday&page= 2004).

Below is a sample poem that I created based on the words and ideas of the article. (Obviously, several different poems are possible from one news article, depending on the choices each poem finder makes.)

### Peace One Day

One way
observing the Day
International Day of Peace
encourage
worldwide

24-hour
peace and nonviolence
21 September
in every house of worship
in every place of spiritual practice
individuals
all men, women, and children
who seek peace in the world
preventing violent conflict
raising public awareness
support a global cease-fire
this worldwide initiative
begins
in your community.

**Peace One Day**

Once you develop the knack of using poetic formulas like biopoems and poetry-building exercises like the construction of found poems, you will begin to see many other possibilities for creating original poems. Dave Morice provides even more options for creating poems in unusual formats in his book *The Adventures of Dr. Alphabet: 104 Unusual Ways to Write Poetry in the Classroom and the Community* (1996). His suggestions are generally quite playful and unorthodox but can be lots of fun, too. Here is just a sampling of the 104 choices:

- Autumn leaf poems
- Postage stamp poems
- Rolodex poems
- Thumb book poems
- Poetry poker
- Poetry checkers
- Poetry mazes
- Social security poems
- Shakespearean sonnet maker

## Poetry Journals

Keeping a poetry journal can be a meaningful exercise for children, especially for aspiring poets. A journal can take the form of a notebook or folder for storing copies of favorite poems, for recording one's responses to individual poems, for gathering favorite words, personal reflections, and one's own poetry writing—or for all three purposes. Poetry journals can assist children to partic-ipate actively in reading poetry, to record personal reactions and preferences, and to develop writing skills. This tool can be especially helpful for students learning English who struggle with new vocabulary and syntax in oral com-munication situations. Sometimes discussing possible journal content may serve as a powerful prewriting technique that prompts children toward more thoughtful responses in their journals. Journal entries may range from freewriting to responses to prompts. Additionally, children may want to con-sider who will read their journals. They may write for an adult, may pair with peers or children of different ages or grade levels, or may exchange thoughts with adult volunteers via buddy journals. One amusing mock journal that ap-pears to be written and gathered by a child writer but is actually the creation of adult author Gary Crew and illustrator Craig Smith is the highly visual pic-ture book *Troy Thompson's Excellent Peotry* [sic] *Book*. Sharon Creech creates another journal-like book with her verse novel *Love That Dog*. Both books are inspiring examples of a child's poetic voice (filtered through an adult author) and useful models of what a poetry journal might look and sound like.

# English Language Learners and Poetry Writing

As children experience frequent poetry read-alouds and choral readings, the realization that they could write their own poetry emerges as a natural extension. And although some English language learners may have limited linguistic proficiency, several poetry-writing formats are ideally suited for them. Because lists are simple and familiar to everyone, for example, the list poem (or catalog verse) is an excellent introduction to the writing of poetry at any age or proficiency level. Simple completions such as "I wish . . ." or "I remember . . ." can lead to funny or poignant student-authored poems. Read-alouds and choral reading activities lay the foundation for composing by providing models of poem structure such as color poetry (green is . . .) or five senses poetry (winter smells like / feels like / tastes like / looks like / sounds like). After hearing various models, children can collaborate to generate similar poems of their own, discussing format, word choice, and style issues. A terrific resource for choosing poem and designing activities is *A Chorus of Cultures: Developing Literacy through Multicultural Poetry*, by Alma Flor Ada, Violet Harris, and Lee Bennett Hopkins (1993). Generally speaking, children are ready to solo only after they have worked on a poem with others in a class or group. But do

## Barbara Esbensen Poetry Portfolio Available

The Children's Literature Research Collections held at the Kerlan Collection of the University of Minnesota offer a unique resource for sharing poetry with children: a portfolio of materials donated by NCTE Poetry Award–winner Barbara Esbensen. The Barbara Esbensen Poetry Portfolio is a multimedia learning tool that uses the work of Barbara Esbensen to highlight her versatility as a writer, poet, and storyteller. The kit is appropriate for grades 2 through 8 and includes lessons, biographical information, supporting documents, and overhead transparencies of manuscript pages and galleys of Esbensen's writing. This can be invaluable for helping children understand the process of writing and publishing poetry. Aspiring writers, in particular, will find this "behind-the-scenes" view fascinating.

SOURCE: http://special.lib.umn.edu/clrc/esbensen/.

not be surprised if your English language learners impress you with their fresh ideas and use of words. Often their developing English vocabulary makes them even more resourceful with word choice and placement.

## Publishing Children's Writing

Children who enjoy writing are often interested in seeing their work in print. One informal approach is to type, print, and post their poetry. Or you can create a photocopied anthology of the poetry of many child writers. But for children who are truly dedicated and ambitious, submitting a poem for publication is a worthy goal. And there are several web and print resources that print children's original poetry. Help child poets become familiar with the protocol for submitting manuscripts (style, format, and so forth), and prepare them for the competitive process and for possible rejection. Let them choose which poems they are most proud of, keep copies of everything submitted, and get parent permission. Then celebrate with them when their work is accepted and appears in print. Congratulate them, publicly showcase their accomplishment, and spread the word. Success inspires success. And, of course, if their work is rejected, offer support and encouragement. The following are among the longest-running publications and websites that feature children's writing:

> *Stone Soup* magazine
> http://www.stonesoup.com
> Children's Art Foundation
> P.O. Box 83
> Santa Cruz, CA 95063

This print publication specializes in showcasing the original art and writing, including poetry, of children from eight to thirteen years of age.

> *Merlyn's Pen*
> http://www.merlynspen.com
> P.O. Box 1058
> East Greenwich, RI 02818

Middle school students can see their writing published in this print magazine.

> Kid News
> http://www.kidnews.com

This website features kids' writing from practically everywhere. It includes poems, short stories, and novellas that children submit via either online form or e-mail. There are also links to various school magazines.

Potato Hill Poetry
http://www.potatohill.com

This website is rich with ideas for sharing poems and poetry writing with children of all ages. Among its offerings are poetry-writing contests for kids, poems written by children of all ages, and teacher resources and workshop information.

Children's Literature Web Guide: Children's Writing
http://www.ucalgary.ca/~dkbrown/writings.html

This web page provides links to a variety of websites where children can see their own writing and art published and enjoy writing and art created by other children. Included are an encyclopedia written by children; a diary project; writing contests; and poetry, story books, and art by children of all ages, from elementary school through high school.

---

### Resources for Young People on Poetry Writing

Kathi Appelt, *Poems from Homeroom: A Writer's Place to Start*

Ralph J. Fletcher, *Poetry Matters: Writing a Poem from the Inside Out*

Paul B. Janeczko, *How to Write Poetry*

X. J. Kennedy and D. Kennedy, comps. *Knock at a Star*

Myra Cohn Livingston, *Poem-Making: Ways to Begin Writing Poetry*

---

## Conclusion

As we work to help children verbalize their responses to poetry and expand their poetry-based experiences through drama, music, art, and writing, we establish a pattern of connecting poetry with our lives in varied ways. We begin by learning how to ask appropriate questions and how to help children help themselves understand poetry. We help children internalize poems through genuine poetry talk. We invite them to extend their experiences of poetry by providing opportunities for verbal and artistic expression. And we open the door to self-expression by giving them opportunities to write their own poetry. As Susan Wooldridge reminds us in her book *Poemcrazy: Freeing Your Life with Words*, "The symbolic language of poetry allows us to express and begin to understand not only our feelings, but our idiosyncrasies, problems, and fears" (1996, 17). That give-and-take between the poem presenter and poem participants provides a shared experience that can create memorable moments as well as bonds that last a lifetime.

> *Human beings can't live without language,*
> *can't live without communication, and they*
> *will create it—somehow.*
>
> —Oliver Sacks, Neurologist

# ∞ *One Final Word*

$\mathcal{M}$ary Ann Hoberman wrote the poem below for the ceremony at which she was given the 2003 National Council of Teachers of English Award for Excellence in Poetry for Children. It then appeared in *Horn Book Magazine* (vol. 81, no. 3 [May / June 2005]: 255) and is used with her permission here. She notes that this poem, "Take Sound," pays homage to the great children's poet David McCord, the first recipient of the NCTE award, by echoing the title and cadence of his poem "Take Sky." It is a lovely tribute to a long tradition of smart, rhythmic, evocative poetry for children—and a fitting end to this book about the pleasures of sharing the sounds and words of poetry with children.

### Take Sound

*by Mary Ann Hoberman*

Each word a poem.
Take *sound*—
Its mysteries abound:
To hear a sound;
To sound to find;
Or to be sound
In body, mind;
A stretch of water
Wide and clear;
To register
Upon the ear—
Each separate meaning
Hovers, tense
Above the more
Intended sense.
Each part of speech
Another trope,
A turn

In the kaleidoscope.
And in this lovely
Layered thing,
The origins
Of language sing,
Alive, ambiguous, absurd—
*In the beginning was the word.*

# ∞ Noteworthy Poets Writing for Young People

Poets' personal websites are listed, when known.

| | |
|---|---|
| Arnold Adoff | http://www.arnoldadoff.com |
| Francisco X. Alarcón | |
| Kathi Appelt | http://www.kathiappelt.com |
| Brod Bagert | http://www.brodbagert.com |
| Calef Brown | http://www.calefbrown.com |
| Joseph Bruchac | http://www.josephbruchac.com |
| John Ciardi | |
| Kalli Dakos | http://www.kallidakos.com |
| Rebecca Kai Dotlich | |
| Barbara Esbensen | |
| Aileen Fisher | |
| Paul Fleischman | http://www.paulfleischman.net |
| Ralph Fletcher | http://www.ralphfletcher.com |
| Douglas Florian | http://www.douglasflorian.com |
| Kristine O'Connell George | http://www.kristinegeorge.com |
| Nikki Giovanni | http://nikki-giovanni.com |
| Joan Bransfield Graham | http://www.joangraham.com |
| Eloise Greenfield | |
| Nikki Grimes | http://www.nikkigrimes.com |
| Georgia Heard | |
| Mary Ann Hoberman | http://www.maryannhoberman.com |
| Sara Holbrook | http://www.saraholbrook.com |
| Lee Bennett Hopkins | |
| Paul Janeczko | http://www.pauljaneczko.com |
| X. J. Kennedy | http://www.xjanddorothymkennedy.com |
| Karla Kuskin | http://www.karlakuskin.com |
| J. Patrick Lewis | http://www.jpatricklewis.com |
| Myra Cohn Livingston | |
| Walter Dean Myers | |
| David McCord | |
| Eve Merriam | |
| Lilian Moore | |
| Pat Mora | http://www.patmora.com |

Naomi Shihab Nye
Susan Pearson
Jack Prelutsky
Alice Schertle
Carol Diggory Shields
Joyce Sidman                    http://www.joycesidman.com
Shel Silverstein                http://www.shelsilverstein.com
Marilyn Singer                  http://www.marilynsinger.net
Sonya Sones                     http://www.sonyasones.com
Gary Soto                       http://www.garysoto.com
Joyce Carol Thomas              http://www.joycecarolthomas.com
Judith Viorst
April Halprin Wayland           http://www.aprilwayland.com
Nancy Willard
Janet Wong                      http://www.janetwong.com
Valerie Worth
Jane Yolen                      http://www.janeyolen.com

## IN PARTICULAR, POETS FROM MANY CULTURES

### African American Poetry for Young People

Gwendolyn Brooks               Eloise Greenfield
Lucille Clifton                Nikki Grimes
Countee Cullen                 Langston Hughes
Paul Laurence Dunbar           Walter Dean Myers
Nikki Giovanni                 Marilyn Nelson

### Latino/Latina Poetry for Young People

Francisco Alarcón              Pat Mora
Lulu Delacre                   José-Luis Orozco
Juan Felipe Herrera            Gary Soto

### Asian Pacific American Poetry for Young People

Minfong Ho                     Janet Wong
Michio Mado

Native American Poetry for Young People

Joseph Bruchac            Virginia Driving Hawk Sneve
Hettie Jones

International Poetry for Young People

John Agard            Dennis Lee
Monica Gunning        Grace Nichols
Lynn Joseph           Michael Rosen

*Appendix B*

# ⌒⌒ Bibliography of Children's Poetry Books

A comprehensive list of all the poetry books cited in the text.

Abeel, Samantha. 1993. *Reach for the Moon*. Duluth, MN: Pfeifer-Hamilton.

Ada, Alma Flor. 1997. *Gathering the Sun*. New York: Lothrop, Lee & Shepard.

Ada, Alma Flor, and Isabel Campoy, comps. 2003. *¡Pio Peep! Traditional Spanish Nursery Rhymes*. New York: HarperCollins.

Adedjouma, D. 1996. *The Palm of My Heart: Poetry by African American Children*. New York: Lee & Low.

Adoff, Arnold. 1982. *All the Colors of the Race*. New York: Lothrop, Lee & Shepard.

———. 1973. *Black Is Brown Is Tan*. New York: Harper & Row.

———, ed. 1968. *I Am the Darker Brother: An Anthology of Modern Poems by Negro Americans*. New York: Macmillan.

———. 1991. *In for Winter, Out for Spring*. San Diego: Harcourt Brace.

———. 1997. *Love Letters*. New York: Scholastic.

———, ed. 1974/1994. *My Black Me: A Beginning Book of Black Poetry*. Reprinted New York: Dutton.

———. 1986. *Sports Pages*. New York: HarperCollins.

———. 1995. *Street Music: City Poems*. New York: HarperCollins.

———. 2000. *Touch the Poem*. New York: Blue Sky.

Agard, John, and Grace Nichols, eds. 1994. *A Caribbean Dozen: Poems from Caribbean Poets*. Cambridge, MA: Candlewick.

———. 1995. *No Hickory, No Dickory, No Dock: Caribbean Nursery Rhymes*. Cambridge, MA: Candlewick.

Akaza, Norihisa. 1994. *Smell of the Rain, Voices of the Stars*. Orlando, FL: Harcourt Brace.

Alarcón, Francisco X. 1999. *Angels Ride Bikes, and Other Fall Poems*. San Francisco: Children's Book Press.

———. 1998. *From the Bellybutton of the Moon, and Other Summer Poems / Del Ombligo de la Luna, y Otros Poemas de Verano*. San Francisco: Children's Book Press.

———. 2001. *Iguanas in the Snow, and Other Winter Poems / Iguanas en la Nieve, y Otros Poemas de Invierno*. San Francisco: Children's Book Press.

———. 1997. *Laughing Tomatoes, and Other Spring Poems / Jitomates Risuenos, y Otros Poemas de Primavera*. San Francisco: Children's Book Press.

———. 2005. *Poems to Dream Together / Poemas para Sonar Juntos*. New York: Lee & Low.

Altman, Susan, and Susan Lechner. 1993. *Followers of the North Star: Rhymes about African American Heroes, Heroines, and Historical Times*. Chicago: Children's Press.

Amon, Aline. 1981. *The Earth Is Sore: Native Americans on Nature*. New York: Atheneum.

Angelou, Maya. 1993. *Life Doesn't Frighten Me*. New York: Steward, Tabori & Chang.

Anholt, Catherine, and Laurence Anholt. 1998. *Big Book of Families*. Cambridge, MA: Candlewick.

Appelt, Kathi. 2004. *My Father's Summers: A Daughter's Memoirs*. New York: Henry Holt.

———. 2002. *Poems from Homeroom: A Writer's Place to Start*. New York: Henry Holt.

Arbuthnot, May Hill. 1961. *The Arbuthnot Anthology of Children's Literature: Single-Volume Edition of Time for Poetry, Time for Fairy Tales, and Time for True Tales*. Chicago: Scott Foresman.

Asch, Frank. 1998. *Cactus Poems*. San Diego: Harcourt Brace.

———. 1996. *Sawgrass Poems: A View of the Everglades*. San Diego: Harcourt Brace.

———. 1999. *Song of the North*. San Diego: Harcourt Brace.

Atwood, Ann. 1971. *Haiku: The Mood of Earth*. New York: Scribner's.

Bagert, Brod. 1993. *Chicken Socks, and Other Contagious Poems*. Honesdale, PA: Wordsong/Boyds Mills.

———. 1997. *The Gooch Machine: Poems for Children to Perform*. Honesdale, PA: Wordsong/Boyds Mills.

———. 1992. *Let Me Be the Boss: Poems for Kids to Perform*. Honesdale, PA: Wordsong/Boyds Mills.

———. 1991. *Steel Cables: Love Poems from Adam Rib*. New Orleans: Juliahouse.

Bangs, Edward. 1976. *Steven Kellogg's Yankee Doodle*. New York: Parent's Magazine Press.

Baring-Gould, William, and Ceil Baring-Gould. 1962. *The Annotated Mother Goose: Nursery Rhymes Old and New*. New York: C. N. Potter.

Bates, Katharine Lee. 1994. *O Beautiful for Spacious Skies*. New York: Chronicle.

Bauer, Caroline Feller, ed. 1986. *Snowy Day: Poems and Stories*. New York: HarperCollins.

Bedard, Michael. 1992. *Emily*. New York: Doubleday.

Begay, Shonto. 1995. *Navajo: Visions and Voices across the Mesa*. New York: Scholastic.

Behn, Harry, comp. and trans. 1964. *Cricket Songs: Japanese Haiku*. New York: Harcourt, Brace & World.

———, trans. 1971. *More Cricket Songs: Japanese Haiku Translated by Harry Behn*. New York: Harcourt, Brace, Jovanovich.

Benjamin, Floella, comp. 1995. *Skip across the Ocean: Nursery Rhymes from Around the World*. New York: Orchard.

Berry, James. 1991. *Isn't My Name Magical? Sister and Brother Poems*. New York: Simon & Schuster.

Bierhorst, John. 1998. *In the Trail of the Wind: American Indian Poems and Ritual Orations*. Rev. ed. New York: Farrar, Straus & Giroux.

———, comp. 1994. *On the Road of Stars: Native American Night Poems and Sleep Charms*. New York: Macmillan.

Blake, Quentin, comp. 1995. *The Penguin Book of Nonsense Verse*. New York: Penguin.

Bober, Natalie S. 1991. *A Restless Spirit: The Story of Robert Frost*. New York: Henry Holt.

Bogan, Louise, and William Jay Smith, eds. 1990. *The Golden Journey: Poems for Young People*. Chicago: Contemporary.

Bontemps, Arna, comp. 1941. *Golden Slippers: An Anthology of Negro Poetry for Young Readers*. New York: Harper & Row.

Booth, David. 1990. *Voices on the Wind: Poems for All Seasons*. New York: Morrow.

Bouchard, David. 1995. *If You're Not from the Prairie . . .* New York: Atheneum.

———. 1996. *Voices from the Wild*. San Francisco: Chronicle.

Brenner, Barbara. 1994. *The Earth Is Painted Green: A Garden of Poems about Our Planet*. New York: Scholastic.

———. 2000. *Voices: Poetry and Art from Around the World*. Washington, DC: National Geographic Society.

Brooks, Gwendolyn. 1956/1984. *Bronzeville Boys and Girls*. Reprinted New York: HarperCollins.

Brown, Calef. 2000. *Dutch Sneakers and Flea Keepers: 14 More Stories*. Boston: Houghton Mifflin.

———. 1998. *Polkabats and Octopus Slacks: 14 Stories*. Boston: Houghton Mifflin.

Brown, Dale S. 1995. *I Know I Can Climb the Mountain*. Columbus, OH: Mountain Books & Music.

Brown, H. Jackson, Jr. 1991. *Live and Learn and Pass It On*. Nashville: Rutledge Hill.

———. 1995. *Live and Learn and Pass It On*. Vol. 2. Nashville: Rutledge Hill.

Bruchac, Joseph. 1996. *Between Earth and Sky: Legends of Native American Sacred Places*. San Diego: Harcourt Brace.

————. 1996. *The Circle of Thanks*. Mahwah, NJ: BridgeWater.

———— 1995. *The Earth under Sky Bear's Feet: Native American Poems of the Land*. New York: Philomel.

————. 1996. *Four Ancestors: Stories, Songs, and Poems from Native North America*. Mahwah, NJ: BridgeWater.

————. 1992. *Thirteen Moons on Turtle's Back: A Native American Year of Moons*. New York: Philomel.

Bryan, Ashley, comp. 1994. *All Night, All Day: A Child's First Book of African American Spirituals*. New York: Atheneum.

————. 1997. *Ashley Bryan's ABC of African American Poetry*. New York: Atheneum.

————, comp. 1978. *I Greet the Dawn: Poems by Paul Laurence Dunbar*. New York: Atheneum.

————. 1992. *Sing to the Sun*. New York: HarperCollins.

Burleigh, Robert. 1997. *Hoops*. San Diego: Silver Whistle.

————. 2004. *Langston's Train Ride*. New York: Scholastic.

Burt, Mary Elizabeth. 1904/1971. *Poems That Every Child Should Know: A Selection of the Best Poems of All Times for Young People*. Reprinted Freeport, NY: Books for Libraries.

Bush, Timothy. 2000. *Ferocious Girls, Steamroller Boys, and Other Poems in Between*. New York: Orchard.

Calmenson, Stephanie. 2002. *Welcome, Baby! Baby Rhymes for Baby Times*. New York: HarperCollins.

Carle, Eric. 1989. *Animals, Animals*. New York: Scholastic.

Carlson, Lori M., ed. 1994. *Cool Salsa: Bilingual Poems on Growing Up Latino in the United States*. New York: Henry Holt.

————. 2005. *Red Hot Salsa*. New York: Henry Holt.

————. 1998. *Sol a Sol: Bilingual Poems*. New York: Henry Holt.

Carlstrom, Nancy White. 1996. *Let's Count It Out, Jesse Bear*. New York: Simon & Schuster.

Carroll, Lewis. 2004. *Jabberwocky*. Illustrated by Stephane Jorisch. Tonawanda, NY: Kids Can Press.

Carson, Jo. 1991. *Stories I Ain't Told Nobody Yet: Selections from the People Pieces*. New York: Theatre Communications Group.

Castillo, Ana. 2000. *My Daughter, My Son, the Eagle, the Dove: An Aztec Chant*. New York: Dutton.

Chandra, Deborah. 1993. *Rich Lizard, and Other Poems*. New York: Farrar, Straus & Giroux.

Christensen, Bonnie. 2001. *Woody Guthrie: Poet of the People*. New York: Knopf.

Ciardi, John. 1966. *The Monster Den; or, Look What Happened at My House—and to It*. Philadelphia: Lippincott. Reprinted Honesdale, PA: Wordsong, 1991.

———. 1970. *Someone Could Win a Polar Bear*. Philadelphia: Lippincott.

———. 1970. *You Know Who*. Philadelphia: Lippincott.

———. 1962. *You Read to Me, I'll Read to You*. Philadelphia: Lippincott. Reprinted New York: HarperTrophy, 1987.

Clifton, Lucille. 1983. *Everett Anderson's Goodbye*. New York: Henry Holt.

———. 1970. *Some of the Days of Everett Anderson*. New York: Holt, Rinehart & Winston.

Clinton, Catherine. 1993/1998. *I, Too, Sing America: Three Centuries of African American Poetry*. Boston: Houghton Mifflin.

Cohn, Amy L., comp. 1993. *From Sea to Shining Sea: A Treasury of American Folklore and Folk Songs*. New York: Scholastic.

Cole, Joanna, comp. 1989. *Anna Banana: 101 Jump-Rope Rhymes*. Illustrated by Alan Tiegreen. New York: HarperTrophy.

Cole, Joanna, and Stephanie Calmenson, comps. 1995. *Yours Till Banana Splits: 201 Autograph Rhymes*. New York: Morrow Junior Books.

Cooling, Wendy. 2004. *Come to the Great World*. New York: Holiday House.

Cooper, Floyd. 1994. *Coming Home: From the Life of Langston Hughes*. New York: Philomel.

Cooper, Kay. 2001. *Too Many Rabbits, and Other Fingerplays about Animals, Nature, Weather, and Children*. New York: Cartwheel.

Creech, Sharon. 2004. *Heartbeat*. New York: HarperCollins.

———. 2001. *Love That Dog*. New York: HarperCollins.

Crew, Gary. 2003. *Troy Thompson's Excellent Peotry* [sic] *Book*. La Jolla, CA: Kane/Miller.

Crews, Nina. 2004. *The Neighborhood Mother Goose*. New York: Greenwillow.

Crist-Evans, Craig. 1999. *Moon over Tennessee: A Boy's Civil War Journal*. Boston: Houghton Mifflin.

Cullinan, Bernice F., ed. 1996. *A Jar of Tiny Stars: Poems by NCTE Award–Winning Poets*. Honesdale, PA: Wordsong/Boyds Mills.

Cumpian, Carlos. 1994. *Latino Rainbow: Poems about Latino Americans*. Chicago: Children's Press.

Curry, Jennifer. 2002. *Animal Poems*. New York: Scholastic.

Cyrus, Kurt. 2005. *Hotel Deep: Light Verse from Dark Water*. Orlando, FL: Harcourt.

———. 2001. *Oddhopper Opera: A Bug's Garden of Verses*. San Diego: Harcourt Brace.

Dakos, Kalli. 1993. *Don't Read This Book, Whatever You Do! More Poems about School*. New York: Trumpet Club.

———. 1996. *The Goof Who Invented Homework, and Other School Poems*. New York: Dial.

———. 1990. *If You're Not Here, Please Raise Your Hand: Poems about School*. New York: Four Winds.

———. 1995. *Mrs. Cole on an Onion Roll, and Other School Poems*. New York: Trumpet Club.

———. 2003. *Put Your Eyes up Here, and Other School Poems*. New York: Simon & Schuster.

De Fina, Allan A. 1997. *When a City Leans against the Sky*. Honesdale, PA: Boyds Mills.

De Gerez, Toni, comp. 1984. *My Song Is a Piece of Jade: Poems of Ancient Mexico in English and Spanish / Mi Canción es un Pedazo de Jade: Poemas del México Antiguo en Inglés y Español*. Boston: Little Brown.

De Regniers, Beatrice Schenk, et al., eds. 1988. *Sing a Song of Popcorn: Every Child's Book of Poems*. New York: Scholastic.

———, eds. 1988. *The Way I Feel Sometimes*. New York: Clarion.

Delacre, Lulu. 2004. *Arrorró Mi Niño: Latino Lullabies and Gentle Games*. New York: Lee & Low.

———, comp. 1992. *Arroz con Leche: Popular Songs and Rhymes from Latin America*. New York: Scholastic.

———, comp. 1992. *Las Navidades: Popular Christmas Songs from Latin America*. New York: Scholastic.

Demi, ed. 1986. *Dragon Kites and Dragonflies: A Collection of Chinese Nursery Rhymes*. San Diego: Harcourt Brace Jovanovich.

———, comp. 1994. *In the Eyes of the Cat: Japanese Poetry for All Seasons*. Translated by Tze-si Huang. New York: Henry Holt.

DePaola, Tomie. 1985. *Tomie DePaola's Mother Goose*. New York: Putnam.

Dotlich, Rebecca Kai. 2003. *In the Spin of Things: Poetry of Motion*. Honesdale, PA: Wordsong/Boyds Mills.

———. 1998. *Lemonade Sun, and Other Summer Poems*. Honesdale, PA: Wordsong/Boyds Mills.

———. 2004. *Over in the Pink House: New Jump-Rope Rhymes*. Honesdale, PA: Wordsong/Boyds Mills.

———. 2001. *When Riddles Come Rumbling: Poems to Ponder*. Honesdale, PA: Wordsong/Boyds Mills.

Dunbar, Paul L. 1999. *Jump Back, Honey: The Poems of Paul Laurence Dunbar*. New York: Hyperion.

Dunning, Stephen, Edward Luders, and Hugh Smith. 1966. *Reflections on a Gift of Watermelon Pickle*. New York: Scholastic.

Esbensen, Barbara. 1984. *Cold Stars and Fireflies: Poems of the Four Seasons*. New York: Crowell.

———. 1995. *Dance with Me*. New York: HarperCollins.

———. 1995. *The Dream Mouse: A Lullaby Tale from Old Latvia*. Boston: Little Brown.

———. 1996. *Echoes for the Eye: Poems to Celebrate Patterns in Nature*. New York: HarperCollins.

———. 1999. *Jumping Day*. Honesdale, PA: Boyds Mills.

———. 1992. *Who Shrank My Grandmother's House? Poems of Discovery*. New York: HarperCollins.

———. 1986. *Words with Wrinkled Knees*. New York: Crowell.

Feelings, Tom. 1993. *Soul Looks Back in Wonder*. New York: Dial.

Field, Edward. 1998. *Magic Words: Poems*. San Diego: Gulliver Books/Harcourt Brace.

Fisher, Aileen. 1991. *Always Wondering: Some Favorite Poems of Aileen Fisher*. New York: HarperCollins.

———. 2002. *I Heard a Bluebird Sing: Children Select Their Favorite Poems by Aileen Fisher*. Honesdale, PA: Boyds Mills.

———. 1980. *Out in the Dark and Daylight*. New York: Harper & Row.

Fleishman, Paul. 2000. *Big Talk: Poems for Four Voices*. Cambridge, MA: Candlewick.

———. 1985. *I Am Phoenix: Poems for Two Voices*. New York: Harper & Row.

———. 1988. *Joyful Noise: Poems for Two Voices*. New York: Harper & Row.

Fletcher, Ralph J. 1994. *I Am Wings: Poems about Love*. New York: Bradbury.

———. 1997. *Ordinary Things: Poems from a Walk in Early Spring*. New York: Atheneum.

———. 2002. *Poetry Matters: Writing a Poem from the Inside Out*. New York: HarperTrophy.

———. 2005. *A Writing Kind of Day: Poems for Young Poets*. Honesdale, PA: Wordsong/Boyds Mills.

Florian, Douglas. 2003. *Autumnblings: Poems & Paintings*. New York: Greenwillow.

———. 1994. *Beast Feast: Poems and Paintings*. San Diego: Harcourt Brace.

———. 1994. *Bing Bang Boing: Poems and Drawings*. San Diego: Harcourt Brace.

———. 1997. *In the Swim: Poems and Paintings*. San Diego: Harcourt Brace.

———. 1998. *Insectlopedia: Poems and Paintings*. San Diego: Harcourt Brace.

———. 1999. *Laugh-eteria: Poems and Drawings*. San Diego: Harcourt Brace.

———. 2000. *Mammalabilia: Poems and Paintings*. San Diego: Harcourt Brace.

———. 1993. *Monster Motel: Poems and Paintings*. San Diego: Harcourt Brace.

———. 1996. *On the Wing: Bird Poems and Paintings*. San Diego: Harcourt Brace.

———. 2002. *Summersaults: Poems and Paintings*. New York: Greenwillow.

———. 1999. *Winter Eyes: Poems and Paintings*. New York: Greenwillow.

———. 2005. *Zoo's Who*. San Diego: Harcourt.

Foreman, Michael. 2002. *Michael Foreman's Playtime Rhymes*. Cambridge, MA: Candlewick.

Foster, John, comp. 1988. *Another Third Poetry Book*. New York: Oxford University Press.

———, comp. 1997. *Let's Celebrate: Festival Poems*. New York: Oxford University Press.

Fox, Dan, ed. 2003. *A Treasury of Children's Songs: Forty Favorites to Sing and Play*. New York: Henry Holt.

Frame, Jeron Ashford. 2003. *Yesterday I Had the Blues*. Berkeley, CA: Tricycle.

Francis, Lee, ed. 1999. *When the Rain Sings: Poems by Young Native Americans*. New York: Simon & Schuster.

Franco, Betsy. 1999. *Counting Caterpillars, and Other Math Poems*. New York: Scholastic.

———. 2003. *Mathematickles!* New York: Simon & Schuster.

Frank, Josette. 1977. *Poems to Read to the Very Young*. New York: Random House.

Frost, Helen. 2003. *Keesha's House*. New York: Farrar, Straus & Giroux.

———. 2004. *Spinning through the Universe*. New York: Farrar, Straus & Giroux.

Frost, Robert.1978. *Stopping by Woods on a Snowy Evening*. Illustrated by Susan Jeffers. Reissued New York: Dutton, 2001.

Geis, Jacqueline. 1992. *Where the Buffalo Roam*. Nashville: Ideals Children's Books.

George, Kristine O'Connell. 2005. *Fold Me a Poem*. San Diego: Harcourt Brace.

———. 1997. *The Great Frog Race, and Other Poems*. New York: Clarion.

———. 2004. *Hummingbird Nest: A Journal of Poems*. New York: Harcourt.

———. 2002. *Little Dog and Duncan*. New York: Clarion.

———. 1998. *Old Elm Speaks: Tree Poems*. New York: Clarion.

———. 2002. *Swimming Upstream: Middle School Poems*. New York: Clarion.

———. 2001. *Toasting Marshmallows: Camping Poems*. New York: Clarion.

Gherman, Beverly. 1996. *Robert Louis Stevenson: Teller of Tales*. New York: Atheneum.

Ghigna, Charles. 1995. *Riddle Rhymes*. New York: Hyperion.

Giovanni, Nikki. 1971. *Spin a Soft Black Song*. New York: Hill & Wang.

———. 1996. *The Sun Is So Quiet*. New York: Henry Holt.

———. 1981. *Vacation Time: Poems for Children*. New York: Morrow.

Glaser, Isabel Joshlin, comp. 1995. *Dreams of Glory: Poems Starring Girls*. New York: Atheneum.

Glenn, Mel. 1982. *Class Dismissed! High School Poems*. New York: Clarion.

———. 1999. *Foreign Exchange: A Mystery in Poems*. New York: Morrow Junior Books.

———. 1997. *Jump Ball: A Basketball Season in Poems*. New York: Lodestar/Dutton.

———. 1991. *My Friend's Got This Problem, Mr. Candler: High School Poems*. New York: Clarion.

———. 1997. *The Taking of Room 114: A Hostage Drama in Poems*. New York: Lodestar/Dutton.

———. 1996. *Who Killed Mr. Chippendale?* New York: Lodestar/Dutton.

Goldstein, Bobbye S., comp. 1993. *Birthday Rhymes, Special Times*. New York: Bantam Doubleday.

———, comp. 1992. *Inner Chimes: Poems on Poetry*. Honesdale, PA: Boyds Mills.

Gollub, Matthew. 1998. *Cool Melons Turn to Frogs: The Life and Poems of Issa*. New York: Lee & Low.

Gonzalez, Ray, ed. 1999. *Touching the Fire: Fifteen Poets of Today's Latino Renaissance*. New York: Anchor/Doubleday.

Gordon, Ruth, comp. 1995. *Pierced by a Ray of Sun: Poems about the Times We Feel Alone*. New York: HarperCollins.

Graham, Joan Bransfield. 1999. *Flicker Flash*. Boston: Houghton Mifflin.

———. 1994. *Splish Splash*. Boston: Houghton Mifflin.

Grandits, John. 2004. *Technically, It's Not My Fault: Concrete Poems*. New York: Clarion.

Greenberg, Jan. 2001. *Heart to Heart: New Poems Inspired by Twentieth-Century American Art*. New York: Abrams.

Greenfield, Eloise. 1977. *Africa Dream*. New York: John Day. Reprinted New York: HarperTrophy, 1992.

———. 1978. *Honey, I Love, and Other Love Poems*. New York: HarperCollins.

———. 1988. *Nathaniel Talking*. New York. Black Butterfly Children's Books.

———. 1996. *Night on Neighborhood Street*. New York: Puffin Pied Piper. Reprinted Jacksonville, IL: Bound to Stay Bound, 1999.

———. 1988. *Under the Sunday Tree*. New York: Harper & Row.

Grimes, Nikki. 2002. *Bronx Masquerade*. New York: Dial.

———. 1996. *Come Sunday*. Grand Rapids, MI: William B. Eerdmans.

———. 2002. *Danitra Brown Leaves Town*. New York: HarperCollins.

———. 1999. *Hopscotch Love: A Family Treasury of Love Poems*. New York: Lothrop, Lee & Shepard.

———. 2000. *Is It Far to Zanzibar? Poems about Tanzania*. New York: Lothrop, Lee & Shepard.

———. 1997. *It's Raining Laughter: Poems*. New York: Dial.

———. 1994. *Meet Danitra Brown*. New York: Lothrop, Lee & Shepard.

———. 1999. *My Man Blue: Poems*. New York: Dial.

———. 2000. *Shoe Magic*. New York: Orchard.

Gunning, Monica. 1993. *Not a Copper Penny in Me House*. Honesdale, PA: Wordsong / Boyds Mills.

———. 1998. *Under the Breadfruit Tree: Island Poems*. Honesdale, PA: Wordsong / Boyds Mills.

Hague, Michael. 1997. *Teddy Bear, Teddy Bear: A Classic Action Rhyme*. New York: Morrow Junior Books.

Hale, Glorya, ed. 1997. *Read-Aloud Poems for Young People: An Introduction to the Magic and Excitement of Poetry*. New York: Black Dog & Leventhal.

Hale, Sarah Josepha. 1990. *Mary Had a Little Lamb*. Illustrated by Bruce McMillan. New York: Scholastic.

Hall, Donald, ed. 1999. *The Oxford Illustrated Book of American Children's Poems*. New York: Oxford University Press.

Hallworth, Grace, comp. 1996. *Down by the River: Afro-Caribbean Rhymes, Games, and Songs for Children*. New York: Scholastic.

Harley, Avis. *Fly with Poetry: An ABC of Poetry*. Honesdale, PA: Wordsong/Boyds Mills.

——— . 2001. *Leap into Poetry: More ABCs of Poetry*. Honesdale, PA: Wordsong / Boyds Mills.

Harrison, David L. 2004. *Connecting Dots: Poems of My Journey*. Honesdale, PA: Wordsong/Boyds Mills.

———. 1993. *Somebody Catch my Homework*. Honesdale, PA: Wordsong/Boyds Mills.

———. 1996. *A Thousand Cousins: Poems of Family Life*. Honesdale, PA: Wordsong/Boyds Mills.

Hass, Robert, comp. 1998. *Poet's Choice: Poems for Everyday Life*. Hopewell, NJ: Ecco.

Hastings, Scott E. 1990. *Miss Mary Mac All Dressed in Black: Tongue Twisters, Jump-Rope Rhymes, and Other Children's Lore from New England*. Little Rock: August House.

Haverlah, B. J. 1993. *Poems from the Heart of Cow Country*. Maljamar, NM: Double Diamond.

Heard, Georgia. 1992. *Creatures of Earth, Sea, and Sky*. Honesdale, PA: Wordsong/Boyds Mills.

———, ed. 2000. *Songs of Myself: An Anthology of Poems and Art*. New York: Mondo.

———. 2002. *This Place I Know: Poems of Comfort*. Cambridge, MA: Candlewick.

Heide, Florence Parry, and Roxanne Heide Pierce. 1996. *Oh, Grow Up! Poems to Help You Survive Parents, Chores, School, and Other Afflictions*. New York: Orchard.

Herrera, Juan Felipe. 1998. *Laughing Out Loud, I Fly: Poems in English and Spanish*. New York: HarperCollins.

Hesse, Karen. 1997. *Out of the Dust*. New York: Scholastic.

———. 2001. *Witness*. New York: Scholastic.

Hines, Anna Grossnickle. *Pieces: A Year in Poems and Quilts*. New York: Greenwillow.

Hirschfelder, Arlene B., and Beverly Singer, comp. 1992. *Rising Voices: Writings of Young Native Americans*. New York: Scribner's.

Ho, Minfong. 1996. *Maples in the Mist: Poems for Children from the Tang Dynasty*. New York: Lothrop, Lee & Shepard.

Hoberman, Mary Ann. 1991. *Fathers, Mothers, Sisters, Brothers: A Collection of Family Poems*. Boston: Joy Street.

———. 1998. *Miss Mary Mack: A Hand-Clapping Rhyme*. New York: Scholastic.

———. 1994. *My Song Is Beautiful: Poems and Pictures in Many Voices*. Boston: Little, Brown.

———. 1997. *The Seven Silly Eaters*. San Diego: Harcourt Brace.

———. 2001. *Very Short Stories to Read Together*. Boston: Little Brown.

Holbrook, Sara. 1996. *Am I Naturally This Crazy?* Honesdale, PA: Boyds Mills.

———. 2003. *By Definition: Poems of Feelings*. Honesdale, PA: Wordsong/Boyds Mills.

———. 1996. *The Dog Ate My Homework*. Honesdale, PA: Boyds Mills.

———. 1996. *I Never Said I Wasn't Difficult*. Honesdale, PA: Boyds Mills.

———. 2003. *Wham! Its a Poetry Jam: Discovering Performance Poetry*. Honesdale, PA: Wordsong / Boyds Mills.

———. 1996. *Which Way to the Dragon! Poems for the Coming-on-Strong*. Honesdale, PA: Boyds Mills.

Holman, Felice. 1985. *The Song in My Head*. New York: Scribner's.

Hopkins, Lee Bennett, comp. 1998. *Around the Neighborhood*. New York: Sadlier-Oxford.

———. 1995. *Been to Yesterdays: Poems of a Life*. Honesdale, PA: Wordsong/Boyds Mills.

———, comp. 1995. *Blast Off: Poems about Space*. New York: HarperCollins.

———, comp. 1987. *Click, Rumble, Roar: Poems about Machines*. New York: Crowell.

———, comp. 1998. *Climb into My Lap: First Poems to Read Together*. New York: Simon & Schuster.

———. 2005. *Days to Celebrate: A Full Year of Poetry, People, Holidays, History, Fascinating Facts, and More*. New York: Greenwillow.

———. 1995. *Dinosaurs*. New York: Random House.

————, comp. 1998. *Families, Families*. New York: Sadlier-Oxford.

————, comp. 1990. *Good Books, Good Times*. New York: Trumpet. Reprinted New York: HarperTrophy, 2000.

————. 1995. *Good Rhymes, Good Times: Original Poems*. New York: HarperCollins.

————, comp. 1994. *Hand in Hand: An American History through Poetry*. New York: Simon & Schuster.

————, ed. 2002. *Hoofbeats, Claws, and Rippled Fins: Creature Poems*. New York: HarperCollins.

————, comp. 1993. *It's About Time*. New York: Simon & Schuster.

————, comp. 1999. *Lives: Poems about Famous Americans*. New York: HarperCollins.

————, comp. 1997. *Marvelous Math: A Book of Poems*. New York: Simon & Schuster.

————, comp. 1998. *Me, Myself, and I!* New York: Sadlier-Oxford.

————. 1999. *Mother Goose and Her Animal Friends*. New York: Sadlier-Oxford.

————. 2000. *My America: A Poetry Atlas of the United States*. New York: Simon & Schuster.

————, comp. 1996. *Opening Days: Sports Poems*. San Diego: Harcourt Brace.

————. 1995. *Pauses: Autobiographical Reflections of 101 Creators of Children's Books*. New York: HarperCollins.

————, comp. 1998. *Places to Visit, Places to See*. New York: Sadlier-Oxford.

————, comp. 1992. *Ring out, Wild Bells: Poems about Holidays and Seasons*. New York: Harcourt Brace.

————, comp. 1996. *School Supplies: A Book of Poems*. New York: Simon & Schuster.

————, comp. 1988. *Side by Side: Poems to Read Together*. New York: Simon & Schuster.

————, comp. 1983. *The Sky Is Full of Song*. New York: Harper & Row.

————, comp. 1995. *Small Talk: A Book of Short Poems*. San Diego: Harcourt Brace.

————, comp. 1997. *Song and Dance*. New York: Simon & Schuster.

————, comp. 1999. *Spectacular Science: A Book of Poems*. New York: Simon & Schuster.

————, comp. 1999. *Sports! Sports! Sports!* New York: HarperCollins.

————, comp. 1984. *Surprises*. New York: HarperTrophy.

————, comp. 1992. *Through Our Eyes: Poems and Pictures about Growing Up*. New York: Trumpet.

————, comp. 1994. *Weather: Poems for All Seasons*. New York: HarperTrophy.

————. 1993. *The Writing Bug*. Katonah, NY: R. C. Owen.

Hudson, Wade, comp. 1993. *Pass It On: African American Poetry for Children*. New York: Scholastic.

Hughes, Langston. 1994. *The Dreamkeeper, and Other Poems*. New York: Knopf.

———. 1994. *The Sweet and Sour Animal Book*. New York: Oxford University Press.

Hummon, David. 1999. *Animal Acrostics*. Nevada City, CA: Dawn Publications.

Izuki, Steven. 1994. *Believers in America: Poems about Americans of Asian and Pacific Islander Descent*. Chicago: Children's Press.

Jacobs, Leland B. 1993. *Just around the Corner: Poems about the Seasons*. New York: Henry Holt.

Janeczko, Paul B. 1999. *How to Write Poetry*. New York: Scholastic.

———, ed. 1994. *A Kick in the Head: An Everyday Guide to Poetic Forms*. Cambridge, MA: Candlewick.

———, comp. 1988. *The Music of What Happens: Poems That Tell Stories*. New York: Orchard.

———, comp. 1990. *The Place My Words Are Looking For*. New York: Bradbury.

———, comp. 1994. *Poetry from A to Z: A Guide for Young Writers*. New York: Bradbury.

———. 1983. *Poetspeak: In Their Work, About Their Work; A Selection*. Scarsdale, NY: Bradbury.

———, comp. 2001. *A Poke in the I: A Collection of Concrete Poems*. Cambridge, MA: Candlewick.

———, comp. 1991. *Preposterous: Poems of Youth*. New York: Orchard.

———, comp. 2002. *Seeing the Blue Between: Advice and Inspiration for Young Poets*. Cambridge, MA: Candlewick.

———. 1993. *Stardust Hotel*. New York: Orchard.

———, comp. 2000. *Stone Bench in an Empty Park*. New York: Orchard.

———. 1998. *That Sweet Diamond: Baseball Poems*. New York: Atheneum.

———, comp. 1987. *This Delicious Day*. New York: Orchard.

———. 2004. *Worlds Afire*. Cambridge, MA: Candlewick.

Johnson, Angela. 1998. *The Other Side: Shorter Poems*. New York: Orchard.

Johnson, Dave, ed. 2000. *Movin': Teen Poets Take Voice*. New York: Orchard.

Johnson, James Weldon. 1995. *Lift Ev'ry Voice and Sing*. New York: Scholastic.

Johnson, Lindsay Lee. 2002. *Soul Moon Soup*. Asheville, NC: Front Street.

Johnston, Tony. 1996. *My Mexico / México Mío*. New York: Putnam's Sons.

———. 1999. *An Old Shell: Poems of the Galapagos*. New York: Farrar, Straus & Giroux.

Jones, Hettie, comp. 1971. *The Tree Stands Shining: Poetry of the North American Indian*. New York: Dial.

Joseph, Lynn. 1990. *Coconut Kind of Day: Island Poems*. New York: Lothrop, Lee & Shepard.

Josephson, Judith Pinkerton. 2000. *Nikki Giovanni: Poet of the People*. Berkeley Heights, NJ: Enslow.

Katz, Bobbi, comp. 1992. *Puddle Wonderful: Poems to Welcome Spring*. New York: Random House.

———. 2001. *A Rumpus of Rhymes: A Book of Noisy Poems*. New York: Dutton.

Kellogg, Steven. 1976. *Steven Kellogg's Yankee Doodle*. New York: Parent's Magazine Press. Reprinted as *Yankee Doodle*. New York: Simon & Schuster, 1996.

Kennedy, Dorothy M., comp. 1993. *I Thought I'd Take My Rat to School: Poems for September to June*. New York: Little Brown.

———, ed. 1998. *Make Things Fly: Poems about the Wind*. New York: Margaret K. McElderry Books.

Kennedy, X. J. 2002. *Exploding Gravy: Poems to Make You Laugh*. Boston: Little Brown.

———. 1975. *One Winter Night in August, and Other Nonsense Jingles*. New York: Scribner's.

Kennedy, X. J., and Dorothy Kennedy, comps. 1982. *Knock at a Star: A Child's Introduction to Poetry*. Boston: Little Brown.

———, comps. 1992. *Talking Like the Rain: A Read-to-Me Book of Poems*. Boston: Little Brown.

Knudson, R. Rozanne, and May Swensen, comps. 1988. *American Sports Poems*. New York: Orchard.

Koch, Kenneth, and Kate Farrell, comps. 1985. *Talking to the Sun*. New York: Henry Holt.

Koertge, Ron. 2003. *Shakespeare Bats Cleanup*. Cambridge, MA: Candlewick.

Korman, Gordon, and Bernice Korman. 1992. *The D? Poems of Jeremy Bloom: A Collection of Poems about School, Homework, and Life (Sort Of)*. New York: Scholastic.

Koss, Amy Goldman. 1987. *Where Fish Go in Winter, and Answers to Other Great Mysteries*. Los Angeles: Price Stern Sloan.

Kurtz, Jane. 2000. *River Friendly, River Wild*. New York: Simon & Schuster.

Kuskin, Karla. 1980. *Dogs and Dragons, Trees and Dreams: A Collection of Poems*. New York: HarperCollins.

———. 2003. *Moon, Have You Met My Mother? The Collected Poems of Karla Kuskin*. New York: HarperCollins.

———. 1975. *Near the Window Tree: Poems and Notes*. New York: HarperCollins.

———. 1985. *Something Sleeping in the Hall: Poems*. New York: Harper & Row.

———. 1995. *Thoughts, Pictures, and Words*. Katonah, NY: R. C. Owen.

Lansky, Bruce, comp. 1994. *A Bad Case of the Giggles: Kids' Favorite Funny Poems*. Deephaven, MN: Meadowbrook.

————, comp. 1998. *Miles of Smiles: Kids Pick the Funniest Poems, Book #3*. New York: Scholastic.

————, comp. 1997. *No More Homework! No More Tests! Kids' Favorite Funny School Poems*. Minnetonka, MN: Meadowbrook.

Lasky, Kathryn. 2003. *A Voice of Her Own: The Story of Phillis Wheatley, Slave Poet*. Cambridge, MA: Candlewick.

Lawrence, Jacob. 1968. *Harriet and the Promised Land*. New York: Simon & Schuster.

Lear, Edward. 1991. *The Owl and the Pussycat*. Illustrated by Jan Brett. New York: Putnam.

————. 1998. *The Owl and the Pussycat*. Illustrated by James Marshall. New York: HarperCollins.

Lee, Dennis. 1991. *The Ice Cream Store*. New York: Scholastic. Reprinted New York: HarperCollins, 1999.

Lessac, Frane, comp. 2003. *Camp Granada: Sing-Along Camp Songs*. New York: Henry Holt.

Levy, Constance. 1998. *A Crack in the Clouds*. New York: Margaret K. McElderry Books.

————. *Splash! Poems of Our Watery World*. New York: Orchard.

Lewis, J. Patrick. 2002. *Arithme-Tickle: An Even Number of Odd Riddle-Rhymes*. San Diego: Harcourt.

————. 1995. *Black Swan White Crow*. New York: Atheneum.

————. 1999. *The Bookworm's Feast: A Potluck of Poems*. New York: Dial.

————. 1998. *Doodle Dandies: Poems That Take Shape*. New York: Atheneum.

————. 2000. *Freedom Like Sunlight: Praisesongs for Black Americans*. Mankato, MN: Creative Editions.

————. 1990. *A Hippopotamusn't, and Other Animal Verses*. New York: Dial.

————. 2005. *Please Bury Me in the Library*. Orlando, FL: Gulliver/Harcourt.

————. 1996. *Riddle-icious*. New York: Scholastic.

————. 1995. *Ridicholas Nicholas: More Animal Poems*. New York: Dial.

————. 2002. *A World of Wonders: Geographic Travels in Verse and Rhyme*. New York: Dial.

Lewis, Richard, comp. 1971. *I Breathe a New Song: Poems of the Eskimo*. New York: Simon & Schuster.

————. 1988. *In the Night Still Dark*. New York: Atheneum.

Lillegard, Dee. 2000. *Wake Up House! Rooms Full of Poems*. New York: Knopf.

Lindbergh, Reeve. 1990. *Johnny Appleseed*. Boston: Joy Street.

Little, Jean. 1989. *Hey World, Here I Am!* New York: Harper & Row.

Little, Lessie Jones. 1988. *Children of Long Ago: Poems*. Reprinted New York: Lee & Low, 2000.

Livingston, Myra Cohn. 1993. *Abraham Lincoln: A Man for All the People; A Ballad*. New York: Holiday House.

———. 1994. *Animal, Vegetable, Mineral: Poems about Small Things*. New York: HarperCollins.

———. 1985. *Celebrations*. New York: Holiday House.

———. 1982. *A Circle of Seasons*. New York: Holiday House.

———. 1990. *Climb into the Bell Tower: Essays on Poetry*. New York: Harper & Row.

———. 1996. *Festivals*. New York: Holiday House.

———, comp. 1989. *Halloween Poems*. New York: Holiday House.

———. 1992. *Let Freedom Ring: A Ballad of Martin Luther King Jr*. New York: Holiday House.

———. 1991. *Poem-Making: Ways to Begin Writing Poetry*. New York: HarperCollins.

———, comp. 1993. *Roll Along: Poems on Wheels*. New York: Margaret K. McElderry Books.

———. 1998. *Space Songs*. New York: Holiday House.

Longfellow, Henry Wadsworth. 1984. *Hiawatha's Childhood*. Illustrated by Errol Le Cain. New York: Farrar, Straus & Giroux.

———. 2001. *The Midnight Ride of Paul Revere*. Illustrated by Christopher Bing. New York: Handprint.

———. 1990. *Paul Revere's Ride*. Illustrated by Ted Rand. New York: Dutton.

Lyne, Sandford, comp. 1996. *Ten-Second Rainshowers: Poems by Young People*. New York: Simon & Schuster.

———, comp. 2004. *Soft Hay Will Catch You: Poems by Young People*. New York: Simon & Schuster.

Lyon, George Ella. 1999. *Where I'm From, Where Poems Come From*. Spring, TX: Absey.

MacLachlan, Patricia. 1995. *What You Know First*. New York: HarperCollins.

Mado, Michio. 1992. *The Animals: Selected Poems*. New York: Margaret K. McElderry Books.

———. 1998. *The Magic Pocket*. New York: Margaret K. McElderry Books.

Manguel, Alberto, comp.1990. *Seasons*. New York: Doubleday.

Mayo, Margaret. 2002. *Wiggle Waggle Fun: Stories and Rhymes for the Very Very Young*. Cambridge, MA: Candlewick.

McCord, David. 1999. *Every Time I Climb a Tree*. New York: Little Brown.

McKissack, Patricia C. 1984. *Paul Laurence Dunbar: A Poet to Remember*. Chicago: Children's Press.

Medearis, Angela Shelf. 1995. *Skin Deep, and Other Teenage Reflections: Poems*. New York: Macmillan.

Medina, Jane. 2004. *The Dream on Blanca's Wall / El sueño pegado en la pared de Blanca: Poems in English and Spanish*. Illustrated by Robert Casilla. Honesdale, PA: Boyds Mills.

———. 1999. *My Name Is Jorge on Both Sides of the River: Poems*. Honesdale, PA: Boyds Mills.

Meltzer, Milton. 1999. *Carl Sandburg: A Biography*. Brookfield, CT: Twenty-first Century.

———. 2004. *Emily Dickinson: A Biography*. Brookfield, CT: Twenty-first Century.

———. 1968. *Langston Hughes: A Biography*. New York: Crowell. Reprinted Brookfield, CT: Millbrook, 1997.

———. 2002. *Walt Whitman: A Biography*. Brookfield, CT: Twenty-first Century.

Merriam, Eve. 1995. *Bam Bam Bam*. New York: Henry Holt.

———. 1970. *Finding a Poem*. New York: Atheneum.

———. 1964. *It Doesn't Always Have to Rhyme*. New York: Atheneum.

———. 1962. *There Is No Rhyme for Silver*. New York: Scribner.

———. 1996. *You Be Good and I'll Be Night*. New York: HarperTrophy.

Michelson, Richard. 2000. *Ten Times Better*. New York: Marshall Cavendish.

Milne, A. A. 1928. *The House at Pooh Corner*. London: Methuen.

———. 1988. *When We Were Very Young*. New York: Dutton.

———. 1958. *The World of Christopher Robin: The Complete When We Were Very Young and Now We Are Six*. New York: Dutton.

Milnes, Gerald. 1990. *Granny Will Your Dog Bite, and Other Mountain Rhymes*. New York: Knopf.

Mitchell, Stephen. *The Wishing Bone, and Other Poems*. Cambridge, MA: Candlewick.

Molloy, Paul, ed. 1968. *Poetry U.S.A.* New York: Scholastic.

Monahan, Sean. 1992. *Multivoice Magic: Poetry as Shared Reading*. Australia: Longman Cheshire.

Moore, Lilian. 2001. *I'm Small, and Other Verses*. Cambridge, MA: Candlewick.

———. 1997. *Poems Have Roots: New Poems*. New York: Atheneum.

———, comp. 1992. *Sunflakes: Poems for Children*. New York: Clarion.

Mora, Pat. 1996. *Confetti: Poems for Children*. New York: Lee & Low.

———. 1998. *Delicious Hullabaloo / Pachanga Deliciosa*. Houston, TX: Pinata.

———. 1994. *The Desert Is My Mother / El Desierto Es Mi Madre*. Houston, TX: Pinata.

———. 2001. *Love to Mama: A Tribute to Mothers*. New York: Lee & Low.

————. 2000. *My Own True Name: New and Selected Poems for Young Adults, 1984–1999*. Houston, TX: Pinata.

————. 1998. *This Big Sky*. New York: Scholastic.

————. 1996. *Uno, Dos, Tres / One, Two, Three*. New York: Clarion.

Morrison, Lillian, comp. 1992. *At the Crack of the Bat: Baseball Poems*. New York: Hyperion.

Morrison, Meighan. 1993. *Long Live Earth*. New York: Scholastic.

Moss, Jeff. 1997. *Bone Poems*. New York: Scholastic.

————. 1997. *The Dad of the Dad of the Dad of Your Dad*. New York: Ballantine.

Most, Bernard. 1990. *Four and Twenty Dinosaurs*. New York: Harper & Row. Reprinted San Diego: Voyager, 1999.

Murphy, Elspeth Campbell. 1988. *Recess: Prayer Meditations for Teachers*. Grand Rapids, MI: Baker Book House.

Murphy, Jim. 1993. *Across America on an Emigrant Train*. New York: Clarion.

Myers, Walter Dean. 1998. *Angel to Angel*. New York: HarperCollins.

————. 2003. *Blues Journey*. New York: Holiday House.

————. 1993. *Brown Angels: An Album of Pictures and Verse*. New York: HarperCollins.

————. 1995. *Glorious Angels: A Celebration of Children*. New York: HarperCollins.

————. 1997. *Harlem: A Poem*. New York: Scholastic.

————. 2004. *Here in Harlem: Poems in Many Voices*. New York: Holiday House.

Newcome, Zita. 2000. *Head, Shoulders, Knees, and Toes, and Other Action Rhymes*. Cambridge, MA: Candlewick.

Newsome, Effie Lee. 1999. *Wonders: The Best Children's Poems by Effie Lee Newsome*. Honesdale, PA: Boyds Mills.

Nicholls, Judith, comp. 1993. *Earthways, Earthwise: Poems on Conservation*. Oxford, NY: Oxford University Press.

Nichols, Grace. 1997. *Asana and the Animals: A Book of Pet Poems*. Cambridge, MA: Candlewick.

Niven, Penelope. 2003. *Carl Sandburg: Adventures of a Poet*. Orlando, FL: Harcourt.

Nye, Naomi Shihab. 2000. *Come with Me: Poems for a Journey*. New York: Greenwillow.

————. 1998. *Fuel*. Rochester, NY: BOA Editions.

————, comp. 2000. *Salting the Ocean: 100 Poems by Young Poets*. New York: Greenwillow.

————, comp. 1998. *The Space between Our Footsteps: Poems and Paintings from the Middle East*. New York: Simon & Schuster.

———, comp. 1992. *This Same Sky: A Collection of Poems from Around the World.* New York: Four Winds.

———, comp. 1995. *The Tree Is Older Than You Are: A Bilingual Gathering of Poems and Stories from Mexico with Paintings by Mexican Artists.* New York: Simon & Schuster.

———, comp. 1999. *What Have You Lost?* New York: Greenwillow.

Nye, Naomi Shihab, and Paul Janeczko, eds. 1996. *I Feel a Little Jumpy around You: A Book of His and Her Poems Collected in Pairs.* New York: Simon & Schuster.

Okutoro, Lydia Omolola, comp. 1999. *Quiet Storm: Voices of Young Black Poets.* New York: Hyperion.

Oliver, Mary. 1992. *New and Selected Poems.* Boston: Beacon.

O'Neill, Mary. 1989. *Hailstones and Halibut Bones: Adventures in Color.* New York: Doubleday.

———. 1968. *Take a Number.* Garden City, NY: Doubleday.

Opie, Iona. 1999. *Here Comes Mother Goose.* Cambridge, MA: Candlewick.

———, ed. 1996. *My Very First Mother Goose.* Cambridge, MA: Candlewick.

———, ed. 1997. *Wee Willie Winkie, and Other Rhymes.* Cambridge, MA: Candlewick.

Opie, Iona, and Peter Opie, eds. 1992. *I Saw Esau: The Schoolchild's Pocket Book.* Cambridge, MA: Candlewick.

Orozco, José-Luis, comp. 1994. *De Colores, and Other Latin American Folk Songs for Children.* New York: Dutton.

———. 2002. *Diez Deditos: Ten Little Fingers, and Other Play Rhymes and Action Songs from Latin America.* New York: Dutton.

———.1994. *Fiestas: A Year of Latin American Songs of Celebration.* New York: Dutton.

Osofsky, Audrey. 1996. *Free to Dream: The Making of a Poet: Langston Hughes.* New York: Lothrop, Lee & Shepard.

Panzer, Nora, ed. 1994. *Celebrate America in Poetry and Art.* New York: Hyperion.

Pappas, Theoni. 1991. *Math Talk: Mathematical Ideas in Poems for Two Voices.* San Carlos, CA: Wide World Publishing/Tetra.

Paraskevas, Betty. 1995. *Gracie Graves and the Kids from Room 402.* San Diego: Harcourt Brace.

Paul, A. W. 1999. *All by Herself: 14 Girls Who Made a Difference; Poems.* San Diego: Browndeer/Harcourt Brace.

Pearson, Susan, comp. 2002. *The Drowsy Hours.* New York: HarperCollins.

———. 2005. *Grimericks.* New York: Marshall Cavendish.

———. 2004. *Squeal and Squawk: Barnyard Talk.* New York: Marshall Cavendish.

———. 2005. *Who Swallowed Harold? and Other Poems about Pets*. New York: Marshall Cavendish.

Perdomo, Willie. 2002. *Visiting Langston*. New York: Henry Holt.

Peters, Lisa Westberg. 2003. *Earthshake: Poems from the Ground Up*. Illustrated by Cathie Felstead. New York: HarperCollins.

Peterson, Isabel, ed. 1954. *The First Book of Poetry*. New York: Franklin Watts.

Philip, Neil, comp. 1996. *Earth Always Endures: Native American Poems*. New York: Viking.

———, ed. 1997. *In a Sacred Manner I Live: Native American Wisdom*. New York: Clarion.

———, ed. 2000. *It's a Woman's World: A Century of Women's Voices in Poetry*. New York: Dutton.

———, ed. 1996. *The New Oxford Book of Children's Verse*. Oxford, NY: Oxford University Press.

———, comp. 1995. *Singing America: Poems That Define a Nation*. New York: Viking.

Pomerantz, Charlotte. 1982. *If I Had a Paka: Poems in Eleven Languages*. New York: Greenwillow.

Prelutsky, Jack comp. 1997. *The Beauty of the Beast*. New York: Knopf.

———, comp. 1997. *Dinosaur Dinner with a Slice of Alligator Pie: Favorite Poems by Dennis Lee*. New York: Scholastic.

———. 1993. *The Dragons Are Singing Tonight*. New York: Scholastic.

———. 2002. *The Frog Wore Red Suspenders*. New York: Greenwillow.

———, comp. 2003. *I Like It Here at School*. New York: Scholastic.

———. 2004. *If Not for the Cat: Haiku*. Illustrated by Ted Rand. New York: Greenwillow.

———. 1977. *It's Halloween*. New York: Greenwillow.

———. 1996. *Monday's Troll*. New York: Scholastic.

———. 1984. *The New Kid on the Block*. New York: Greenwillow.

———. 1976. *Nightmares: Poems to Trouble Your Sleep*. New York: Greenwillow. Reprinted New York: Mulberry, 1993.

———. 1994. *A Pizza the Size of the Sun*. New York: Greenwillow.

———, comp. 1983. *The Random House Book of Poetry for Children*. New York: Random House.

———, comp. 1986. *Read-Aloud Rhymes for the Very Young*. New York: Knopf.

———. 1986. *Ride a Purple Pelican*. New York: Greenwillow.

———. 1980. *Rolling Harvey Down the Hill*. New York: Greenwillow. Reprinted New York: Mulberry, 1993.

————. 1990. *Something BIG Has Been Here*. New York: Scholastic.

————, comp. 1999. *The 20th-Century Children's Poetry Treasury*. New York: Knopf.

————. 1993. *Tyrannosaurus Was a Beast: Dinosaur Poems*. New York: Greenwillow.

Reef, Catherine. 2000. *Paul Laurence Dunbar: Portrait of a Poet*. Berkeley Heights, NJ: Enslow.

————. 1995. *Walt Whitman*. New York: Clarion.

Rich, Mary Perrotta, ed. 1998. *Book Poems: Poems from National Children's Book Week, 1959–1998*. New York: Children's Book Council.

Robb, Laura, comp. 1997. *Music and Drum: Voices of War and Peace, Hope and Dreams*. New York: Philomel.

Roberts, Elizabeth, and Elias Amidon. 1991. *Earth Prayers: 365 Prayers, Poems, and Invocations for Honoring the Earth*. San Francisco: HarperCollins.

————. 1996. *Life Prayers: 365 Prayers, Blessings, and Affirmations to Celebrate the Human Journey from Around the World*. San Francisco: HarperCollins.

Rochelle, Belinda, comp. 2001. *Words with Wings: A Treasury of African-American Poetry and Art*. New York: HarperCollins.

Roemer, Heidi. 2004. *Come to My Party, and Other Shape Poems*. New York: Henry Holt.

Rogasky, Barbara, comp. 2001. *Leaf by Leaf*. New York: Scholastic.

————, comp. 1994. *Winter Poems*. New York: Scholastic.

Rosen, Michael, comp. 1998. *Classic Poetry: An Illustrated Collection*. Cambridge, MA: Candlewick.

————. 1992. *Itsy-Bitsy Beasties: Poems from Around the World*. Minneapolis, MN: Carolrhoda.

————, comp. 1995. *The Kingfisher Book of Children's Poetry*. London: Kingfisher.

————, comp. 1995. *Walking the Bridge of Your Nose*. London: Kingfisher.

————, comp.1991. *A World of Poetry*. London: Kingfisher.

Rosen, Michael, J., ed. 1996. *Food Fight: Poets Join the Fight against Hunger with Poems about Their Favorite Foods*. San Diego: Harcourt Brace.

————, ed. 1992. *Home: A Collaboration of Thirty Distinguished Authors and Illustrators of Children's Books to Aid the Homeless*. New York: HarperCollins.

Rosenberg, Liz, ed. 1998. *Earth-Shattering Poems*. New York: Henry Holt.

————, ed. 1996. *The Invisible Ladder: An Anthology of Contemporary American Poems for Young Readers*. New York: Henry Holt.

————, ed. *Light-Gathering Poems*. New York: Henry Holt.

Rosenthal, Betsy R. 2004. *My House Is Singing*. Illustrated by Margaret Chodos-Irvine. New York: Harcourt.

Rylant, Cynthia. 1991. *Appalachia: The Voices of Sleeping Birds*. San Diego: Harcourt Brace Jovanovich.

———. 1984. *Waiting to Waltz: A Childhood*. Scarsdale, NY: Bradbury.

———. 1996. *The Whales*. New York: Scholastic.

Sandburg, Carl. 1998. *Grassroots: Poems by Carl Sandburg*. San Diego: Browndeer/Harcourt Brace.

Schertle, Alice. 1995. *Advice for a Frog*. New York: Lothrop, Lee & Shepard.

———. 1994. *How Now, Brown Cow?* San Diego: Browndeer/Harcourt Brace.

———. 1999. *A Lucky Thing*. San Diego: Harcourt Brace.

Schickendanz, Judith, Mary Lynn Pergantis, Jan Kanosky, Annmarie Blaney, and Joan Ottinger. 1997. *Curriculum in Early Childhood: A Resource Guide for Preschool and Kindergarten Teachers*. Boston: Allyn & Bacon.

Schmidt, Annie M. G. 1981. *Pink Lemonade: Poems for Children*. Translated and adapted from the Dutch by Henrietta ten Harmsel. Grand Rapids, MI: Eerdmans.

Schnur, Steven. 1999. *Spring: An Alphabet Acrostic*. New York: Clarion.

Schwartz, Alvin. 1992. *And the Green Grass Grew All Around: Folk Poetry from Everyone*. New York: HarperCollins.

Seuss, Dr. 1996. *My Many Colored Days*. New York: Knopf.

Shakur, Tupac. 1999. *A Rose That Grew from Concrete*. New York: Pocket Books.

Shannon, George, comp. 1996. *Spring: A Haiku Story*. New York: Greenwillow.

Shaw, Alison, comp. 1995. *Until I Saw the Sea: A Collection of Seashore Poems*. New York: Henry Holt.

Shields, Carol Diggory. 2003. *Almost Late to School, and More School Poems*. New York: Dutton.

———. 2002. *BrainJuice: American History, Fresh Squeezed!* Brooklyn, NY: Handprint.

———. 2003. *BrainJuice: Science, Fresh Squeezed!* Brooklyn, NY: Handprint.

———. 1995. *Lunch Money, and Other Poems about School*. New York: Dutton.

Sidman, Joyce. 2005. *Song of the Water Boatman, and Other Pond Poems*. Boston: Houghton Mifflin.

———. 2003. *The World According to Dog: Poems and Teen Voices*. Boston: Houghton Mifflin.

Siebert, Diane. 2000. *Cave*. New York: HarperCollins.

———. 1989. *Heartland*. New York: Crowell.

———. 1988. *Mojave*. New York: Crowell.

———. 1991. *Sierra*. New York: HarperCollins.

———. 1990. *Train Song*. New York: Crowell. Reprinted New York: HarperCollins, 1993.

———. 1984. *Truck Song*. New York: Crowell.

Siegen-Smith, Nikki. 2001. *First Morning: Poems about Time*. New York: Barefoot Books.

Sierra, Judy. 1998. *Antarctic Antics: A Book of Penguin Poems*. New York: Scholastic.

———. 2005. *Schoolyard Rhymes: Kids' Own Rhymes for Rope Skipping, Hand Clapping, Ball Bouncing, and Just Plain Fun*. New York: Knopf.

Silverstein, Shel. 1996. *Falling Up: Poems and Drawings*. New York: HarperCollins.

———. 1981. *A Light in the Attic*. New York: Harper & Row.

———. 1974. *Where the Sidewalk Ends*. New York: Harper & Row.

Simon, Seymour. 1995. *Star Walk*. New York: Morrow.

Singer, Marilyn. 1996. *All We Needed to Say: Poems about School from Tanya and Sophie*. New York: Atheneum.

———. 2005. *Monday on the Mississippi*. New York: Henry Holt.

———. 1989. *Turtle in July*. New York: Macmillan.

Slapin, Beverly, and Doris Seale, eds. 1998. *Through Indian Eyes: The Native American Experience in Books for Children*. Berkeley, CA: Oyate.

Slier, Deborah, ed. 1991. *Make a Joyful Sound: Poems for Children by African American Poets*. New York: Checkerboard.

Smaridge, Norah. 1977. *School Is Not a Missile Range*. Nashville: Abingdon.

———. 1968. *Teacher's Pest*. New York: Hawthorn.

Smith, Charles R., Jr. 2004. *Hoop Kings*. Cambridge, MA: Candlewick.

Smith, Hope Anita. *The Way a Door Closes*. New York: Henry Holt.

Smith, William Jay, comp. 1982. *A Green Place: Modern Poems*. New York: Delacorte.

Sneve, Virginia Driving Hawk, comp. 1989. *Dancing Teepees: Poems of American Indian Youth*. New York: Holiday House.

Sones, Sonya. 2004. *One of Those Hideous Books Where the Mother Dies*. New York: Simon & Schuster.

———. 1999. *Stop Pretending: What Happened When My Big Sister Went Crazy*. New York: HarperCollins.

———. 2001. *What My Mother Doesn't Know*. New York: Simon & Schuster.

Soto, Gary. 1995. *Canto Familiar*. San Diego: Harcourt Brace.

———. 2002. *Fearless Fernie: Hanging Out with Fernie and Me*. New York: Putnam.

———. 1990. *A Fire in My Hands*. New York: Scholastic.

———. 1992. *Neighborhood Odes*. San Diego: Harcourt Brace Jovanovich.

Spier, Peter. 1970. *The Erie Canal*. Garden City, NY: Doubleday.

———. 1967. *London Bridge Is Falling Down!* Garden City, NY: Doubleday.

———. 1973. *The Star-Spangled Banner*. Garden City, NY: Doubleday.

Stepanek, Mattie J. T. 2001. *Journey through Heartsongs*. Alexandria, VA: VSP.

Steptoe, Javaka, comp. 1997. *In Daddy's Arms I Am Tall: African Americans Celebrating Fathers*. New York: Lee & Low.

Stevenson, James. 1998. *Popcorn: Poems*. New York: Greenwillow.

———. 1995. *Sweet Corn: Poems*. New York: Greenwillow.

Stevenson, Robert Louis. 2005. *Block City*. Illustrated by Daniel Kirk. New York: Simon & Schuster.

———. 1999. *A Child's Garden of Verses*. New York: Simon & Schuster.

Still, James. 1998. *An Appalachian Mother Goose*. Lexington: University Press of Kentucky.

Strickland, Dorothy S., ed. 1982. *Listen, Children: An Anthology of Black Literature*. New York: Bantam Doubleday.

Strickland, Dorothy S., and Michael R. Strickland, comps. 1994. *Families: Poems Celebrating the African-American Experience*. Honesdale, PA: Wordsong/Boyds Mills.

Strickland, Michael R. 1996. *African-American Poets*. Springfield, NJ: Enslow.

———, comp. 1993. *Poems That Sing to You*. Honesdale, PA: Wordsong/Boyds Mills.

Strong, Amy. 2003. *Lee Bennett Hopkins: A Children's Poet*. New York: Franklin Watts.

Sullivan, Charles, ed. 1994. *Here Is My Kingdom: Hispanic-American Literature and Art for Young People*. New York: Abrams.

———, comp. 1989. *Imaginary Gardens: American Poetry and Art for Young People*. New York: Abrams.

Swamp, Chief Jake. 1995. *Giving Thanks: A Native American Good Morning Message*. New York: Lee & Low.

Swann, Brian. 1998. *The House with No Door: African Riddle-Poems*. San Diego: Browndeer.

———. 1998. *Touching the Distance: Native American Riddle-Poems*. San Diego: Browndeer.

Sword, Elizabeth Hauge, and Victoria Flournoy McCarthy, eds. 1995. *A Child's Anthology of Poetry*. New York: Franklin Watts. Reprinted New York: Trumpet, 1998.

Tashjian, Virginia, comp. 1969. *Juba This and Juba That: Story Hour Stretches for Large or Small Groups*. Boston: Little Brown.

Tedlock, Dennis. 1972. *Finding the Center: Narrative Poetry of the Zuni Indians*. New York: Dial.

Testa, Maria. 2002. *Becoming Joe DiMaggio*. Cambridge, MA: Candlewick.

Thayer, Ernest Lawrence. 2000. *Ernest L. Thayer's Casey at the Bat: A Ballad of the Republic Sung in the Year 1888*. Illustrated by Christopher Bing. San Francisco: Handprint.

Thomas, Joyce Carol. 1993. *Brown Honey in Broomwheat Tea: Poems*. New York: HarperCollins.

———. 1995 *Gingerbread Days*. New York: HarperCollins.

———. 1998. *I Have Heard of a Land*. New York: HarperCollins.

Thomas, Shelley Moore. 1998. *Somewhere Today: A Book of Peace*. Morton Grove, IL: Albert Whitman.

Thompson, Brian, comp. 1989. *Catch It If You Can*. London: Viking Kestral.

Thurston, Cheryl Miller. 1987. *Hide Your Ex-Lax under the Wheaties: Poems about Schools, Teachers, Kids, and Education*. Fort Collins, CO: Cottonwood.

Tran, Ngoc-Dung, comp. 1998. *To Swim in Our Own Pond / Ta Ve Ta Tam Ao Ta: A Book of Vietnamese Proverbs*. Fremont, CA: Shen's Books.

Turner, Ann. 1993. *Grass Songs*. San Diego: Harcourt Brace Jovanovich.

———. 1997. *Mississippi Mud: Three Prairie Journals*. New York: HarperCollins.

Ulrich, George. 1995. *My Tooth Ith Loothe: Funny Poems to Read Instead of Doing Your Homework*. New York: Bantam Doubleday.

Untermeyer, Louis, comp. 1959. *The Golden Treasury of Poetry*. New York: Golden Press.

Viorst, Judith. 1972. *Alexander and the Terrible, Horrible, No Good, Very Bad Day*. New York: Atheneum.

———. 1981. *If I Were in Charge of the World, and Other Worries: Poems for Children and Their Parents*. New York: Atheneum.

———. 1995. *Sad Underwear, and Other Complications: More Poems for Children and Their Parents*. New York: Atheneum.

Volavkova, Hana, ed. 1993. *I Never Saw Another Butterfly: Children's Drawings and Poems from Terezin Concentration Camp, 1942–1944*. New York: Schocken.

Warren, Robert Penn. 1946. *All the King's Men*. Reprinted Birmingham, AL: Southern Living Gallery, 1984.

Wayland, April Halprin. 2002. *Girl Coming In for a Landing: A Novel in Poems*. New York: Knopf.

Westcott, Nadine Bernard, comp. 1994. *Never Take a Pig to Lunch, and Other Poems about the Fun of Eating*. New York: Orchard.

———. 1987. *Peanut Butter and Jelly: A Play Rhyme*. New York: Dutton.

Whipple, Laura, comp. 1994. *Celebrating America: A Collection of Poems and Images of the American Spirit*. New York: Philomel.

———, comp. 1989. *Eric Carle's Animals, Animals*. New York: Scholastic.

Whitman, Walt. 1991. *I Hear America Singing*. New York: Philomel.

Wilbur, Richard. 1998. *The Disappearing Alphabet*. San Diego: Harcourt Brace.

Willard, Nancy. 1981. *A Visit to William Blake's Inn: Poems for Innocent and Experienced Travelers*. San Diego: Harcourt.

———. 1987. *The Voyage of the Ludgate Hill: Travels with Robert Louis Stevenson*. San Diego: Harcourt.

Williams, Vera B. 2001. *Amber Was Brave, Essie Was Smart*. New York: Greenwillow.

Winter, Jeanette. 2002. *Emily Dickinson's Letters to the World*. New York: Frances Foster Books/Farrar, Straus & Giroux.

Winters, Kay. 2000. *Tiger Trail*. New York: Simon & Schuster.

Wise, William. 2000. *Dinosaurs Forever*. New York: Dial.

Wolf, Allan. 2003. *The Blood-Hungry Spleen, and Other Poems about Our Parts*. Illustrated by Greg Clark. Cambridge, MA: Candlewick.

Wong, Janet S. 1999. *Behind the Wheel: Poems about Driving*. New York: Margaret K. McElderry Books.

———. 1994. *Good Luck Gold, and Other Poems*. New York: Margaret K. McElderry Books.

———. 2003. *Knock on Wood: Poems about Superstitions*. New York: Margaret K. McElderry Books.

———. 2003. *Minn and Jake*. New York: Farrar, Straus & Giroux.

———. 2000. *Night Garden: Poems from the World of Dreams*. New York: Margaret K. McElderry Books.

———. 1999. *The Rainbow Hand: Poems about Mothers and Children*. New York: Margaret K. McElderry Books.

———. 1996. *A Suitcase of Seaweed, and Other Poems*. New York: Margaret K. McElderry Books.

Wood, Nancy. 1995. *Dancing Moons*. New York: Doubleday.

———. 1998. *Sacred Fire*. New York: Doubleday.

———. 1993. *Spirit Walker*. New York: Doubleday.

Woodson, Jacqueline. 2003. *Locomotion*. New York: Putnam.

Worth, Valerie. 1994. *All the Small Poems and Fourteen More*. New York: Farrar, Straus & Giroux.

Wyndham, Robert, comp. 1968. *Chinese Mother Goose Rhymes*. Cleveland: World. Reprinted New York: PaperStar, 1998.

Yep, Laurence, ed. 1993. *American Dragons: Twenty-five Asian American Voices*. New York: HarperCollins.

Yolen, Jane. 2000. *Color Me a Rhyme: Nature Poems for Young People*. Honesdale, PA: Wordsong/Boyds Mills.

———. 2000. *How Do Dinosaurs Say Good Night?* New York: Blue Sky.

———, comp. 1997. *Once upon Ice, and Other Frozen Poems*. Honesdale, PA: Wordsong/Boyds Mills.

————. 1996. *Sacred Places*. San Diego: Harcourt Brace.

————. 1998. *Snow, Snow: Winter Poems for Children*. Honesdale, PA: Wordsong/ Boyds Mills.

————, ed. 1992. *Street Rhymes from Around the World*. Honesdale, PA: Wordsong/ Boyds Mills.

————. 1995. *Water Music*. Honesdale, PA: Wordsong/Boyds Mills.

Young, Ed. 1997. *Voices of the Heart*. New York: Scholastic.

Zehares, Wade. 2001. *Big, Bad, and a Little Bit Scary: Poems That Bite Back!* New York: Viking.

Ziefert, Harriet. 1997. *Mother Goose Math*. New York: Viking.

# ∞ References

This list identifies professional reference tools for the adult who wants to learn more about sharing poetry with children. It also provides full publication information for sources cited in the text.

Ada, Alma Flor, Violet Harris, and Lee Bennett Hopkins. 1993. *A Chorus of Cultures: Developing Literacy through Multicultural Poetry*. Carmel, CA: Hampton-Brown.

Anderson, Nancy A. 2006. *Elementary Children's Literature: The Basics for Teachers and Parents*. 2nd ed. New York: Pearson.

Bagert, B. 1992. Act It Out: Making Poetry Come Alive. In *Invitation to Read: More Children's Literature in the Reading Program*. Newark, DE: International Reading Association.

Barton, Bob, and David Booth. 2004. *Poetry Goes to School: From Mother Goose to Shel Silverstein*. Markham, Ontario, Canada: Pembroke Publishers.

Bauer, C. F. 1995. *The Poetry Break: An Annotated Anthology with Ideas for Introducing Children to Poetry*. New York: H. W. Wilson.

Booth, David, and Bill Moore. 2003. *Poems Please! Sharing Poetry with Children*. 2nd ed. Markham, Ontario, Canada: Pembroke Publishers.

Brountas, Maria. 1995. The Versatility of Poetry. *Teaching PreK–8* 25 (March): 40–42.

Bryant, P. E., L. Bradley, M. MacLean, and J. Crossland. 1989. Nursery Rhymes, Phonological Skills, and Reading. *Journal of Child Language* 16:407–28.

Burleson, Marcie Lynn. 2002. Seeing the "Sights" with Poetry. *Teaching PreK–8* 32 (April): 60–61.

Bush, Gail. 1997. Speak, Muses. *School Library Journal* 43 (September): 139.

Chatton, B. 1993. *Using Poetry across the Curriculum*. Phoenix: Oryx.

Copeland, Jeffrey S. 1993. *Speaking of Poets: Interviews with Poets Who Write for Children and Young Adults*. Urbana, IL: National Council of Teachers of English.

Copeland, Jeffrey, S., and Vicky S. Copeland. 1995. *Speaking of Poets 2: More Interviews with Poets Who Write for Children and Young Adults*. Urbana, IL: National Council of Teachers of English.

Cullinan, Bernice. 1999. Lessons from Mother Goose. *Instructor-Primary* 108 (March): 55.

Cullinan, B., M. Scala, and V. Schroder. 1995. *Three Voices: An Invitation to Poetry across the Curriculum*. York, ME: Stenhouse.

Esbensen, Barbara J. 1995. *A Celebration of Bees: Helping Children to Write Poetry*. New York: Henry Holt.

Fisher, C. J., and M. A. Natarella. 1982. Young Children's Preferences in Poetry: A National Survey of First, Second, and Third Graders. *Research in the Teaching of English* 16 (4): 339–54.

Fox, Mem. 2001. *Reading Magic: Why Reading Aloud to Our Children Will Change Their Lives Forever*. San Diego: Harcourt.

Glover, M. K. 1999. *A Garden of Poets: Poetry Writing in the Elementary School*. Urbana, IL: NCTE.

Goforth, F. S. 1998. *Literature and the Learner*. Belmont, CA: Wadsworth.

Graham, Jorie. 2005. Comments on Kristine O'Connell George Website. http://64.77.108.137/poetry_thinks.htm.

Hadaway, N., S. M. Vardell, and T. Young. 2002. *Literature-Based Instruction with English Language Learners*. New York: Allyn & Bacon Longman.

Hadaway, N. L., S. M. Vardell, and T. A. Young. 2001. Scaffolding Oral Language Development through Poetry for Students Learning English. *Reading Teacher* 54:796–806.

Heard, Georgia. 1994. *For the Good of the Earth and Sun: Teaching Poetry*. Portsmouth, NH: Heinemann.

———. 1999. *Awakening the Heart: Exploring Poetry in Elementary and Middle School*. Portsmouth, NH: Heinemann.

Holbrook, Sara. 2002. *Wham! It's a Poetry Jam: Discovering Performance Poetry*. Honesdale, PA: Wordsong/Boyds Mills.

———. 2005. *Practical Poetry: A Nonstandard Approach to Meeting Content-Area Standards*. Portsmouth, NH: Heinemann.

Hopkins, Lee Bennett. 1986. *Pass the Poetry Please*. 3rd ed. New York: HarperCollins.

———. 1995. *Pauses: Autobiographical Reflections of 101 Creators of Children's Books*. New York: HarperCollins.

Huck, Charlotte, Barbara Kiefer, Susan Hepler, and Janet Hickman. 2003. *Children's Literature in the Elementary School*. New York: McGraw Hill.

Jacobs, James, and Michael Tunnell. 2004. *Children's Literature, Briefly*. 3rd ed. New York: Merrill.

Koch, Kenneth. 1970. *Wishes, Lies, and Dreams: Teaching Children to Write Poetry*. New York: Chelsea House.

———. 1973. *Rose, Where Did You Get That Red?* New York: Random House.

Korbeck, Sharon. 1995. Children's Poetry: Journeying beyond the Road Less Traveled. *School Library Journal* 41 (April): 43–44.

Kordigel, M. 1995. "Every Poet a Big Child": The Slovene Poet Boris A. Novak. *Bookbird* 33 (1): 36–37.

Kutiper, K., and P. Wilson. 1993. Updating Poetry Preferences: A Look at the Poetry Children Really Like. *Reading Teacher* 47 (1): 28–34.

Livingston, Myra Cohn. 1984. *The Child as Poet: Myth or Reality?* Boston: Horn Book.

Manning, Maryann, and Gary Manning. 1997. Talk about Poetry. *Teaching PreK–8* 27 (February): 100–101.

McCaslin, Nellie. 2000. *Creative Drama in the Classroom and Beyond.* 7th ed. New York: Addison Wesley Longman.

McClure, A. 1990. *Sunrises and Songs: Reading and Writing Poetry in the Classroom.* Portsmouth, NH: Heinemann.

Morice, D. 1996. *The Adventures of Dr. Alphabet: 104 Unusual Ways to Write Poetry in the Classroom and the Community.* New York: Teachers and Writers Collaborative.

Nye, Naomi Shihab. 2005. Spiral Staircase. *Horn Book Magazine* 81, no. 3 (May/June): 251–54.

Raymond, Allen. 1999. Lee Bennett Hopkins Is Still the "Little Kid from Newark." *Teaching PreK–8* 29 (January): 58–61.

Routman, Regie. 2000. *Kids' Poems: Teaching First-Graders to Love Writing Poetry.* New York: Scholastic.

Sloan, Glenna. 2003. *Give Them Poetry: A Guide for Sharing Poetry with Children K–8.* New York: Teachers College Press.

Steinbergh, Judith. 1994. *Reading and Writing Poetry: A Guide for Teachers.* New York: Scholastic.

Terry, Ann. 1974. *Children's Poetry Preferences: A National Survey of Upper Elementary Grades.* Urbana, IL: National Council of Teachers of English.

Tiedt, Iris McClellan. 2002. *Tigers, Lilies, Toadstools, and Thunderbolts: Engaging K–8 Students with Poetry.* Newark, DE: International Reading Association.

Vardell, S. M. 2003. Poetry for Social Studies: Poems, Standards, and Strategies. *Social Education* 67 (4): 206–11.

———. 2005. Lift Ev'ry Voice and Sing: Multicultural Poetry for Children and Young Adults. *Versed* (Bulletin of the Office for Diversity, American Library Association): March/April. http://www.ala.org/ala/diversity/versed/versedbackissues/march 2005abc/mar05.htm.

Vardell, S. M., and J. M. Jacko. 2005. Folklore for Kids: Exploring the Rhymes, Songs, and Games of Childhood. *Book Links* 14 (4): 29–33.

Vardell, S., N. Hadaway, and T. Young. 2002. Choosing and Sharing Poetry with ESL Students. *Book Links* 11 (5): 51–56.

Wilson, P., and K. Kutiper. 1994. Beyond Silverstein and Prelutsky: Enhancing and Promoting the Elementary and Middle School Poetry Collection. *Youth Services in Libraries* (Spring 1994): 273–81.

Wooldridge, Susan Goldsmith. 1996. *Poemcrazy: Freeing Your Life with Words*. New York: Three Rivers Press.

Zipes, Jack, Lissa Paul, Lynne Vallone, Peter Hunt, and Gillian Avery. 2005. *The Norton Anthology of Children's Literature: The Traditions in English*. New York: Norton.

# ⌒ *Index*

*Page numbers in italics indicate a profile of the poet.*

**Sylvia M. Vardell** is currently a professor at Texas Woman's University in the School of Library and Information Studies, where she teaches graduate courses in children's and young adult literature. She received her PhD from the University of Minnesota in 1983. Vardell has published articles in *Book Links*, *Language Arts*, *English Journal*, *Reading Teacher*, *New Advocate*, *Young Children*, *Social Education*, and *Horn Book*, as well as several chapters and books on language and literature. Vardell helped establish the annual Texas Poetry Festival, held every spring, and organizes the Poetry Round-Up at the Texas Library Association Conference, modeled after the ALSC Poetry Blast held at the ALA Annual Conference. She served on the National Council of Teachers of English committee that established the Orbis Pictus Award for Outstanding Nonfiction for Children and as cochair of the NCTE Poetry Award Committee. She has presented at many state, regional, national, and international conferences, and has received grants from the Middle East Policy Council, the Ezra Jack Keats Foundation, the National Council of Teachers of English, the ALAN Foundation, the Texas Library Association, and the National Endowment for the Humanities. She also taught at the University of Zimbabwe in Africa as a Fulbright scholar in 1989. She is married, has two children, and is a naturalized American citizen.